W9-ARB-584

HARPER FORUM BOOKS

Martin E. Marty, General Editor

RELIGIOUS ISSUES
IN
AMERICAN HISTORY

HARPER FORUM BOOKS

Martin E. Marty, *General Editor*

Published:

IAN G. BARBOUR
SCIENCE AND RELIGION: New Perspectives on the Dialogue

A. ROY ECKARDT
THE THEOLOGIAN AT WORK: A Common Search for Understanding

JOHN MACQUARRIE
CONTEMPORARY RELIGIOUS THINKERS: From Idealist
Metaphysicians to Existential Theologians

GIBSON WINTER
SOCIAL ETHICS: Issues in Ethics and Society

JAMES M. GUSTAFSON & JAMES T. LANEY
ON BEING RESPONSIBLE: Issues in Personal Ethics

EDWIN SCOTT GAUSTAD
RELIGIOUS ISSUES IN AMERICAN HISTORY

SAMUEL SANDMEL
OLD TESTAMENT ISSUES

RELIGIOUS

ISSUES

IN

AMERICAN

HISTORY

edited by

Edwin Scott Gaustad

1817

HARPER & ROW, PUBLISHERS
NEW YORK, EVANSTON, AND LONDON

1- United States -Religion -Collections

RELIGIOUS ISSUES IN AMERICAN HISTORY. *Copyright © 1968 by Edwin Scott Gaustad. Printed in the United States of America. All rights reserved. For information address Harper & Row, Publishers, Incorporated, 49 East 33rd Street, New York, N.Y. 10016.*

FIRST EDITION

LIBRARY OF CONGRESS CATALOG CARD NUMBER: 68-17601

F-S

Published as a Harper Forum Book, 1968, by Harper & Row, Publishers, Incorporated, New York, Evanston, and London.

HARPER FORUM BOOKS

Often dismissed with a shrug or accepted with thoughtless piety in the past, religion today belongs in the forum of study and discussion. In our society, this is particularly evident in both public and private colleges and universities. Scholars are exploring the claims of theology, the religious roots of culture, and the relation between beliefs and the various areas or disciplines of life. Students have not until now had a series of books which could serve as reliable resources for class or private study in a time when inquiry into religion is undertaken with new freedom and a sense of urgency. *Harper Forum Books* are intended for these purposes. Eminent scholars have selected and introduced the readings. Respectful of the spirit of religion as they are, they do not shun controversy. With these books a new generation can confront religion through exposure to significant minds in theology and related humanistic fields.

MARTIN E. MARTY, GENERAL EDITOR
The Divinity School
The University of Chicago

ACKNOWLEDGMENTS

It is a pleasure to express appreciation to the John Randolph Haynes and Dora Haynes Foundation for a summer fellowship which gave initial impetus to the present volume. A University of California intramural grant also assisted in securing some of the scarcer items.

The courtesy of publishers or individuals who have graciously permitted the reprinting of materials on which they hold the copyright is also gratefully acknowledged. These include the following:

Harvard University Press for Charles Finney's *Lecturers on Revivals of Religion* (see Chap. 8) and for Josiah Strong's *Our Country* (see Chap. 14);

Alexander L. Abbott for Lyman Abbott's *Reminiscences* (see Chap. 12);

The Macmillan Company (Crowell-Collier) for Walter Lippmann's *Preface to Morals* (see Chap. 15);

Beacon Press for John Dewey's *Reconstruction in Philosophy* (see Chap. 16);

Princeton University Press for Will Herberg's essay in *Religious Perspectives in American Culture* (see Chap. 16);

West Publishing Company for the texts of United States Supreme Court decisions (see Chap. 17);

Sheed and Ward for John C. Murray's *We Hold These Truths* (see Chap. 18);

The Christian Scholar and William Hamilton for an essay reprinted in *Radical Theology and the Death of God* (see Chap. 18).

I happily express both gratitude and affection to my daughter, Susan, for bearing the major portion of the typing burden. Lance Woeltjen assisted in doggedly checking typescript against the original documents. In the overall preparation of this volume as in all other undertakings, my wife has not escaped unscathed. Remarkably, she has not attempted to.

E. S. G.

CONTENTS

INTRODUCTION

No Thirty Years' War, no *cujus regio, ejus religio* has marred America's history. No pogroms, no Inquisition, no armed crusade has in the name of sect or creed taken the lives or property of heterodox thousands. No military campaigns led by bishops or cardinals, no wars of conversion or baptism of armies. No mass excommunication, interdicts, or expulsions. Religion in America must be a tame affair.

Not really. While it is possible in medieval or modern Europe to find holy wars on a scale not discoverable in the United States, the latter has not been without its blood. And even more clearly has it not been without its persecution, prejudice, harassment, rancor, intolerance, deception, hypocrisy, subversion, and mayhem—all in the name of religion. From the seventeenth-century hanging of Quakers in Boston to the eighteenth-century imprisonment of Baptists in Virginia, to the nineteenth-century sacking of Catholic churches in Philadelphia, to the twentieth-century exclusion of Jews from "better" clubs and neighborhoods everywhere, religious conflict has been an integral part of the American scene.*

The issues here reviewed do not necessarily center on the external clashes or overt persecutions. While these can be the most dramatic confrontations, they are less likely to be the most significant in determining the direction that the nation takes. Persecution is usually of a weak and despised minority; open conflict and flagrant bigotry generally conceal a more fundamental cleavage within the social order itself. The chapters that

* See the useful compendium edited by Earl Raab, *Religious Conflict in America: Studies in the Problems Beyond Bigotry* (New York: Doubleday Anchor Book, 1964). Raab's introductory word is noteworthy: "There is reason to believe that interreligious conflict in America will finally prove to be a more knotty, more durable, and in some ways more significant problem than interracial conflict" (p. 1).

follow, therefore, seek to record more the subterranean tremors, less the collapse of particular structures.

Nor do the chapters of this volume attempt to delineate that intramural denominational warfare with which America's history is replete. Church schisms and separations, ecclesiastical quarrels and trials, do comprise a lengthy and fascinating chapter in the national story. So frequently however these are purely domestic spats, household contests that disturb neither the peace nor the common pursuits of the total community. In fact, the community is ordinarily unaware of most battles that rage within sectarian walls, or, if aware, is unsure whether any substantial question is at stake.

By contrast, the aim here has been to concentrate on issues that have involved the larger community, issues in whose outcome men's interest was widespread and sharp. What is sought are those major cultural shifts, those pivotal choices—conscious or otherwise—that come in what William James called the forked-road situations of life. Though it is not always possible to see history turning its corners, it is usually possible to recognize options that are live, forced, and momentous (to stay with James' vocabulary a bit longer). The ripples and reverberations flowing from these contrasting options shape the nation we live in today.

This volume's eighteen issues are presented in the form of debate. Sometimes the opposing sides are fully aware of each other, are indeed attacking each other with precision and vigor. In other instances, however, the debate is a more artificial construct in that the contenders may not be addressing each other directly nor responding explicitly to the other's argument. The debate then belongs to the larger audience, either of their day or this; it belongs to the nation itself.

A debate has its limitations, limitations aggravated if the reader permits himself to become partisan too soon. The case for or against any particular point of view is not a case of "good guys" versus "bad guys," of wise men versus fools, of true believers versus heretics. While one's sympathies may certainly register as they are inclined, it should be remembered that the persons quoted are never presented in the full roundness of their thought. A single point of view, a limited perspective, a partial defense is normally all that is permitted to any one of them. In fairness, therefore, the reader should look for the inherent logic, the personal integrity of each position, remembering that villainy or heroism is something more than managing to be, at any given point, on history's winning side.

The very clash of opposites, moreover, may be a means of moving men to new levels of understanding. Without adopting an Hegelian stance, one can see a nation choosing neither *A* nor *B*, but embracing in a more sophisticated, judicious manner what is best in both. Of course, it does not always work that way—else we would all be Hegelians! It is also possible to select the worst of both, as John F. Kennedy used to say of the nation's capital city: that it successfully combined northern charm with southern efficiency. But a commitment to the democratic process includes the confidence that public discussion, even acrimonious debate, is one of the more suitable means for settling differences among men.

In addition to the general principles of selection noted above, each chapter's introduction offers some rationale for the inclusion of that particular issue. Legitimate and perhaps puzzled queries may remain. Also honest differences are to be expected and voiced regarding the editorial judgment exercised. A book about great national debates could scarcely wish to eliminate all debate. But perhaps a few of the minor puzzles can be clarified now.

Why no Scopes trial here? Isn't that the outstanding religious issue in American history—at least in the present century? No, it is not. The Scopes trial was a funeral oration in honor of theological giants who fell in earlier battles. The real war was not fought in Dayton, Tennessee in 1925, but in the universities and seminaries, lecture halls and ordination services, decades before. The confrontation, therefore, between men like Lyman Abbott and Charles Hodge (see Chap. 12) is far more a national issue—though Dayton was admittedly far more a national spectacle.

What of fundamentalism and modernism—where are these terms to be found? Does not this issue transcend most others? The fundamentalist-modernist division is unfortunately not a single issue but many. The different ground on which the opposing forces stand, the different world view held by each, are more critical issues than any narrow doctrinal dispute in any specific year. And these underlying divergences do deserve attention (see for example Chaps. 7, 8, and 12 through 15).

Surely federal aid to education, specifically to parochial and church-related schools, is the central religious issue in our time: where is the chapter on that? So far as political decision-making is concerned, this may indeed be the current contest of greatest note. But the fissures deep within the body social are related to long-standing conflicts of opinion (see Chaps. 2, 14, 16, 17, and 18). Again, the debates over prohibition, over representation at the Vatican, over the Al Smith or John Kennedy campaigns, over Sabbath laws and school prayers, are only surface symptoms of half-hidden tremors. And it is to these profounder rumblings—sometimes painfully disruptive, sometimes remarkably creative—that attention is here directed.

In a glowing seventeenth-century report on the state of Virginia's society, an optimistic—or careless—Anglican wrote that the inhabitants "all live in peace and love." This was not true of seventeenth-century Virginia, nor of the twelve other colonies a hundred years later, nor of thirty states in mid-nineteenth century, nor is it the case in our fifty-states of the present day. The readings offered here do not reveal a tranquil land where all live together in peace and love. The book is dedicated, however, to the proposition that better understanding of our divisions may help us simply to live together. Which is a notion that occurred to a few Americans some time ago: *e pluribus unum.*

                                                                E. S. G.

1

MERCANTILISM

OR

MISSION

THE DEGREE of religious motivation in England's entry into the New World is a much-mooted point in American history. With good reason. Motives are always complex and obscure—our own no less than those we plumb for in others. Complexity is confounded when the historian must sift the always fragmentary evidence from centuries past, hoping to discern not only what happened but why. Charlemagne was crowned on Christmas Day, 800 A.D.—why? What were his motives, or the motives of Pope Leo III, or of those who encouraged or of those who resisted? Sir Walter Raleigh, we know, sent ships to the Carolina coast in 1584—but why? In this instance Raleigh provides his own answer: "Men have traveled, as they have lived, for religion, for wealth, for knowledge, for pleasure, for power and the overthrow of rivals." The complexity is built in.

In America's colonization, further variety is introduced by the very separateness of the several efforts to settle in the New World. From Nova Scotia to Barbados, from Plymouth to Savannah, motives and methods vary greatly. Mission more than mercantilism has been seen as the predominant motivation in the settlement of New England, Pennsylvania, and Maryland. But even Virginia's tobacco-raising patriarch had undertaken, said Perry Miller, "not a mercantile investment but a medieval pilgrimage." Pilgrims may also be planters, and merchants need not eschew piety.

In Raleigh's half-brother, Sir Humphrey Gilbert (c. 1539–1583), the mixture of motive can likewise be found, though the economic concern is controlling. This concern is evident throughout his career as he sought to open new trade routes, to discover a Northwest Passage, to establish colonies in Ireland and North America, and "to annoy the King of Spain." Gilbert planned and proposed on a grand scale, often displaying more of daring imagination than of prudential execution. His many attempts personally to view the New World culminated in June 1583 when he set out with five ships for Newfoundland. Landfall was made in early August, and Gilbert grandly claimed all he saw for England (the French, Spanish, and Portuguese fishermen continued unperturbed their habits of many years). On the return voyage in September, Gilbert was lost at sea.

In the document below, written six years before his death, Gilbert argues for the aggrandizement of England's economic and political fortunes at the expense of Spain. One may annoy in several ways: by seizing Spanish fishing fleets around Newfoundland, thus weakening the merchant marine and giving Spain no opportunity "to recover breath whereby to repair their decayed losses." Or, one may intercept gold-laden ships setting out from Mexico and South America—making Spain "weak and poor" but England "strong and rich." If a little hypocrisy is required to enable England to get away with all this, no bother: "I hold it as lawful in Christian policy to prevent a mischief betime as to revenge it too late."

Richard Hakluyt the Younger (c. 1552–1616) more than any other individual is identified with England's voyages of discovery and colonization. A propagandist without peer, Hakluyt exhorted, edited, cajoled, and inspired until Englishmen's feet were firmly planted on New World soil. And though he never stepped on that soil himself, he was named honorary rector of the first permanent English parish in America: Jamestown. For Hakluyt was, in addition to all else, an Anglican minister, a minister eager to see Christianity reach the Western world in its "pure form." The mission to the heathen could not, therefore, be left to the devices of Catholic France or Catholic Spain.

While best known as the compiler-editor of the remarkable work, *Principal Navigations* (1589 and following), Hakluyt had earlier submitted to Queen Elizabeth *A Discourse on Western Planting* (1584) that urged immediate colonization. Written "at the request and direction of Mr. Walter Raleigh, now knight," the *Discourse* marshaled all the crucial, urgent reasons why the Queen should loosen her purse strings and encourage her people to colonize. In Chapter 20, Hakluyt summarizes his arguments in the form of twenty-three reasons, the sixteenth of which reads: "We shall by planting there enlarge the glory of the gospel, and from England plant sincere religion and provide a safe and sure place to receive people from all parts of the world that are forced to flee for the truth of God's word." It was no afterthought. For the very first chapter of the *Discourse,* reprinted below, was a proclamation of England's mission.

A

[The text is taken from David Beers Quinn, The *Voyages and Colonising Enterprises of Sir Humphrey Gilbert* (London: Hakluyt Society, 1940), Vol. I, pp. 170–75.]

A Discourse How Hir Majestie
May Annoy the King of Spayne

I am bowld (most excellent Soveraigne) to exercise my pen touching matters of state, because I am a syllie member of this

Common Weale of England, and doe not offer myself therein as an Instructor, or a reformer, but as a Welwiller to your Majestie and my Countrie, wherein the meanest or simplest ought not to yeeld them selves second to the best, or wisest. In which respect I hope to be pardoned, if through want of judgement I be mistaken herein. And so to the matter.

The safety of Principates, Monarchies, and Common Weales rest chiefly in making theire enemies weake, and poore, and themselves strong and rich, Both which god hath specially wrought for your majestes safety, if your highness shall not overpas good opportunities for the same, when they are offered. For your neighboures infelicities through civill warres, hath weakened and impoverished them both by sea, and land, And hath strengthened your Majestes Realme both by thone, and thother, which thinge is so manyfest, that it weare more then in vayne, to go about to prove the same. And for that that this your Majestes Realme of England requireth other consideracions then those which are of ther continent, I will omit them, and sypnn a threed propper for our English loomes.

First your highnes owght undoubtedly to seeke the kingdome of heaven, and upon that fowndacion to beleeve that there can never be constant, and firme league of amytie betwene those princes, whose division is planted by the woorme of thier consciences. So that their leagues and fayre wordes, ought to be held but as mermaydes songes, sweet poysons, or macquesites, that abuse with outward plawsabilityie, and gay showes. For in troth as in such leagues there is no assuraunce, so Christian princes ought not for any respect to combyne themselves in amytie, with such as are at open and professed warres with god himselfe. For non est consilium omnino contra deum. So that no state or common weale can florishe, where the first and principall care is not for goddes glorie, and for thadvaunsing of the pollisies of his spirituall kingdom, which donn, your majestie is to thinck that it is more then tyme to pare theire nayles by the stumpes, that are most readie prest to plucke the crowne (as it were in despite of god) from your highnes head, not only by

foraine force: also by stirring up of home factions. And therefore the best waie is first to purge, or at least wise to redresse
your owne kingdome of theire suspected adherentes, I meane
not by banishment, or by fire, and sworde, but by diminishing
their habilities by purse, creditt and force. Then to foresee by
all diligente meanes, that your suspected neighbors may not have
opportunity to recover breath whereby to repayre theire decayed
losses; which for your safetie is principally to be don, by the
farther weakening of theire navies, and by preserving and increasing of your owne.

And the deminishing of their forces by sea is to be done
eyther by open hostilytie, or by some colorable meanes; as by
geving of lycence under lettres patentes to discover and inhabyte
some strange place, with speciall proviso for their safetyes
whome pollisy requyreth to have most annoyed by which meanes
the doing of the contrarie shalbe imputed to the executors fawlt;
your highnes lettres patentes being a manyfest shewe that it was
not your Majestes pleasure so to have it. After the publick
notyse of which fact, your Majestie is either to avowe the same
(if by the event thereof it shall so seme good) or to disavowe
both them and the fact, as league breakers, leaving them to
pretend yt as done without your pryvitie, either in the service of
the prince of Orange or otherwise.

This cloake being had for the raigne, the way to worke the
feate is to sett forth under such like colour of discoverie, certayne
shippes of warre to the N.L. [New Land] which with your good
licence I will undertake without your Majestes charge; in which
place they shall certainely once in the yeere meete in effecte
all the great shipping of Fraunce, Spayne, and Portyngall, where
I would have take and bring awaye with theire fraygthes and
ladinges, the best of those shippes and burn the woorst, and
those that they take to carrie into Holland or Zeland, or as
pirattes to shrowd them selves for a small time uppon your
Majestes coastes, under the frendship of some certayne vice-
admirall of this Realme; who may be afterwardes committed to
prison, as in displeasure for the same, against whose returnes,

six monthes provision of bread, and fower of drinck to be layd
in some apt place: together with municion to serve for the number of five or six thousand men, which men with certaine other
shippes of warr being in a readyness, shall pretend to inhabit
St. Lawrence Island, the late discovered Contries in the North,
or elswhere, and not to joyne with the others but in some certaine
remote place at sea.

The setting forth of shipping for this service will amounte to
no great matter, and the retourne shall certainely be with greate
gayne, For the N.F.[Newland Fish]is a principall and rich and
everie where vendible merchaundise: and by the gayne thereof,
shipping, victuall, munition, and the transporting of five or six
thousand soldiors may be defrayed.

It may be sayd that a fewe shippes cannot possibilie distres so
many: and that although by this service yow take or destroy all
the shipping you find of theirs in those places: yet are they but
subjectes shippes, theire owne particular navies being nothing
lessoned therby, and therefore theire forces shall not so much be
diminyshed, as yt is supposed, whereunto I answere.

There is no doubt to performe it without dawnger. For although they may be many in number, and great of burthen, yet
are they furnished with men, and munition, but like fishers,
and when they come upon the coastes, they do alwaies disperse
them selves into sundry portes, and do disbarke the moste of
their people into small boates for the taking and drying of
theire fish, leaving fewe or none aborde theire shippes, so that
there is as little doubt of the easye taking, and carrying of them
away: as of the decaying hereby of those princes forces by sea.
For theire owne proper shippinges are very fewe, and of small
forces in respect of the others, and theire subjectes shipping
being once destroyed, yt is likely that they will never be repaired,
partly through the decaye of the owners, and partly through the
losses of the trades whereby they mainteyned the same / For
everie man that is hable to build shippes doth not dispose his
wealth that waye, so that their shipping being once spoyled, yt
is likely that they will never be recovered to the like number and

strength, but if they should yt will requiei [*sic*] a long time to
season timber for that purpose, all which space we shall have
good opportunity to proceed in our farther enterprises / And all
the meane tyme the forsayd princes shall not only be disapointed
of their forces as aforesaid, but also leese great revenues, which
by traffick they formerly gayned; and shall therewithall endure
great famine for want of such necessarie victualles &c. as they
former enjoyed by those voyages.

It may also be objected that although this may be done in act,
yet it is not allowable, being against your Majestes league: for
although by the reach of reason mens Ies may be obscured, yet
unto God nothing is hidden, which I answere thus.

I hold it as lawfule in christen pollicie, to prevent a mischief
betime: as to revenge it to late, especiallie seing that god him
selfe is a party in the common quarrelles now a foote, and his
ennemy malitiouse disposition towardes your highnes, and his
Church manifestlie seen, although by godes mercifull providence
not yet throughlie felt /

Further it may be saide that if this should be done by Englishmen under what colour soever they should shrowd themselves,
yet will that cut us off from all trafficke with those that shalbe
annoyed by such meanes; and thereby utterlie undoe the state of
merchandise, decaye the mayntenaunce of the shipping of this
Realme and also greatly diminishe your Majestes customes to
which I replie thus.

To prevent theise daungers (that although your highnes may
at the first distres both the FRENCH, SPANYSHE, and
PORTINGALL yet there needeth none to be towched but the
SPANIARDES, and PORTINGALL, or the SPANIARDES
alone) by the want of those whose traffick there is no necessity
of such decaye and losses as partly appeared by the late re-
strainte betwene your Majesty and them. And the forces of the
SPANIARDS and PORTINGALLS, being there so much decayed as aforesaid; The FRENCH of necessitie shalbe brought
under your highnes lye / assuring your majesty the case being
as it is, it were better a thousand folde thus to gayne the start of

them, rather then yerely to submitt our selves subject to have all the marchauntes shippes of this Realme stayed in their handes: whereby they shalbe armed at our costes, to beate us with roddes of our owne making, and ourselves thereby spoyled both of our owne wealth and strength.

And touching the contynuaunce of traffick wherewith to increase and maintaine our shipping, and your majestes revenues, and also to provide that the prices of sotherne wares shall not be so inhaunced to the detriment of the Comon weale: there may be good meanes found for the preventing thereof, as hereafter followeth /

It is true if we shold indure the losse of those trades, and not recover those commodities by some other meanes: that then your Majesty might be both hindred in shippinge, and customes, to the great decaie of the comon Weale. But if your highnes will permit me, with my associates eyther overtly or covertly to perfourme the aforesaide enterprise: then with the gayne thereof there may be easely such a competent companie transported to the W.I.[West Indies] as may be hable not only to disposses the S.[Spaniards] thereof, but also to possesse for ever your Majestie and Realme therewith, and thereby not only be countervaile, but by farr to surmounte with gaine, the aforesaid supposed losses: besides the gowld and silver Mynes, the profitt of the soyle, and the inward and outward customs from thence, By which meanes your highnes doubtfull frendes, or rather apparaunte enemyes, shall not be only made weake and poore, but therewith your selfe, and Realme made strong and rich, both by sea, and by lande, as well there, as here. And where both is wrought under one, it bringeth a most happy conclusion, So that if this may be well brought to passe (where of there is no doubt) then have we hitt the mark we shott at, and wonn the goale of our securities to the immortall fame of your Majestie /

For when your enemyes shall not have shipping, nor meanes left them whereby to maintayne shipping, to annoye your Majestie nor your subjectes be any longer enforced for want of other trades to submitt them selves to the daunger of theire arrestes,

then of force this Realme being an Iland shall be discharged
from all forraine perills, if all the MONARCHIES of the world
should joyne against us, so long as IRELAND shal be in salf
keping, the league of SCOTLAND maintayned, and further
amitie concluded with the prince of ORANGE and the King
of DENMARK. By which meanes also your majestie shall in-
graffe and glewe to your crowne, in effect all the Northerne
and Southerne viages of the world, so that none shalbe then
well hable to crosse the seas, but subject to your highnes devo-
cion: considering the great increase of shipping that will growe,
and be maynetayned by those long vyages, extending themselves so many sundrie wayes. And if I may perceave that your
highnes shall like of this enterprise, then will I most willinglie
expresse my simple opinion, which waye the W.I. [West Indies]
maye without difficultie be more surprised, and defended, without which resolucion it were but labour lost. But if your Majestie
like to do it at all, then wold I wish your highnes to consider
that delay doth often tymes prevent the perfourmaunce of good
thinges: for the Winges of mans life are plumed with the feathers
of Death. And so submitting my self to your Majesties favourable judgement I cease to trouble your highnes any further.
Novembris: 6. 1577.

Your Majestes most faithfull
servaunt and subject.
H. GYLBERTE

B

[The text is taken from Charles Deane, ed., *Documentary History of the State of Maine* (Cambridge, Mass.: John Wilson and Son, 1877), Vol. II, pp. 7–12.]

A Discourse on Western Planting
Chapter I

That this Westerne discoverie will be greately for thinlargemente of the gospell of Christe, whereunto the princes of the Refourmed Relligion are chefely bounde, amongeste whome her Majestie ys principall.

Seinge that the people of that parte of AMERICA from 30. degrees in Florida northewarde unto 63. degrees (which ys yet in no Christian princes actuall possession) are idolaters; and that those which Stephen Gomes broughte from the coaste of NORUMBEGA in the yere 1524, worshipped the sonne, the moone, and the starres, and used other idolatrie . . . and that those of Canada and Hochelaga in 48. and 50. degrees worshippe a spirite which they call Cudruaigny, as we reade in the tenthe chapiter of the seconde relation of Jaques Cartier, whoe saieth: This people beleve not at all in God, but in one whome they call Cudruaigny; they say that often he speaketh with them, and telleth them what weather shall followe, whether goodd or badd, &c., and yet notwithstandinge they are very easie to be perswaded, and doe all that they sawe the Christians doe in their devine service, with like imitation and devotion, and were very desirous to become Christians, and woulde faine have been baptized, as Verarsanus witnesseth in the laste wordes of his relation, and Jaques Cartier in the tenthe chapiter before recited—it remayneth to be thoroughly weyed and considered by what meanes and by whome this moste godly and Christian work may be perfourmed of inlarginge the glorious gospell of Christe, and reducinge of infinite multitudes of these simple people that are in errour into the righte and perfecte way of their saluation. The blessed Apostle Paule, the converter of the Gentiles, Rom: 10. writeth in this manner: Whoesoever shall call on the name of the Lorde shall be saved. But howe shall they call on him in whom they have not beleved? and howe shall they beleve in him of whom they have not hearde? and howe shall they heare withoute a preacher? and howe shall they preache excepte they be sente? Then it is necessary for the salvation of those poore people which have sitten so longe in darkenes and in the shadowe of deathe, that preachers should be sent unto them. But by whome shoulde these preachers be sente? By them no doubte which have taken upon them the protection and defence of the Christian faithe. Nowe the Kinges and Queenes of England have the name of Defendours of the Faithe. By which title I thinke they are not onely chardged to mayneteyne and patronize the faithe of Christe, but also to inlarge and advaunce the same. Neither oughte this to be their laste worke, but rather the principall and chefe of all others, accordinge to the comaundemente of our Saviour, Christe, Mathewe 6, Ffirste seeke the kingdome of God and the righteousnes thereof, and all other thinges shalbe mynistred unto you.

Nowe the meanes to sende suche as shall labour effectually in this busines ys, by plantinge one or twoo colonies of our nation upon that fyrme, where they may remaine in safetie, and firste learne the language of the people nere adjoyninge (the gifte of tongues beinge nowe taken awaye), and by little and little acquainte themselves with their manner, and so with discretion and myldenes distill into their purged myndes the swete and lively liquor of the gospel. Otherwise, for preachers to come unto them rashly with oute some suche preparation for their safetie, yt were nothinge els but to ronne to their apparaunte and certaine destruction, as yt happened unto those Spanishe ffryers, that, before any plantinge, withoute strengthe and company, landed in Fflorida, where they were miserablye massacred by the savages. On the other side, by meane of plantinge firste, the small nation of the Portingales towardes the

Southe and Easte have planted the Christian faithe accordinge
to their manner, and have erected many bisshoprickes and col-
ledges to traine upp the youthe of the infidells in the same, of
which acte they more vaunte in all their histories and chronicles,
then of anythinge els that ever they atchieved. And surely if
they had planted the gospell of Christe purely, as they did not,
they mighte justly have more rejoyced in that deede of theires,
then in the conqueste of the whole contrie, or in any other thinge
whatsoever. The like may be saied of the Spaniardes, whoe . . .
have established in the West Indies three archebisshopricks, to
witt, Mexico, Luna, and Onsco, and thirtene other bisshopricks
there named, and have builte above CC. houses of relligion
in the space of fyftie yeres or thereaboutes. Now yf they, in
their superstition, by meanes of their plantinge in those partes,
have don so greate thinges in so shorte space, what may wee
hope for in our true and syncere relligion, proposinge unto ourselves in this action not filthie lucre nor vaine ostentation, as
they in deede did, but principally the gayninge of the soules of
millions of those wretched people, the reducinge of them from
darkenes to lighte, from falsehoodde to truthe, from dombe
idolls to the lyvinge God, from the depe pitt of hell to the
highest heavens. In the 16. of the Actes of the Apostles, when
Paule soughte to preache in Asia and to goe into Bithinia, the
Holy Ghoste suffered him not. But at Troas a vision appered
unto him by night. There stoode a man of Macedonia and prayed
hym, sayenge: Come into Macedonia and helpe us. And after
he had seene the vysion, ymmediatly he prepared to goe into
Macedonia, beinge assured that the Lorde had called him to
preache the gospell unto them. Even so wee, whiles wee have
soughte to goe into other countries (I woulde I might say to
preache the gospell), God by the frustratinge of our actions
semeth to forbydd us to followe those courses, and the people
of **AMERICA** crye oute unto us, their nexte neighboures, to
come and helpe them, and bringe unto them the gladd tidinges
of the gospell. Unto the prince and people that shalbe the occasion of this worthie worke, and shall open their cofers to the

furtheraunce of this most godly enterprise, God shall open the bottomles treasures of his riches, and fill them with aboundaunce of his hidden blessinges; as he did to the goodd Queene Isabella, which beinge in extreme necessitie, laied her owne jewells to gage for money to furnishe out Columbus for the firste discovery of the West Indies.

And this enterprise the princes of the relligion (amonge whome her Majestie ys principall) oughte the rather to take in hande, because the papistes confirme themselves and drawe other to theire side, shewinge that they are the true Catholicke churche because they have bene the onely converters of many millions of infidells to Christianitie. Yea, I myselfe have bene demaunded of them, how many infidells have been by us converted? Whereunto, albeit I alleaged the example of the mynisters which were sente from Geneva with Villegagnon into Bresill, and those that wente with John Ribault into Florida, as also those of our nation that went with Ffrobisher, Sir Fraunces Drake, and Ffenton; yet in very deede I was not able to name any one infidell by them converted. But God, quoth I, hath his tyme for all men, whoe calleth some at the nynthe, and some at the eleventh houer. And if it please him to move the harte of her Majestie to put her helpinge hande to this godly action, she shall finde as willinge subjectes of all sortes as any other prince in all Christendome. And as for the boastinge of your conversion of such multitudes of infidells, yt may justly be compted rather a perversion, seeinge you have drawen them as it were oute of Sylla into Charibdis, that is to say, from one error into another. Nowe therefore I truste the time ys at hande when by her Majesties forwardnes in this enterprise, not only this objection and suche like shalbe aunswered by our frutefull labor in Godds harvest amonge the infidells, but also many inconveniences and strifes amongest ourselves at home, in matters of ceremonies, shalbe ended. For those of the clergye which by reason of idlenes here at home are nowe alwayes coyninge of newe opynions, havinge by this voyadge to set themselves on worke in reducinge the savages to the chefe principles of our faith, will become lesse contentious, and be contented with the truthe in relligion alreadie established by authoritie. So they that shall beare the name of Christians shall shewe themselves worthye of their vocation, so shall the mouthe of the adversarie be stopped, so shall contention amongest brethren be avoyded, so shal the gospell amonge infidells be published.

2

DIVERSITY

OR

CONFORMITY

To CHURCHMEN and statesmen all over Europe, the scandal of America was not that religious diversity was sometimes endured, but that it was in some instances actively encouraged. Colonization presented sufficient difficulties and dangers without courting disaster in quite unnecessary ways. Forsaking the safety of England was hazardous; living amid a "swarm of sectaries" was ridiculous. Government would collapse, morals would disappear, and all pretense of piety would go.

Most colonists, fortunately, could be depended on to be reasonable men, seeing in "toleration" only another name for libertinism and unbelief. Yet a few men did insist on courting disaster: notably, Roger Williams on the shores of Narragansett Bay and William Penn along the Delaware River and to the west. Of the two colonies, Penn's, founded in 1682, was the more scandalous only because its invitation to diversity found more abounding and varied acceptance.

William Penn (1644–1718) did not arrive at his libertarian views as a result of breathing the "free, democratic air" of

America. It was not a Frontier Spirit but an Inner Light which provoked Penn's rejection of religious persecution, his embrace of religious freedom. The Society of Friends (Quakers), of which he was a member, bore testimony to that Light in ways that embarrassed or infuriated properly constituted authority. Fines were levied, ears were cropped, jails were filled, lives were lost. "Religious liberty" was not a slogan; "freedom of conscience" was not a mere catchy phrase. These were, rather, matters of life and death.

Six years before Charles II granted that huge New World domain to William Penn, the latter wrote *The Great Case of Liberty of Conscience* (1670). English persecution was the villain of the piece, and England's future as a nation the long-range concern of the author. "The Lord God Almighty destroyed Sodom," Penn reminds his readers, and let no man delude himself that wickedness will go unpunished even in this day. God will "hasten to make desolate this wanton land, and not leave an hiding-place for the oppressor." But beyond the severity of his language and the passion of his defense, a further fact stands out: When Penn himself came to rule a realm almost the size of England, he did not abandon the frightening principles set forth here.

Thomas Barton (1730?–1780), a graduate of Dublin University, arrived in America in 1751 where he soon set up a school in Norriton, Pennsylvania. Three years later he returned to England to receive ordination in the Church of England. As a missionary for the Society for the Propagation of the Gospel in Foreign Parts (S.P.G.), Barton once more sailed for America, working chiefly in Pennsylvania as before. Though he became the rector of St. James' in Lancaster, he maintained close contact with the S.P.G. Barton's impact on early American science is perhaps greater than his impact on religion. He was the tutor (and later brother-in-law) of the clockmaker and astronomer David Rittenhouse, and the father of Benjamin Smith Barton, Philadelphia's outstanding botanist.

In the letters given below, Barton is addressing the Secretary of the S.P.G.* whose sympathies the Pennsylvania cleric can rely on. The seeds planted by William Penn in the latter decades of the seventeenth century have now produced their harvest, and an unlovely, unsettling harvest it is for Thomas Barton. He sees "national religion and common sense" forsaken for enthusiasm and fanaticism. He sees true religion choked by the "swarm of sectaries" that abound in a profligate Pennsylvania. He sees diversity not as a blessing bestowed by heaven but as a regrettable postponing of the glad day when the Church of England "must certainly prevail at last." In short, he sees—as did most of his contemporaries—a deliberately encouraged diversity in religion as madness, a required conformity as mere sanity in an otherwise hopelessly chaotic world.

A

[The text is taken from *The Select Works of William Penn* (3d ed.; London: James Phillips, 1782), Vol. III, pp. 1–13.]

The Great Case of Liberty of Conscience
Chapter I

That imposition, restraint, and persecution for conscience sake, highly invade the Divine prerogative, and divest the Almighty of a right, due to none besides himself, and that in five eminent particulars.

The great case of Liberty of Conscience, so often debated and defended (however dissatisfactorily to such as have so little conscience, as to persecute for it) is once more brought to pub-lick view, by a late act against Dissenters, and Bill, or an addi-

---

* From 1739 to 1761 the Reverend Philip Bearcroft, D.D., was Secretary of the S.P.G.; he also served as chaplain to the king as well as holding other offices. He was succeeded by the Reverend Daniel Burton, D.D., who served until his death in 1773.

tional one, that we all hoped the wisdom of our rulers had long since laid aside, as what was fitter to be passed into an act of perpetual oblivion. The kingdoms are alarmed at this procedure, and thousands greatly at a stand, wondering what should be the meaning of such hasty resolutions, that seem as fatal as they were unexpected. Some ask what wrong they have done? others, what peace they have broken? and all, what plots they have formed to prejudice the present government, or occasions given to hatch new jealousies of them and their proceedings? being not conscious to themselves of guilt in any such respect.

For mine own part, I publickly confess myself to be a very hearty Dissenter from the established worship of these nations, as believing Protestants to have much degenerated from their first principles, and as owning the poor despised Quakers, in life and doctrine, to have espoused the cause of God, and to be the undoubted followers of Jesus Christ, in his most holy, strait, and narrow way, that leads to the eternal rest. In all which I know no treason, nor any principle that would urge me to a thought injurious to the civil peace. If any be defective in this particular, it is equal both individuals and whole societies should answer for their own defaults; but we are clear.

However, all conclude that union very ominous and unhappy, which makes the first discovery of itself "by a John Baptist's head in a charger." They mean that feast which some are designed to make upon the liberties and properties of free-born Englishmen: Since to have the entail of those undoubted hereditary rights cut off, for matters purely relative of another world, is a severe beheading in the law: which must be obvious to all, but such as measure the justice of things only, by that proportion they bear with their own interest. A sort of men that seek themselves, though at the apparent loss of whole societies; like to that barbarous fancy of old, which had rather than Rome should burn, than it be without the satisfaction of a bon-fire. And sad it is, when men have so far stupefied their understandings with the strong doses of their private interest, as to become insensible of the public's. Certainly such an over-fondness for self, or that strong inclination to raise themselves in the ruin of what does not so much oppose them, as that they will believe so, because they would be persecuting, is a malignant enemy to that tranquility, which all dissenting parties seem to believe would be the consequence of a toleration.

In short we say, there can be but two ends in persecution; the one to satisfy (which none can ever do) the insatiable appetites of a decimating clergy (whose best arguments are fines and imprisonments); and the other, as thinking therein they do God good service: but it is so hateful a thing upon any account, that we shall make it appear, by this ensuing discourse, to be a declared enemy to God, religion, and the good of human society.

The whole will be small, since it is but an epitome of no larger a tract than fourteen sheets; yet divides itself into the same particulars, every of which we shall defend against imposition, restraint, and persecution, though not with that scope of reason (nor consequently pleasure to the readers) being by other contingent disappointments limited to a narrow stint.

The terms explained, and the question stated.

First, By Liberty of Conscience, we understand not only a mere Liberty of the Mind, in believing or disbelieving this or that principle or doctrine; but "the exercise of ourselves in a visible way of worship, upon our believing it to be indispensably required at our hands, that if we neglect it for fear or favour of any mortal man, we sin, and incur divine wrath." Yet we would be so understood to extend and justify the lawfulness of our so meeting to worship God, as not to contrive, or abet any contrivance destructive of the government and laws of the land, tending to matters of an external nature, directly or indirectly; but so far only as it may refer to religious matters, and a life to come, and consequently wholly independent of the secular affairs of this, wherein we are supposed to transgress.

Secondly, By imposition, restraint, and persecution, we do not only mean the strict requiring of us to believe this to be true, or that to be false; and upon refusal, to incur the penalties enacted in such cases; but by those terms we mean thus much, "any coercive lett or hindrance to us, from meeting together to perform those religious exercises which are according to our faith and persuasion."

The question stated.

For proof of the aforesaid terms thus given, we singly state the question thus;

Whether imposition, restraint, and persecution, upon persons for exercising such a liberty of conscience as is before expressed, and so circumstantiated, be not to impeach the honor of God, the meekness of the Christian religion, the authority of Scripture, the privilege of nature, the principles of common reason, the well being of government, and apprehensions of the greatest personages of former and latter ages?

First, Then we say, that Imposition, Restraint, and Persecution, for matters relating to conscience, directly invade the divine prerogative, and divest the Almighty of a due, proper to none besides himself. And this we prove by these five particulars:

First, If we do allow the honour of our creation due to God only, and that no other besides himself has endowed us with those excellent gifts of Understanding, Reason, Judgment, and Faith, and consequently that he only is the object, as well as the author, both of our Faith, Worship, and Service; then whosoever shall interpose their authority to enact faith and worship in a way that seems not to us congruous with what he has discovered to us to be faith and worship (whose alone property it is to do it) or to restrain us from what we are persuaded is our indispensable duty, they evidently usurp this authority, and invade his incommunicable right of government over conscience: "For the Inspiration of the Almighty gives understanding: and faith is the gift of God," says the divine writ.

Secondly, Such magisterial determinations carry an evident

claim to that infallibility, which Protestants have been hitherto so jealous of owning, that, to avoid the Papists, they have denied it to all but God himself.

Either they have forsook their old plea; or if not, we desire to know when, and where, they were invested with that divine excellency; and whether imposition, restraint, and persecution, were ever deemed by God the fruits of his Spirit. However, that itself was not sufficient; for unless it appear as well to us that they have it, as to them who have it, we cannot believe it upon any convincing evidence, but by tradition only; an anti-protestant way of believing.

Thirdly, It enthrones man as king over conscience, the alone just claim and privilege of his Creator; whose thoughts are not as mens thoughts, but has reserved to himself that empire from all the Caesars on earth: For if men, in reference to souls and bodies, things appertaining to this and the other world, shall be subject to their fellow-creatures, what follows, but that Caesar (however he got it) has all, God's share, and his own too? And being Lord of both, both are Caesar's, and not God's.

Fourthly, It defeats God's work of Grace, and the invisible operation of his eternal Spirit, (which can alone beget faith, and is only to be obeyed, in and about religion and worship) and attributes mens conformity to outward force and corporal punishments. A faith subject to as many revolutions as the powers that enact it.

Fifthly and lastly, Such persons assume the judgment of the great tribunal unto themselves; for to whomsoever men are imposedly or restrictively subject and accountable in matters of faith, worship and conscience; in them alone must the power of judgment reside: but it is equally true that God shall judge all by Jesus Christ; and that no man is so accountable to his fellow-creatures, as to be imposed upon, restrained, or persecuted for any matter of conscience whatever.

Thus, and in many more particulars, are men accustomed to intrench upon Divine Property, to gratify particular interests in the world; and (at best) through a misguided apprehension to imagine "they do God good service," that where they cannot give faith, they will use force; which kind of sacrifice is nothing less unreasonable than the other is abominable: God will not give his honour to another; and to him only, that searches the heart and tries the reins, it is our duty to ascribe the gifts of understanding and faith, without which none can please God.

B

[The text is taken from William S. Perry, *Historical Collections Relating to the American Colonial Church* (Hartford?, 1871), Vol. II, pp. 343, 366–68, 448–51.]

Letters to the Secretary, Society for the Propagation of the Gospel

Lancaster in Pennsylvania, Novr. 8th, 1762.

REV^d SIR,
* * * We are surrounded by multitudes of Dissenters of every kind who are all brought up in such narrow principles that they can be no friends to the National Church, which notwithstanding the opposition she daily meets with, kind Heaven has hitherto preserved and enlarged; and I make no doubt but thro' the Divine Blessing she will soon advance to the remotest parts of this vast Continent.

Popery has gained considerable ground in Pennsylvania of late years. The professors of that Religion here are chiefly Germans who are constantly supplied with missionarys from the Society of Jesus, as they are pleased to stile themselves. One of that order resides in this place, and had influence enough last Summer to get a very elegant Chapel of hewn Stone erected in this Town. Their behaviour in outward appearance is quiet and

inoffensive but they have been often suspected during this war*
of communicating intelligence to the Enemies of our Religion
and Country.

I know of no Heathens or Infidels among us except a few
Indians that live near the River Susquehanna.

I remain, Revd Sir,

THO^S BARTON.

Lancaster in Pennsylvania, Novr 16th, 1764

REV^d SIR,

* * * This mission then takes in the whole of Lancaster
county (80 miles in length and 26 in breadth), part of Chester
County and part of Berks, so that the circumference of my stated
mission only, is 200 miles. The County of Lancaster contains up-
wards of 40,000 Souls; of this Number not more than 500 can
be reckon'd as belonging to the Church of England; the rest are
German Lutherans, Calvinists, Mennonists, Moravians, New
Born, Dunkars, Presbyterians, Seceders, New Lights, Covenan-
ters, Mountain Men, Brownists, Independents, Papists, Quakers,
Jews, &c. Amidst such a swarm of Sectaries, all indulged and
favored by the Government, it is no wonder that the National
Church should be borne down. At the last Election for the
county to choose Assemblymen, Sheriff, Coroner, Commissioners, Assessors, &c., 5000 Freeholders voted, and yet not a
single member of the Church was elected into any of these
offices. Notwithstanding these and the like discouragements, I
have the satisfaction to assure the Honble Society that my people
have continued to give proofs of that submission and obedience
to civil authority, which it is the glory of the Church of England to inculcate; and whilst faction and party strife have been
rending the province to pieces, they behaved themselves as became peaceable and dutiful subjects, never intermeddling in the
least. Suffer me to add, Sir, that in the murder of the Indians in

* Seven Years' War, or more familiarly, the French and Indian War
(1754–1763).—ED.

this place and the different insurrections occasioned by this inhuman act, not one of them was ever concerned.* Justice demands this testimony from me in their favour; as their conduct
upon this occasion has gained them much credit and honour.
Upon the whole, the Church of England visibly gains ground
throughout the province. The mildness and Excellency of her
Constitution, her moderation and charity, even to her Enemies,
and (I hope I may be indulged to say), the indefatigable labours
of her Missionaries, must at length recommend her to all except those who have an hereditary prejudice and aversion to her.

The German Lutherans have frequently in their coetus's proposed a union with the Church of England; and several of their
clergy, with whom I have conversed are desirous of addressing
his Grace My Lord Bishop of Canterbury, and my Lord Bishop
of London, upon this subject. A large and respectable congregation of Dutch Calvinists in Philadelphia have already drawn up
Constitutions, by which they oblige themselves to conform to the
canons and constitutions of the National Church, and to use her
Liturgy and forms and none else, provided they be approved
of, and received at home; and that My Lord Bishop will grant
ordination to such gentlemen as they shall present to him.

The Germans in general are well affected to the Church of
England, and might easily be brought over to it. A Law oblig-
ing them to give their Children an English Education, which
could not be deemed an abridgement of their liberty (as British
subjects) would soon have this effect.

The Presbyterians are in much disrepute with all the other
Sects and seem to be at a stand. They gain no accessions except
from the Importations of their own Society from the North of
Ireland, and yet what is strange Numbers of their young Men are
daily emancipated by the Colleges of New England and the
Jersey who are Licens'd by their Presbyteries, and sent by scores
into the world in search of a Flock. But they are a people who
are unsteady and much given to change, fond of Novelty, and

* This is a reference to the thoughtless massacre of twenty peaceable
Conestoga Indians in 1763.—ED.

easily led away by every kind of Doctrine. This disposition will ever be a bar to their encrease. The Seceders are making great Havock among them and are proselyting them by thousands to their opinions. These last, however, are a set of Men who under a Monarchial Government I think cannot subsist long. Their interest upon their own principles must undoubtedly destroy itself.

The Church of England then must certainly prevail at last. She has hitherto stood her Ground amidst all the rage and wildness of fanaticism; and whilst Methodists and New Lights have roamed over the Country, "leading captive silly women" and drawing in thousands to adopt their strange and Novel doctrines the Members of this Church (a few in Philadelphia excepted) have "held fast the professions of their faith without wavering," and if deprived, as she is, of any legal estabilshment in her favour, and remote from the Immediate Influence and direction of her lawful Governors the Bishops, she has stood unmoved and gained a respectable footing, what might be expected if these were once to take place?

The Establishment of Episcopacy in America has been long talked of and long expected; and I humbly beg the Hon'ble Society's pardon if I should take the liberty to observe that this could never in any former time be introduced with more success than at present. Many of the principal Quakers wish for it in hopes it might be a check to the growth of Presbyterianism, which they dread, and the Presbyterians, on the other hand would not chuse to murmur at a time when they are obliged to keep fair with the Church whose assistance they want against the Combinations of the Quakers who would willingly crush them. I hope to be indulged if with all humility I should further observe that it is thought the lands lately belonging to the Romish Clergy in Canada, are sufficient to support a Bishop in America, and a number of Missionaries in the new Conquests without adding to the burden of the Mother Country; and that His Majesty if properly applied to would be graciously pleased to appropriate them to this use. These things perhaps have been already mentioned to and considered by the Society. But the Affection which I bear to the Church of England would not suffer me to omit any hint that I thought might be an advantage to her.* * *

I am, Revd Sir, &c.,

THO^s BARTON.

Lancaster in Pennsylvania, December 17, 1770
REV^d AND VERY WORTHY SIR,

With regard to the Churches then under my care I am happy enough to assure the Society that they have suffered no diminution from the ill-natured opposition they have lately met with but have stood firm amidst the wild tho' *popular* systems of religion which extravagant Enthusiasts have propagated around them. The progress of Fanaticism however in some parts of this Province is become very considerable. *A broken officer,* an *English Baker,* a *Dutch Shoemaker,* & a *crazy Planter,* besides a number of strolling Methodists have all in their turns been followed &' admired whilst national religion & common sense have been rejected & forsaken. Nay, some of those fanaticks have had influence enough to get large Meeting houses erected for them. The new dispensation set up by these people contradicts some of the most comfortable doctrines of the Gospel. It discourages its Proselytes from the pursuit of virtuous & moral actions. It teaches them that "the Baptism administered to them by those called *clergy* was no Baptism," in consequence of which numbers have suffered themselves to be rebaptized. Instead of instructing the people to "serve the Lord with *gladness*" & to have "*joy* in the Holy Ghost," these miserable teachers advance a gloomy and dreadful religion which has thrown its followers into dereliction & despair & has made many of them fitter objects for a *Hospital* than a *Church.* They have set up nocturnal Societies, travelled from House to House. Their *Meetings* have often continued till midnight; & it is said some extravagancies have been acted in these Meetings equal to any that we read of among the ancient Bacchanalians.

Boys of 10 and 12 years old have been sent about the country to pray and exhort publickly. In short the raving notions & ridiculous freaks that are every day spread & acted among us under the name of Religion is beyond the power of description. The extreme absurdity however of these dispensations is the only security we have from their becoming dangerous. Such madness & folly cannot possibly last long and tho' they may & undoubtedly will unhinge the rational principles of people for the present; yet when they return to their senses, as I trust they will soon do, they will be more cautious of being led into future delusions by *false profits* and pretended Saints.* * *

And I assure you, Revd Sir, &c.,
THO^s BARTON.

3

SCHISM

OR

ORDER

THE WAVE of religious excitement sweeping over the American colonies in the mid-eighteenth century had palpable and enduring effects on national and ecclesiastical life. In New England where the Great Awakening was concentrated in time and encompassing in its scope, these effects may be most clearly seen.

The transition from medieval to modern comes in differing forms and at varying times. But one mark of it is the collapse of the traditional pattern of parish life. The lines of ecclesiastical authority, the purity of episcopal instruction, the stability of apostolic succession—these and much else besides were shattered in the Great Awakening. Piety more than position and clerical results more than clerical pedigree became the standard for approval and support. When parish walls broke down, the church entered the world in a far riskier and more freewheeling manner. Instability and innovation (and sometimes irrelevance) characterized the churches' life within the nation.

That transition received a powerful shove on March 8, 1740

in Nottingham, Pennsylvania. There Gilbert Tennent preached a sermon whose novelty and bluntness aroused resentment and widespread fear. Tennent (1703–1764), a native of Ireland, was the eldest son of a famous and influential Presbyterian family in the middle colonies. The father, William Tennent (1673–1746), established in 1736 the significant Log College, a progenitor of the College of New Jersey. Gilbert's vigorous activity during the Great Awakening in both the middle colonies and New England entitles him, like his friend George Whitefield, to all the encomiums or opprobrium heaped upon the notorious novelty of itinerant preaching.

In the sermon excerpted below, Tennent challenges the revered notion that parish lines should not be crossed—neither by minister nor by parishioner. On the contrary, this itinerant argues, one must go where the spiritual food is. If a minister is himself spiritually undernourished, it is not likely that he can offer real sustenance. So what is a starving sinner or even saint to do? ". . . if they go a few miles farther than ordinary to enjoy those which they most profit by, who do they wrong?" Traveling those few miles, however, helped move the nation into the modern era.

John Hancock (1702–1744) was pastor of the First Church in Braintree, Massachusetts, when Tennent unleashed his angry words. Of the Harvard class of 1719, this John Hancock was the father of the better-known John, many times governor of the state of Massachusetts. The elder Hancock's death in 1744 cut short a career that held increasing promise. His congregation included some of New England's sturdiest pillars, among them John Adams, whom he baptized in 1735.

In the sermon cited below, John Hancock takes deadly aim at Gilbert Tennent. If Tennent is afraid of a ministry without heart, Hancock is apprehensive about a ministry without brains. If Tennent worries about a moribund spirituality, Hancock is concerned about "prostituting the holy Ministry" by "opening a wide Door of Entrance . . . to every bold Intruder." An able and learned ministry is, argued Hancock, a "Hedge" which protects the Church of God from "Ignorance, Error, Heresy, Superstition, Confusion, and every evil Work. . . ." But such a ministry is also a great preserver of the social order, a useful servant of authority and stability (the sermon was preached in the colony of Connecticut, that land of steady habits), and a mighty foe "of those scandalous separations, wherewith some of our Churches have been lately torn." Properly trained, regularly ordained clergymen are not "Busy-bodies in other Men's Matters, or Bishops in another Man's Diocese."

A

[The text is taken from Gilbert Tennent, *The Danger of an Unconverted Ministry, Considered in a Sermon on Mark 6:34 . . . from the Second Edition Printed at Philadelphia* (Boston: Rogers & Fowle, 1742), pp. 10, 11–12, 13–14, 16–17, 17–18, 19–20.]

The Danger of an Unconverted Ministry

* * * My Brethren, We should mourn over those, that are destitute of faithful Ministers, and sympathize with them. Our Bowels should be moved with the most compassionate Tenderness, over those dear fainting Souls, that are as Sheep having no Shepherd; and that after the Example of our blessed LORD.

Dear Sirs! we should also most earnestly pray for them, that the compassionate Saviour may preserve them, by his mighty Power, thro' Faith unto Salvation; support their sinking Spirits, under the melancholy Uneasiness of a dead Ministry sanctify and sweeten to them the dry Morsels they get under such blind Men, when they have none better to repair to. . . .

And indeed, my Brethren, we should join our Endeavours to our Prayers. The most likely Method to stock the Church with a faithful Ministry, in the present Situation of Things, the publick Academies being so much corrupted and abused generally, is,

To encourage private Schools, or Seminaries of Learning, which are under the Care of skilful and experienced Christians; in which those only should be admitted, whoupon strict Examination, have in the Judgment of a reasonable Charity, the plain Evidences of experimental Religion. Pious and experienced Youths, who have a good natural Capacity, and great Desires after the Ministerial Work, from good Motives, might be sought for, and found up and down in the Country, and put to Private Schools of the Prophets; especially in such Places, where the Publick ones are not. This Method, in my Opinion, has a noble Tendency, to build up the Church of God. And those who have any Love to Christ, or Desire after the Coming of his Kingdom, should be ready, according to their Ability, to give somewhat, from time to time, for the Support of such poor Youths, who have nothing of their own. And truly, Brethren, this Charity to the Souls of Men, is the most noble kind of Charity—O! if the Love of God be in you, it will constrain you to do something, to promote so noble and necessary a Work. It looks Hypocrite-like to go no further, when other Things are required, than cheap Prayer. Don't think it much, if the Pharisees should be offended at such a Proposal; these subtle selfish Hypocrites are wont to be scar'd about their Credit, and their Kingdom; and truly they are both little worth, for all the Bustle they make about them. If they could help it, they wo'dn't let one faithful Man come into the Ministry; and therefore their Opposition is an encouraging Sign. Let all the Followers of the Lamb stand up and act for GOD against all Opposers: Who is upon GOD's Side? who?

THE IMPROVEMENT of this Subject remains. And

1. If it be so, That the Case of those, who have no other, or no better than Pharisee-Teachers, is to be pitied: Then what a Scrole & Scene of Mourning, and Lamentation, and Wo, is opened! because of the Swarms of Locusts, the Crowds of Pharisees, that have as covetously as cruelly, crept into the Ministry, in this adulterous Generation! who as nearly resemble the Character given of the old Pharisees, in the Doctrinal Part of this Discourse, as one Crow's Egg does another. It is true

some of the modern Pharisees have learned to prate a little more
orthodoxly about the New Birth, than their Predecessor Nico-
demus, who are, in the mean Time, as great Strangers to the
feeling Experience of it, as he. They are blind who see not this
to be the Case of the Body of the Clergy, of this Generation.
And O! that our Heads were Waters, and our Eyes a Fountain
of Tears, that we could Day and Night lament, with the utmost
Bitterness, the doleful Case of the poor Church of God, upon
this account.

2. From what has been said, we may learn, That such who
are contented under a dead Ministry, have not in them the
Temper of that Saviour they profess. It's an awful Sign, that
they are as blind as Moles, and as dead as Stones, without any
spiritual Taste and Relish. And alas! isn't this the Case of Multitudes? If they can get one, that has the Name of a Minister, with
a Band, and a black Coat or Gown to carry on a Sabbathdays
among them, although never so coldly, and insuccessfully; if he
is free from gross Crimes in Practice, and takes good Care to
keep at a due Distance from their Consciences, and is never troubled about his Insuccessfulness; O! think the poor Fools, that is
a fine Man indeed; our Minister is a prudent charitable man, he
is not always harping upon Terror, and sounding Damnation in
our Ears, like some rash-headed Preachers, who by their un-
charitable Methods, are ready to put poor People out of their
Wits, or to run them into Despair; O! how terrible a Thing is
that Dispair! Ay, our Minister, honest Man, gives us good Caution against it. Poor silly Souls consider seriously these Passages,
of the Prophet, Jeremiah 5. 30, 31.

3. We may learn, the Mercy and Duty of those that enjoy a
faithful Ministry. Let such glorify GOD, for so distinguishing a
Privilege, and labour to walk worthy of it, to all Well-pleasuring;
left for their Abuse thereof, they be exposed to a greater
Damnation.

4. If the Ministry of natural Men be as it has been represented; Then it is both lawful and expedient to go from them
to hear Godly Persons; yea, it's so far from being sinful to do

this, that one who lives under a pious Minister of lesser Gifts, after having honestly endeavour'd to get Benefit by his Ministry, and yet gets little or none, but doth find real Benefit and more Benefit elsewhere; I say, he may lawfully go, and that frequently, where he gets most Good to his precious Soul, after regular Application to the Pastor where he lives, for his Consent, and proposing the Reasons thereof; when this is done in the Spirit of Love and Meekness, without Contempt of any, as also without rash Anger or vain Curiosity. * * *

It is also an unquestionable Truth, that ordinarily GOD blesses most the best Gifts, for the Hearers Edification, as by the best Food he gives the best Nourishment. Otherwise the best Gifts would not be desirable, and GOD Almighty in the ordinary Course of his Providence, by not acting according to the Nature of Things, would be carrying on a Series of unnecessary Miracles; which to suppose, is unreasonable. The following Places of holy Scripture, confirm what hath been last observed. I Cor. 14. 12. I Tim. 4. 14, 15, 16. 2 Tim. I. 6 & Acts II. 24.

If God's People have a Right to the Gifts of all God's Ministers, pray, why mayn't they use them, as they have Opportunity? And if they should go a few Miles farther than ordinary, to enjoy those, which they profit most by; who do they wrong? Now, our LORD does inform his People, I Cor. 3. 22. That whether Paul, or Apollos, or Cephas; all was theirs.

But the Example of our Dear Redeemer, will give farther Light in this Argument. Tho' many of the Hearers, not only of the Pharisees, but of John the Baptist, came to hear our Saviour, and that not only upon Week-days, but upon Sabbathdays, and that in great Numbers, and from very distant Places; yet he reproved them not: And did not our Lord love the Apostle John more than the rest, and took him with him, before others, with Peter and James, to Mount Tabor, and Gethsemany? Matt. 17. and Chap. 26.

To bind Men to a particular Minister, against their Judgment and Inclinations, when they are more edified elsewhere, is carnal with a Witness; a cruel Oppression of tender Consciences, a com-

pelling of Men to Sin: For he that doubts, is damn'd if he eat;
and whatsoever is not of Faith, is Sin. * * *

Undoubtedly it is a great Duty, to avoid giving just Cause of
Offence to any; and it is also highly necessary, that pious Souls
should maintain Union and Harmony among themselves; notwithstanding of their different Opinions in lesser Things. And
no doubt this is the Drift of the many Exhortations which we
have to Peace and Unity in Scripture.

Surely, it cannot be reasonably suppos'd, that we are exhorted,
to a Unity in any Thing that is wicked, or inconsistent with the
Good, or greater Good of our poor Souls: For that would be like
the Unity of the Devils, a Legion of which dwelt peaceably in
one Man: Or like the Unity of Ahab's false Prophets; all these
four Hundred Daubers were very peaceable and much united,
and all harped on the pleasing String: Ay, they were moderate
Men, and had the Majority on their Side. * * *

Again it may be objected, That the aforesaid Practice tends to
grieve our Parish-Minister, and to break Congregations in Pieces.

I answer, If our Parish-Minister be grieved at our greater
Good, or prefers his Credit before it; then he has good Cause to
grieve over his own Rottenness, and Hypocrisie. And as for
Breaking of Congregations to Pieces, upon the Account of People's Going from Place to Place, to hear the Word, with a View
to get greater Good; that spiritual Blindness and Death, that so
generally prevails, will put this out of Danger. It is but a very
few, that have got any spiritual Relish; the most will venture
their Souls with any Formalist, and be well satisfied with the
sapless Discourses of such dead Drones.

Well, doesn't the Apostle assert, That Paul and Apollos are
nothing? Yes, it is true, they & all others are nothing as Efficient
Causes; they could not change Men's Hearts. But were they
nothing as Instruments? The Objection insinuates one of these
two Things, either that there is no Difference in Means, as to
their Suitableness; or that there is no Reason to expect a greater
Blessing upon the most suitable Means: Both which are equally
absurd, and before confuted.

I would conclude my present Meditations upon this Subject, by Exhorting.

All those who enjoy a faithful Ministry, to a speedy and sincere Improvement of so rare and valuable a Privilege; lest by, their foolish Ingratitude the Righteous GOD be provok'd, to remove the Means they enjoy, or his Blessing from them, and so at last to expose them in another State to Enduring and greater Miseries. For surely, these Sins which are committed against greater Light and Mercy, are more presumptuous, ungrateful, and inexcusable; there is in them a greater Contempt of GOD's Authority, and Slight of his Mercy; those Evils do awfully violate the Conscience, and declare a Love to Sin as Sin; such Transgressors do rush upon the Bosses of GOD's Buckler, they court Destruction without a Covering, and embrace their own Ruin with open Arms. And therefore according to the Nature of Justice, which proportions Sinners Pains, according to the Number and Heinousness of their Crimes, and the Declaration of Divine Truth, you must expect an enflamed Damnation: Surely, it shall be more tolerable for Sodom and Gomorrah, in the Day of the LORD, than for you, except ye repent.

And let gracious Souls be exhorted, to express the most tender Pity over such as have none but Pharisee-Teachers; and that in the Manner before described: To which let the Example of our LORD in the Text before us, be an inducing and effectual Incitement; as well as the gracious and immense Rewards, which follow upon so generous and noble a Charity, in this and the next State.

And let those who live under the Ministry of dead Men, whether they have got the Form of Religion or not, repair to the Living, where they may be edified. . . .

And O! that vacant Congregations would take due care in the Choice of their Ministers! Here indeed they should hasten slowly. The Church of Ephesus is commended, for Trying them which said they were Apostles, and were not; and for finding them Liars. Hypocrites are against all Knowing of others, and Judging, in order to hide their own Filthiness; like Thieves they flee

a Search, because of the stolen Goods. But the more they endeavour to hide, the more they expose their Shame. Does not
the spiritual Man judge all Things? Tho' he cannot know the
States of subtil Hypocrites infallibly; yet may he not give a near
Guess, who are the Sons of Sceva, by their Manner of Praying,
Preaching, and Living? Many Pharisee-Teachers have got a long
fine String of Prayer by Heart, so that they are never at a Loss
about it; their Prayers and Preachings are generally of a Length,
and both as dead as a Stone, and without all Savour. I beseech
you, my dear Bretheren, to consider, That there is no Probability of your getting Good, by the Ministry of Pharisees. For they
are no Shepherds (no faithful ones) in Christ's Account. They
are as good as none, nay, worse than none, upon some Accounts.
For take them first and last, and they generally do more Hurt
than Good. They strive to keep better out of the Places where
they live; nay, when the Life of Piety comes near their Quarters,
they rise up in Arms against it, consult, contrive and combine
in their Conclaves against it, as a common Enemy, that discovers and condemns their Craft and Hypocrisie. And with what
Art, Rhetorick, and Appearances of Piety, will they varnish their
Opposition of Christ's Kingdom? As the Magicians imitated the
Works of Moses, so do false Apostles, and deceitful Workers,
the Apostles of Christ.

I shall conclude this Discourse with the Words of the Apostle
Paul, 2 Cor. 11. 14. 15.

And no Marvel; for Satan himself is transformed into an
Angel of Light: Therefore it is no great Thing if his Ministers
also be transformed as the Ministers of Righteousness; whose
End shall be according to their Works.

B

[The text is taken from John Hancock, *The Danger of an Unqual-ified Ministry, Represented in a Sermon* . . . (on Malachi 2:7, Romans 11:13) (Boston: Rogers & Fowle, 1743), Preface, pp. 18–24, 27–29.]

The Danger of an Unqualified Ministry

N. B. Though there has been a great Cry of late, That the Church is in Danger from an unconverted Ministry; Particularly in an outrageous Sermon of Mr. Gilbert Tennent upon the Danger of an unconverted Ministry, preached at Nottingham, printed and re-printed at Philadelphia and Boston, and indus-triously spread through many Parts of America, to the Hindrance of the Gospel;—Nothing, as the Author of the following Dis-course remembers, has been published, in this Time, upon the Danger of an unqualified Ministry which threatens the Destruc-tion of pure and undefiled Religion in these Churches: which encourages him to hope the present Discourse may be both seasonable and useful at this Day, though he wishes the Argu-ment had been handled by a more skilful and masterly Pen.

* * * The Apostles of our Lord have been very careful to give the Churches of Christ all the necessary Qualifications of good Ministers of Jesus Christ, that they may be furnished at all Times with able and faithful Pastors, and so be kept pure from a cor-rupt and bad Ministry.

Indeed, whosoever has a just Apprehension of the Greatness, Difficulty and Importance of the evangelical Ministry, needeth not Arguments to convince him of the Necessity of encouraging and supporting learned and godly Pastors in the Churches. It is therefore owing to Ignorance, Pride, and Want of Consideration and Judgment, that any think and speak contrariwise, That Men of mean Abilities and Attainments in Knowledge, are able to preach the unsearchable Riches of Christ, open the great Mysteries of Godliness, and defend the Gospel.

Alas! It requires no small Compass of Reason and Learning to be able to preach and defend the Gospel; for Ministers are set to defend, as well as preach the everlasting Gospel: And if Need be, they must contend earnestly for the Faith, which was once delivered to the Saints. The Servant of the Lord must also be patient, in Meekness instructing those that oppose themselves. . . .

For GOD's Sake, Brethren, what would have become of the Christian Religion long ago, had it not been for the wise and learned Defenders of it against its ablest Adversaries? Such as the Apostle Paul, Origen, Justin Martyr, and others among the Fathers; and many since the Time of the Reformation of the Church from Popery.

God has raised up able Advocates and Apologists to espouse and defend his own Cause from Age to Age, who have been valiant for the Truth, and quitted themselves like Men in the Cause of God, so that Truth has not fallen in the Streets, but still prevails in the Earth.

And indeed the Revival of Learning, since the glorious Reformation, has been a great Elucidation and Establishment of the Truths of our holy Religion: So that the Enemies of good Literature are Enemies to the true Interest of Christianity, whether they know it or not. . . .

Were the Gospel-Treasure put into broken Vessels, it would soon run out and perish. If the Teaching and Government of the Church were committed to unskilful and unfaithful Guides, Ignorance would soon be the Mother of Devotion; and Heresy and Confusion, the Doctrine and Discipline of the Christian Church. For to this Purpose testifieth the Apostle Peter, by the Spirit of Prophecy, There shall be false Teachers among you, who privily shall bring in damnable Heresies,—and many shall follow their pernicious Ways, by Reason of whom the Way of Truth shall be Evil spoken of. And through Coveteousness shall they with feigned Words, make Merchandize of you.—

How is it possible for a Novice to magnify his Office, and recommend Religion to the Esteem and Practice of Men? He that teacheth Man Knowledge, should not he know? Because the Preacher was wise, he still taught the People Knowledge, and sought to find out acceptable Words. But how shameful is it, for weak, raw, illiterate Men to exalt themselves to the Priesthood, and set up for Teachers in the Church? who have Need that one teach them, which be the first Principles of the Oracles of God? And have Need of Milk, and should as new-born Babes desire the sincere Milk of the Word, that they may grow thereby?

Moreover, the setting up and sending forth such Teachers in the Church of Christ, is the great Reproach to Christianity, and the direct Way to promote the Contempt of the Clergy, than which a greater Injury can scarce be offered to the true Interest of Religion.

Thus I have finished the doctrinal Part of my Subject, and shall now close it with several useful Reflections.—

First, We may learn, from what has been offered upon this Argument, the great Care that the glorious Head of the Church, has taken for its Instruction and Support.

For to this End, Christ was pleased to raise up a Succession of inspired Prophets and Teachers in the Jewish Church, and at sundry Times, and in divers Manners, spake unto the Fathers by them. In the Fulness of Time, he manifested himself to Israel, full of Grace and Truth, as the Lord who teacheth us to Profit, as the great Teacher of the Church, who spake as never Man spake. When he had finished the Work of GOD, and ascended up on High, he gave Gifts unto Men, Some Apostles, and some Prophets, and some Evangelists, and some Pastors and Teachers, for the perfecting of the Saints, for the Work of the Ministry, for the edifying of the Body of Christ.

Moreover, the Highest himself has established the Security and Safety of the Church in Opposition to the confederated Powers of Earth and Hell, in that glorious Promise, That the Gates of Hell shall not prevail against it. Its Defence is of GOD. GOD is in the midst of her, therefore the burning Bush is not consumed. We have a strong City, Salvation will GOD appoint for Walls and Bulwarks.

How beautiful and safe is the Church in the Favour and Protection of the Almighty, under all the Imperfection that cleaves to his Ministers and Members in this militant State? This is our Hope, and this our Confidence, that God will help her, and that right early.

Secondly, This Doctrine gives a Rule of Conduct to the Ministers of Christ in admitting Persons into the sacred Ministry; that they proceed with great Care and Caution in such a weighty Affair, as they would approve themselves faithful to Christ and his Interest. They are forbid to put a Novice into the evangelical Ministry. Lay Hands suddenly on no Man.

For any of the Ministers of Christ then, to give their Credentials to unworthy Men, is to act directly in the Face of Scripture Canons, and betray the Cause of Christ. It is really to expose their own Souls and the Souls of all they are concerned with to Condemnation, and doing infinite Mischief to the true Interest of Religion.

I would use here great Plainness of Speech, for I apprehend the case requires it, and freely say, that I can't see how Ministers can answer to GOD and their own Consciences, their admitting raw, indiscreit [sic], rash, illiterate and blind Novices into their Pulpits, and commending them to these Churches, as useful Instruments of carrying on the Work of GOD, as hath been the Manner of some more lately.

The Overseers of the Flocks of Christ, are indispensably obliged, by his holy Word, to commit this sacred Treasure to faithful Men who shall be able to teach others also, and not to cast these holy Things to the Dogs of the Flock.

It is to be feared, that there has been too much Indifference and Coldness among the Clergy of New England, as well as elsewhere, in this important Article, of examining and introducing Candidates into the Ministry; especially, in the Years last past, has the sacred Ministry been laid too common, as if it were not a sacred Enclosure, and any bold Intruder might take this Honour to himself, without due qualifications, or a regular Call; which in the Nature of Things bodes very Ill to the Church of Christ: Whereas the Scripture faith, No Man taketh this Honour unto himself, but he that is called of God, as was Aaron.

Were the Ministry of the Gospel committed to ignorant, conceited Novices, 'tis not unlikely that, within two seven Years, the Church would be reduced to a State of Heathenism, thick Darkness would cover the Earth, and gross Darkness the People.

And the present unbounded License of publick Teaching, I apprehend to be a leading Step to the scandalous Disorders and Confusions of these Times: And its high Time to correct and reform this shameful Abuse of the ministerial Authority.

But to the praise of the Government of this Colony [Connecticut], be it spoken, that they have expressed an examplary Care in this Matter of introducing Candidates into the holy Ministry, above all the Provinces in New-England: And it is doubtless a great Part of the Beauty and Strength of your good Constitution. We rejoice, beholding your Order, and the Stedfastness of your Faith in Christ. Upon this very Thing depends the Safety and Prosperity of these Churches.

Suffer me then, my reverend Fathers and Brethren, (though most unworthy) to press it upon you to shew all good Fidelity in this important Affair. For this Power of examining and putting Men into the Ministry, is committed to you to exercise for the Good of the Church. Oh let it not be in vain, but approve yourselves faithful to Christ, and the Souls of Men, that you may both save your own Souls, and be happily instrumental, in this Way, of promoting the common Salvation.

Thirdly, This Doctrine also admonisheth the Churches of Christ, to take Heed of committing their Souls to the Care of unskilful Novices. For hereby the Souls of Men are exposed to eternal Ruin. Who then in his Wits would be careless and unconcerned in the Choice of a Guide and Pastor to his Soul? There is surely no Affair in the whole Circle of Life that requires more serious Care and assiduous Prayer, than this of choosing able, faithful, skilful Guides for our Souls. And as Christ has given these Churches Power of choosing their own Pastors, so let them be exhorted to stand fast in the Liberty wherewith he hath made them free, and not abuse it in a criminal Manner.

Let the Churches be advised to act with prudent Care and Caution in the Exercise of this Power. Be not fond of Novelties, but covet earnestly the best Gifts. Ask Counsel of God, and take the best Advice of the faithful Ministers of Christ; who are commonly most able and ready to serve your best Interest. Oh beware of heaping to yourselves Teachers, and leaning to your own Understanding. For the Time will come, saith the Apostle, when they will not endure sound Doctrine, but after their own Lusts shall they heap to themselves Teachers, having itching Ears; and they shall turn away their Ears from the Truth, and shall be turned unto Fables.

Verily, 'tis to be feared, we are fallen into this Time, now so many of unstable Minds are ready to forsake their own faithful and approved Pastors, and the assembling themselves together, to follow the sounding brass of ignorant, conceited Novices. Verily, verily I say unto you, saith our Savior, the good Shepherd, he that entereth not in by the Door into the Sheepfold, but climbeth up some other Way, the same is a Thief, and a Robber. But he that entereth in by the Door, is the Shepherd of the Sheep. To him the Porter openeth, and the Sheep hear his Voice.

Fourthly, This Doctrine ministers Reproof to every NOVICE that is thrusting himself into the Ministry. For do but consider the infinite Danger of so doing; Lest being lifted up with Pride, he fall into the Condemnation of the Devil. Such know not what they ask and seek, whilst they are striving for the Mastery, to enter into the sacred Ministry. My Brethren, be not many Masters, don't be too forward and hasty, in setting up for Teachers, lest ye receive the greater Condemnation.

Yet strange it is, that so many, in these Days, apprehend themselves well qualified for the ministerial Office without Learning, or Study, or any Qualification for this good Work; except Ignorance, and Confidence may be accounted such. It is to be suspected, that Pride and Self-Conceit is at the Bottom of such a stupid and wild Conduct. What other Cause but Pride can be assigned for the very scandalous Intrusions of illiterate Lay-Men, and raw Novices into the Labours of GOD's faithful Ministers, in one Place and another, to the great Vexation and Disturbance of the Churches of Christ in this Land? Only by Pride cometh Contention. . . .

Fifthly, This Doctrine may also serve to admonish all young unexperienced Converts to take Heed to themselves, watch and be sober; lest being lifted up with Pride, they come into Condemnation. GOD resisteth the Proud, but he giveth Grace unto the Humble. Be cloathed with Humility. Learn of Christ who was meek & lowly in Heart, & has laid Humility in the Foundation of his heavenly Doctrine. Blessed are the poor in Spirit, for theirs is the Kingdom of Heaven. I say to every Man that is among you, not to think of himself more highly than he ought to think, but to think soberly. This will be the best Antidote against many Irregularities and Scandals that prevail in the present Times, and even among many of those, who have been the Subjects of the late religious Commotion in the Land. Particularly, a Spirit of rash, censoring Judging which is gone forth, and rages in the Country? than which nothing can be more contrary to the Spirit of Christ and his Gospel.

It is a just Observation of one [Charles Chauncy] who has Understanding in the Times; says he, "I shall not exceed the literal Truth, when I say, that there never was a Time; since the Settlement of New-England, wherein there were so much bitter and rash Judging: And what may be worth a Note, the Places where this Appearance has been most remarkable, have commonly been most filled with Uncharitableness in all the Expressions of it.

"It would be endless to reckon up the monstrous Sayings which many who call themselves, the Converts of the present Times, have uttered; especially against some of the most valuable Ministers in the Country, out of a Spirit of mere Jealousy."

If these Persons are Christians indeed, then there may be Christianity without Charity, contrary to the Apostle's express

Declaration, If I have no Charity I am nothing. If any Man among you seem to be religious, and bridleth not his Tongue—this Man's Religion is vain. If such Persons have performed the Commandment of the Lord, what meaneth then this Bleating of the Sheep in our Ears, and the lowing of the Oxen which we hear? So much Clamour and evil Speaking among high Professors?

Nay, my Brethren, this is not a vain and trivial Matter, it ought not to be passed over with such a gentle Rebuke as the Manner of some is, in the cold Language of Eli to his wicked Sons, Why do ye such Things? Nay, my Sons, for it is no good Report that I hear. But it was a very bad one, and such an Antichristian Spirit of rash Judging ought to be rebuked sharply. For the great Founder of our holy Religion has expressly said, Judge not.

And now from whence comes such a Spirit of rash Judging? Cometh it not hence, even of this Lust of Pride? And such as indulge it are in Danger of falling into the Condemnation of the Devil.

There has been, of late, much Talk about Religion, and a remarkable Work of GOD in the Country; but it must be remembered, that the Kingdom of GOD is not in Word but in Power: And, for my own Part, I have been waiting to see the Work prove it self in the Power of Godliness, and the genuine Fruits of the Spirit of GOD, in all Goodness, Righteousness and Truth.

But indeed the unwearied Pains taken by the Friends of the late religious Commotion among us, to perswade People, that GOD has remarkably revived his Work in the Land, is so far from being a Confirmation of it, that, in my Opinion, 'tis more apt to bring a Suspicion upon it.

If there be such a happy Revival of GOD's Work, as some contend earnestly for, what Need of calling of Assemblies, and so much Preaching and Writing to possess the Minds of People with the Belief of it? For the Work of GOD will prove itself, by producing a visible and glorious Reformation among the happy Subjects of it, which the Lord hasten in his Time.

Sixthly, Let the Ministers of Christ consider what Reason they have to be humbled for the Remainder of Pride in them.

Though the Work of the Ministry be attended with many humbling Circumstances and pressing Difficulties, particularly at this Time; yet have our Hearts, dear Brethren, been truly humbled to this Day? Are we clothed with Humility down to the Foot? Has not Pride, that Root of Bitterness, been springing and operating in us to our Shame? Is not Knowledge apt to puff us up, and make us Superstitious and Imperious? Ready to lord it over GOD's Heritage, and make us Busy-bodies in other Men's Matters, or Bishops in another Man's Diocess [*sic*]?

Doth not the empty Applause of Men, serve to exalt us above Measure, and feed the Pride and Vanity of our Minds.

Are we not too apt to spend our precious Time in vain Disputes and Wranglings, instead of studying to profit the Souls of our People both in Word and Doctrine.

Are we patient and penitent when we hear the Defaming of many? Oh let us examine ourselves, and labour to keep under and subdue this dangerous Lust, Lest that by any Means when we have preached to others, we ourselves should be castaways. * * *

4

EPISCOPACY

OR

LIBERTY

IN THE 1760's the issue seemed that simple: episcopacy or liberty. Under the umbrella of the former term gathered such freighted notions as English imperialism and ecclesiastical tyranny. Specifically, "episcopacy" raised the question whether England's church in America should be permitted bishops residing in America. That seemed a modest enough desire: an episcopal church by definition is a church dependent on bishops, dependent on them for discipline, for government, for doctrine, indeed for survival itself through ordination. How could tolerant, fair-minded Americans object?

Vigorously, and with effect. The objectors argued that full liberty for Anglicans imperiled the full liberty of other Americans. For England's bishops were never mere spiritual leaders. They wielded vast political power in Parliament and out; they asserted the privileges of an established (i.e., state-supported) church in a manner that compromised the religious freedoms of all others; they made no nice distinctions between civil and ecclesiastical liberties, thereby threatening both. Such objections were weighty at any time and in any place, but in the American colonies in the 1760's and 1770's they took on tremendous import. So much so that the American Revolution must be seen—in no small part—as a religious war (see Carl Bridenbaugh, *Mitre & Sceptre* [New York: Oxford University Press, 1962]).

Many combatants joined the battle between episcopacy and liberty, and words flew with fury: tracts, newspapers, broadsides, sermons, petitions, and plots sped back and forth across the Atlantic. Anglicans were of course the advocates on one side, though not all Anglicans—particularly in the southern colonies—were eager to have a resident bishop. On the other side, Congregationalists in New England and Presbyterians in the middle colonies first sounded the alarm regarding "a formal design to carry on a spiritual siege of our churches." Each side accused the other of tiresome repetition of its arguments—and each was right. But the issue was not merely academic nor was it merely ecclesiastical: it concerned, said a newly formed Society of Dissenters in New York in 1769, "civil and religious liberty [which] is justly esteemed amongst the greatest of human blessings. . . . No one duely sensible of its inestimable value, but will acknowledge it our indispensable duty by every lawful means to preserve it to ourselves and transmit it to posterity."*

Thomas Bradbury Chandler (1726–1790), Yale 1745, gave major impetus to that war of words soon to become a war of blood. Ordained as an Anglican priest in 1751—in England, of course—Chandler took up parish duties in Elizabethtown, New Jersey. His lengthy *Appeal,* extracted below, appeared in 1767, sparking public controversy in pulpit, press, and colonial assembly. It also suggested that Chandler's sympathies would more likely be with the empire than with the colonies should

* *New York Gazette and the Weekly Mercury,* July 24, 1769. See the bitter newspaper battle between the "American Whig" (William Livingston) and "Timothy Tickle, Esq." (Thomas Chandler, Charles Inglis, and Samuel Seabury), the latter constituting "A Whip for an American Whig": *New York Gazette or Weekly Post-Boy,* beginning March 14, 1768; *New York Gazette and the Weekly Mercury,* beginning April 4, 1768.

a break occur. Such was the case. As Chandler became more outspokenly Tory, New Jersey became more relentlessly inhospitable. In 1775 he left for England, returning to New Jersey two years after the conclusion of the Revolution.

Narrowly conceived, Chandler's *Appeal* was "To the Most Reverend Father in God, Thomas, Lord Archbishop of Canterbury," to whom it is specifically addressed. But as the title makes perfectly clear, Chandler had a far broader audience in mind. The good cleric hoped to reach men not yet inflamed by prejudicial passions—to reach Americans willing to respond to the evident "Reasonableness of the Cause"; to reach Englishmen capable of seeing "Episcopacy as the surest Friend of Monarchy."

William Livingston (1723–1790) was willing to respond. Also of Yale, 1741, and an almost exact contemporary of Chandler's, Livingston found reasonableness to lie in a quite different direction. A Presbyterian lawyer and part-time newspaperman, he was the *bête noire* of Anglican interests. Whether the issue was the founding of King's College (later Columbia University), or sending for English bishops, or the weakening of colonial prerogatives, Livingston was ready to speak or write or obstruct. His service to the American cause was extensive: in the First and Second Continental Congresses, in the Constitutional Convention, even briefly in the militia. Nowhere, however, does his courageous leadership appear more fully than in the letter extracted below.

He replied directly to Chandler in the columns of the *New York Gazette and Weekly Mercury,* and Chandler with others responded to him. But when the far away Bishop of Landaff presumed to tell Americans what was best for them, Livingston carried the argument across the ocean. The bishop (and that he *was* a bishop did not help) based most of his remarks on information supplied by Chandler and other Anglican clergy residing in America. Thus, Livingston's target is both the pliable citizenry of the middle colonies and the misinformed citizenry of Britain. If these were his targets, his concern was "the sake of truth, and the cause of religion."

A

[The text is taken from Thomas Bradbury Chandler, *An Appeal to the Public, in Behalf of the Church of England in America . . .* (New York: James Parker, 1767), pp. i–ii, 1–2, 107–17.]

An Appeal to the Public

The Arguments for sending Bishops of the Church of England to America, are so strong and convincing, that an Appeal may be made to the World for the Reasonableness of sending them. The general Plan which has been long settled for the Regulation of their Authority when sent, is so well calculated to secure the religious Privileges of every Denomination of Christians, that nothing more than a proper Explanation can be needful, to recommend it to the Approbation of every candid and unprejudiced Person. For Want of this, many are still averse to an American Episcopate, and some are industriously employed in misrepresenting the Matter, and in propagating their Prejudices and Objections against it. It is therefore the general Opinion here, that it is at length become necessary, to explain this Plan, and thereby, as the most effectual Method, to remove these Prejudices and Objections.* * *

That Application has been lately made to our Superiors, by the Clergy of several of the Colonies, requesting one or more Bishops to be sent to America, is a Matter now generally known, and was never intended to be kept as a Secret. As there is great Reason to hope, both from a Review of the Arguments that were transmitted on the Occasion, and from the favourable Disposition of many in Authority, that this Request in due Time will be granted; it has been thought proper, in a public Manner, to inform all who may imagine themselves to be any Ways concerned in the Event of our Application, candidly and explicitly, for what Reasons, and with what Views, an American Episcopate is so earnestly desired by the Clergy, and the other Friends and Members of the Church.

Some Persons are said to have been alarmed by this Conduct of the Clergy; but when the Case shall be duly explained and understood, it is not apprehended that any Uneasiness will remain, or that any Opposition can be formed against the Execution of a Plan, so reasonable in itself, so necessary to the Church here, and so universally harmless to others of every Denomination. As no Invasion of the civil or religious Privileges of any, whether Churchmen or Dissenters, is thereby intended, it is hoped that every Objection, or even Doubt or Suspicion of that Nature, will, by this Method, be intirely obviated. But should any Objections continue which shall be thought to deserve Notice, the Objectors are invited to propose them in such a Manner, that they may be fairly and candidly debated, before the Tribunal of the Publick; and if none shall be offered, it will be taken for granted that all Parties acquiesce and are satisfied.* * *

. . . . As Ignorance is ever suspicious, it may farther be asked, Shall we not be taxed in this Country for the Support of Bishops, if any shall be appointed? I answer, Not at all. But should a general Tax be laid upon the Country, and thereby a Sum be raised sufficient for the Purpose: and even supposing we should have three Bishops on the Continent, which are the most that have been mentioned; yet I believe such a Tax would not amount to more than Four Pence in One Hundred Pounds. And this would be no mighty Hardship upon the Country. He that could think much of giving the Six Thousandth Part of his Income to any Use, which the Legislature of his Country should assign, deserves not to be considered in the Light of a good Subject, or Member of Society.

But no such Tax is intended, nor, I trust, will be wanted. It has been proposed from the very beginning, that the American Bishops should be supported without any Expence to this Country. A Fund accordingly has been established, for this particular Purpose, for more than half a Century past, under the Influence and Direction of the Society for the Propagation of the Gospel; and many worthy Persons have contributed generously and largely to the Increase of it. . . . If this Stock is not sufficient for the Support of a proper Episcopate in America, I imagine the Difficulty in making it sufficient, will not be great. For, as many have given liberally on the remote Prospect of its being needed, it is not to be doubted but Benefactors will be raised up, when Assistance shall be called for by a present Necessity.

Another Objection has been made by some Persons, to the following Purport; That if Bishops are once settled in America, although in the Manner we now propose, there will probably be an Augmentation of their Power, as soon as Circumstances will admit of it: and what is easy and inoffensive in its Beginning, may become burthensome and oppressive in its End. But at this Rate there can be no End of objecting. For if every possible ill Effect of a Thing, although confessedly proper in itself and harmless in its natural Tendency, may be made an Argument against it, there is nothing that can escape. Arguments of this Sort may be as fairly and properly alleged—against a religious Toleration, which is now generally esteemed by Protestants, to be a natural Right of Men, and a very important one of Christians—against admitting those who dissent from the national Religion to any Degree of civil or military Power, to which, indeed, they have no natural Right—against allowing the common People the Use of the Holy Scriptures, or the Liberty of examining any Points of Religion or Government—against suffering any to receive a learned Education, &c. for none can tell what ill Consequences and Abuses may follow, in some future Period, from these Concessions and Indulgences. The Truth is, Men are not to be terrified or influenced by Fears of such Consequences as are barely possible; but to consider what is reasonable and proper in itself, and what Effects will probably and naturally follow.

That an American Episcopate is reasonable and proper in itself, and that such an Episcopate as is now proposed has a natural Tendency to produce no ill Consequences, has, I trust, been sufficiently proved. There is not the least Prospect at present, that Bishops in this Country will acquire any Influence or Power, but what shall arise from a general Opinion of their Abilities and Integrity, and a Conviction of their Usefulness; and of this, no Persons need dread the Consequences. But should the Government see fit hereafter to invest them with some Degree of civil Power worthy of their Acceptance, which it is impossible to say they will not, although there is no Appearance that they ever will; yet as no new Powers will be created in Favour of Bishops, it is inconceivable that any would thereby be injured. All that the Happiness and Safety of the Public require, is, that the legislative and executive Power be placed in the Hands of such Persons, as are possessed of the greatest Abilities, Integrity and Prudence: and it is hoped that our Bishops will always be thought to deserve this Character.

To explain in what Manner civil Power, if vested in American Bishops, would be most likely to operate, I beg Leave to put the following plain and familiar Case. Let us suppose a Clergyman in this Country, of any Denomination, made a Justice of the Peace, or a Judge of the Quorum: Would the Persons who are immediately concerned in his Proceedings, be otherwise affected, than if he was a meer Layman? It cannot be pretended. Whether it would be proper to give such a Commission to any of the Clergy, is another Point. In most Parts of this Country there can now be no Occasion for it, and where it is not evidently necessary for the Good of the Public, I know that some of the Clergy would refuse it, and I believe there are but very few that would desire it. If then it could be of no great Consequence to the Public or to Individuals, whether a Justice of the Peace be a Clergyman or a Layman, supposing their Abilities and personal Characters to be equal; so, if Bishops should be invested with a proportionable Degree of civil Authority, neither would there be any great Reasons for Complaint. But after all, nothing of this Kind is at present foreseen or intended; and it is absolutely determined that no Powers shall be given them, that can interfere with the civil or religious Rights of any.

But there is no Occasion for dwelling on Particulars of this Nature. The real and only Plan on which it is agreed to settle

Bishops in America, when his Majesty shall see fit to appoint them, has been fairly stated and explained in the preceding Pages. This Plan is now proposed to the Public, to see whether any reasonable Objections can be offered against it. But whatever may be objected against any different Plan, is not to the Purpose. The Friends of the Church are desirous to know, what can be said or suggested against an American Episcopate, in the Form wherein it is proposed to settle it; and they who have any Thing to offer, are requested to confine themselves to this particular Point: For to object against Bishops in this Country, under a Form wherein it is determined not to settle them, is as foreign to the Purpose, as to object against the Authority of the Archbishop of Gnesena, or the Pope of Rome.

I have now taken Notice of all the Objections that have been made against sending Bishops to America, so far as they have come to my Knowledge; and it must be left to the Reader to Judge, whether, with Regard to the Episcopate in Question, they are not unreasonable and groundless. It is indeed possible that other Objections may have been offered, or may be hereafter suggested, against American Bishops; but I am persuaded that upon Examination they will generally be found to be Proofs, rather of the Dexterity or Ill-Will of the Inventors, than of the real Fears and Uneasiness of the Inhabitants. Artful Men may raise Objections and Difficulties in the plainest Cases, and can make any Thing an Argument against any Thing, in a Way that shall appear plausible, to those who are unacquainted with the Legerdemain of Cavilers and Sophists. But whoever employs his Talents in this Exercise, is as unworthy of the public Attention, as the Child that engages in Crambo or Push-Pin.

Thus, having represented the Distress the Church of England in America is under, for Want of an Episcopate—having attempted to prove, by various Arguments and Considerations, the Propriety and Fitness and Necessity of relieving it, and of allowing it the same Advantages which are granted to all other Denominations of Christians in his Majesty's American Dominions—and having explained the Nature and Extent of that

Authority with which our Bishops will be invested, when it shall be thought proper to send them, and shewn that such an Appointment can produce no Harm to the Dissenters, nor afford just grounds of Uneasiness or Complaint to any; I must now hasten to a Conclusion, submitting what has been offered to the Judgment of the Reader. Nothing has been asserted, in the Course of this Work, but what the Author believes, upon good Evidence, to be true; no Argument has been advanced, but with a full Persuasion of its being pertinent and conclusive. He looks upon the Subject to be of the utmost Importance; and he has no Disposition to trifle with it, or with the Public to which he appeals.

If these Papers should have the Honour of coming into the Hands of any of those Persons, from whose Power or Influence an American Episcopate is in any Measure expected; the Author humbly begs, that the Cause which he has undertaken to plead, may not suffer, in their Estimation, from the Unskilfulness of its present Advocate. Although he greatly distrusts his own Management, he has no Diffidence of the Cause itself. He believes it to be the Cause of Truth, of Justice, and of Christianity, and as such he most respectfully and submissively recommends it, imploring their Attention to so extraordinary and important a Case, as that of the Church of England in America.

It need not be repeated, that unless Bishops should be speedily sent us, we can foresee nothing but the Ruin of the Church in this Country. It need not be suggested, that such an Event is too much to be hazarded, when no Good can be expected to arise from such a Risque, and much Evil will probably follow it— Evil, which it is the unquestionable Duty of those to prevent, who are intrusted with the Interests of the Nation. The Church of England here, is so inseparably connected with the Church at Home, or rather, is so essentially the same with it, that it must ever subsist or perish, by the same Means. The Causes indeed, which destroy it here, may be local, and not immediately operate in England; but then, that Inattention and Negligence in our national Superiors, which would suffer it to be destroyed in the

Colonies, must have a general Effect, and can produce no Good to the same Church in the Mother-Country. Here, the Church has been long struggling under such an increasing Load of Difficulties, and is now in such a State of Oppression, as to deserve the Compassion of the whole Christian World. From our own Nation, and the Guardians of its Interest, it conceives itself to be intitled to more; as there is a Concurrence of every Kind of Motive for prevailing upon them, to afford it the Relief which is so essentially needed. The common Principles of Justice, and the most sacred Obligations of the Christian Religion, have been shewn to require this at their Hands.

Nor need the Author use many Words to prove, that Considerations even of a political Nature, are sufficient in this Case, to prevail with those who are insensible to other Motives. The Church of England, in its external Polity, is so happily connected and interwoven with the Civil Constitution, that each mutually supports and is supported by the other. The greatest Friendship and Harmony have ever subsisted between them; and in that memorable Period, wherein the Ruin of the one was affected, the Destruction of the other immediately followed. The Resurrection of the one, afterwards closely attended the Restoration of the other; and he that has a Regard for the Happiness of either, can never wish to see the Experiment repeated, either in England or her Colonies.

It is not pretended that the Character and Manners of the present Times are, in this Respect, the same, as in the Period referred to; nor that those who are Enemies to Episcopacy in this Age, are Enemies to Monarchy, as was frequently the Case formerly. The contrary is evident, in innumerable Instances. There are many British Subjects, both at Home and in the Plantations, who reject Episcopacy, and yet are warm Advocates for our happy Civil Constitution. It is therefore rash and injurious to charge any with Disaffection to the Government, at this Day, because they dissent from the national Religion. But notwithstanding, Episcopacy and Monarchy are, in their Frame and Constitution, best suited to each other. Episcopacy can never thrive in a Republican Government, nor Republican Principles in an Episcopal Church. For the same Reasons, in a mixed Monarchy, no Form of Ecclesiastical Government can so exactly harmonize with the State, as that of a qualified Episcopacy.

And as they are mutually adapted to each other so they are mutually introductive of each other. He that prefers Monarchy in the State, is more likely to approve of Episcopacy in the Church, than a rigid Republican. On the other Hand, he that is for a Parity and a popular Government in the Church, will more easily be led to approve of a similar Form of Government in the State, how little soever he may suspect it himself. It is not then to be wondered, if our Civil Rulers have always considered Episcopacy as the surest Friend of Monarchy; and it may reasonably be expected from those in Authority, that they will support and assist the Church in America, if from no other Motives, yet from a Regard to the State, with which it has so friendly and close an Alliance.

But there is no Reason to doubt, but every proper Motive will have its Effect, upon those wise and illustrious Patriots, who now conduct our public affairs. We no more suspect the Goodness of their Disposition, than the Reasonableness of the Cause, for which we are so anxious. All that we can be justly apprehensive of, is, that to those who reside at such a Distance, the Necessity of relieving the Church in America, with all possible Speed, may not be so evident, as to those who are Eye-Witnesses of its suffering Condition. We therefore beg Leave to suggest this— and earnestly to request, that the Relief, which we doubt not is intended, may be speedily granted. The ill Effects of delaying it, may be irretrievable. The present favourable Opportunity may be soon lost, and then Despair will succeed our disappointed Expectation.

To those who have been averse to American Bishops, and hitherto have shewn a Disposition to oppose their Settlement, I have but a Word more to offer. Their Prejudices, we charitably believe, must have arisen altogether from Misapprehensions of the Case, and from the Fears which, from thence, have been conceived, of their becoming Sufferers, either in their Property or Privileges, by the Episcopate in Question. The Subject is here placed in its true Light, and thereby, it is trusted, their Misapprehensions are fairly removed, and their consequent Fears are shewn to be groundless. Instead therefore of distressing themselves, or of opposing the Church in the Case before us, we flatter ourselves that they will act the Part which Generosity and Candour prescribe, and behave towards us as Fellow-Christians and Protestants ought to behave to one another. If they have been led by Ignorance or Misinformation to oppose a Cause, which they now find to be just; their Duty obliges them to be careful for the future, at the very least, not to obstruct it. If they are in Reality the Friends of Truth, and Justice, and Liberty, which they pretend and we are willing to believe them to be, they must be heartily disposed to act a friendly Part towards us, with Regard to an Episcopate; which Disposition will add greatly to their own Happiness, as well as to ours. They know, by Experience, the inestimable Value of those Advantages, for which we have petitioned; and if we are as fairly intitled to them as any other Christian Societies, they ought not to envy, but to take Pleasure in, our Enjoyment of them.

If all the religious Denominations in America, by the general Constitution of the British Colonies, are to be treated on the Footing of a perfect Equality, for which some have contended; then, the Church of England is as fully intitled to the compleat Enjoyment of its own Discipline and Institutions, as any other Christians. If any one Denomination is intitled to a Superiority above others, as is believed by many; then, the Claim of the Church of England to this Preference, is not to be disputed. One of these must be undoubtedly the Case; and on either Supposition, to endeavour to prevent the Episcopate we have asked for, is Injustice and Cruelty.

B

[The text is taken from William Livingston, *A Letter to the Right Reverend Father in God, John, Lord Bishop of Landaff* . . . (Boston: Kneeland and Adams, 1768), pp. 3–6, 12–14, 25–26.]

A Letter to the Bishop of Landaff

MY LORD,

On reading Dr. Chandler's appeal to the public, in behalf of the church of England in America, I met with a long quotation in favour of an American episcopate, from a sermon preached by your lordship before the incorporated society, for the propagation of the gospel in foreign parts, at their anniversary meeting in the parish church of St. Mary-le-bow, on the 20th of February, 1767—This raised my curiosity to procure the sermon itself; and your lordship will pardon me for saying, that the perusal of it excited at once my indignation and sorrow;—my indignation, that any man should so grosly have abused your lordship's confidence in his veracity, by the most unparralleled misrepresentation of facts; and my sorrow, that a person of your lordship's good sense and distinguished character, should have placed any confidence in so impudent an informer. For indeed, my lord, I question whether there be a pamphlet in the nation, that in proportion to the length of the sermon, contains so great a number of aberrations from the truth. And as the facts alleged are extremely injurious to the characters of men, and many of them, to the memory of the most excellent persons deceased, (whom we have the greatest reason to believe, have, long since, received the approbation of their and your lordship's final judge) whoever abused your lordship's credulity, is on this account, the more inexcusably culpable. How far your lordship is yourself to blame, for preaching and publishing so many interesting facts, on such incompetent testimony as your lordship has relied on, I will not presume to determine. This however, I think

I may venture to say without offence, that as the charges
adduced by your lordship, affect the reputation of great numbers
of his majesty's loyal subjects in these colonies, proportionable
deliberation and pains were necessary to investigate the truth.
And tho' the most sedulous and impartial inquirer may be deceived by misinformation; yet in the present case, it was so easy
a matter to have attained to the utmost certainty, that directly
the reverse of many assertions in your lordship's sermon was
true; that it is not a little surprizing your lordship should have
suffered yourself to have been so palpably misled. And if a
prelate of your lordship's abilities and candour, was so unhappily induced to take up an ill report against your neighbour,
from the mouth or pen of some malicious deceiver, how much
easier may we imagine, will a misjudging and censorious world
adopt, what has been preached and printed by so distinguished
a personage as the bishop of Landaff. It cannot therefore, I
humbly presume, be deemed officious or impertinent, in vindication of the characters so unjustly defamed in your lordship's
sermon, to remove those prejudices you have unfortunately
imbibed; or to prevent their being farther diffused, and more
deeply rivetted, by a discourse, which from the dignity of its
author, must naturally carry great weight, and make very durable impressions. And it appears truly wonderful to me, that
amongst the great numbers in this country, who are capable of
performing this benevolent task, not one that I know of, except
Dr. Chauncy of Boston (to whom I am obliged for several facts
and observations) hath hitherto attempted it. The passages in
your sermon, my lord, which I would be understood to have
particularly in view, are those which relate to the American
colonies. Your lordship says, page 6, "Since the discovery of
the new world, the same provision hath not been made of ministers, necessary to the support of christianity among those who
removed thither, especially in the British colonies." This, my
lord, affirmed of the colonies without discrimination, is so contrary to the truth, that with respect to many of them, they exceed
perhaps in such provision, every other part of the christian

world. In the New-England colonies particularly, they have from their earliest settlement been peculiarly attentive to the most ample provision of a gospel ministry. Their legislative acts, from the commencement of those colonies, abundantly evince this attention. By these provision is always made for the establishment and support of the gospel ministry in every new-erected township; and without such establishment, within three years from the settlement, the grants are liable to an absolute forfeiture. In consequence of this provision, with the divine blessing on their pious endeavours, christianity has not been supported, but so faithfully preached, and so zealously inculcated, that I will venture to affirm, there is not a more virtuous, not a more religious people upon the face of the earth. Indeed, my lord, from the most authentic accounts respecting the state of religion in England, I have reason to think, they surpass both in the theory and practice of christianity, those who have the advantage of enjoying it under the supports of a legal establishment, and are perpetually basking in the full sunshine of episcopal preeminence. Nay, I doubt not your lordship will readily admit, that notwithstanding the millions expended on the dignitaries of the church, and the boasted advantage of episcopal ordination, the people of England do not outshine in purity of morals, either the protestant cantons of Switzerland, the republic of Holland, or the church of Scotland; all which however know nothing about episcopacy, except, as these colonies, I mean, at a convenient and comfortable distance. And though recrimination, my lord, is reputed to be just; yet it is so very disagreeable, that I shall not attempt to heighten the lustre of the lives and examples of the New-England clergy, by the foil of those in the mother country. Let it suffice to inform your lordship, as what may be depended upon for matter of fact, that there are now within the bounds of New-England, not less than five hundred and fifty ministers, some of the presbyterian, but the greater part of the congregational persuasion, regularly set apart to the pastoral charge of as many christian congregations, having been previously qualified with divine and human literature in the course of a liberal education, at some of their colleges. They are

moreover, men of irreproachable lives, and orthodox in principle, who discharge their sacred function in a manner that does
honour to the holy religion they profess. And can it be said, my
lord, with the least appearance of truth, of such a country as this,
(a country so thinly inhabited, and so recently emerging out of a
state of political nonexistence) that it has "not made a provision
of ministers necessary for the support of christianity?" In truth,
my lord, however the people of Britain, may, on account of
their remote situation from us, be prevailed on to credit such
marvellous reports, the North-Americans could not be more
astonished, should your lordship assert, that this part of the
world is not inhabited by any of the human species, but only
by Satyrs, and Centaurs, and Griffins.* * *

But in what sense, my lord, did those adventurers abandon
their native religion? If your lordship means by their native religion, the doctrines of christianity as contained in the thirty-nine
articles of your church; they were so far from abandoning it,
that it were to be wished it had been as inviolably preserved by
those who they left behind them. These were the very doctrines
which they, in their time, universally believed, constantly taught,
and warmly inculcated. These are the doctrines which their
posterity, to this day, believe, teach and inculcate. Nay, they
believe, teach and inculcate them, in the same scriptural and
unadulterated sense, in which they were believed, taught and
inculcated at the time of the reformation. They believe, teach,
and inculcate them, without those sophisticating glosses, by
which they have since, in the mother-country, been wrested to
favour the heresy of Arminius; which your lordship well knows
was not their native sense; and consequently, as far as the English clergy do now pervert them to any such meaning; so far have
they "abandoned their native religion." And if there be any
among the descendants of those adventurers, who have, in this
sense, I mean in a perversion of those articles, abandoned their
native religion, they generally happen, I know not by what
fatality, to be members of the episcopal churches. Few, my lord,
very few of any other denominations amongst us, have hitherto
professed that wonderful dexterity in taylorship, of making robes

of righteousness, and garments of salvation, out of—filthy rags.

Your lordship's charge, is certainly so groundless, that there never was a people in the world, who have been more assiduous in preserving their native religion, and in transmitting it, pure and incorrupt, to their posterity. If catechisms are conducive to this end, they have published as judicious and elaborate ones as any part of the protestant world hath ever produced. Let any impartial man read their productions of this kind; a lesser and a larger one by Mr. Norton, the like by Mr. Mather, several by Mr. Cotton, one by Mr. Davenport, one by Mr. Stone, one by Mr. Norris, one by Mr. Noyes, one by Mr. Fisk, several by Mr. Elliot, one by Mr. Sea-Born Cotton, and a large one by Mr. Fitch; and then let him say, whether true divinity was ever better handled; or whether they were not the most genuine sons of the church of England, who thus maintained her fundemental articles: Articles, so often subscribed, and afterwards denied, by some who are most prompt to monopolize that name to themselves. Have ecclesiastical councils any tendency this way? I find one at Cambridge so early as the year 1648, adopting the Westminster Confession of faith; and another at Boston in 1680, settling the doctrine and discipline of their churches. The resolutions of the latter, my lord, are comprized in a work of great theological erudition; and which required a little more towards its composition, than the skill of construing a chapter in the Greek testament, or reading a sermon of another man's writing, *à la mode D'Angleterre.* Ecclesiastical synods or con-sociations have ever since been in use among them; and what may appear extraordinary to an English prelate, they have been so conducted as never to give any just umbrage to the civil power.

But if your lordship means by their native religion, an implicit submission to ecclesiastico-political power arbitrarily assumed, and tyrannically exercised; or, a recognition of any man on earth, as supreme head of the christian church, in derogation of the transcendent authority of him, to whom angels and authorities, and powers are made subject; or a superstitious attachment to rights and ceremonies of human invention, to the neglect of vital piety and purity of heart; it is agreed, my lord, that in this sense, they did in good earnest abandon their native religion; and 'tis devoutly to be wished, their posterity may never be so infatuated as to resume it. * * *

It must indeed, be admitted, that some of our colleges, for want of professors, and the comparative smallness of their libraries; and others, through a very slender philosophical apparatus, cannot pretend to vie with the universities at home. Considering, however, the infancy of the country, they are far from being contemptible; nor has it ever been remarked, that the clergy of the church of England, who have received their education at any of those seminaries, several of whom have been honoured with the degree of doctors of divinity, in England, are inferior in literary accomplishments, to those who have been educated in the English universities. Be this as it may, it is notorious, that the American colleges are friendly to liberty, and our excellent constitution; and so firmly attached to revolution principles and the illustrious house of Hanover, that none one of them, as far as I have been able to learn, hath ever produced (with all humble submission to the famous university of Oxford) a single Jacobite or Tory.

With this, my lord, I shall humbly take my leave, hoping that for the sake of truth, and the cause of religion, especially remembring how greatly your lordship has been deceived in the present case, you will be so gracious for the future, in whatever concerns the American colonies, as to require the highest evidence of which the nature of the thing is capable. And heartily wishing, my lord, (it being easy to see for what purpose these kind of misinformations are calculated) that your lordship may be so successful, and so throughly satisfied in the discharge of your episcopal function, within the limits of your present diocese, as never to think it your duty, to exchange the See of Landaff, for an American Bishoprick.

> I am, my Lord,
> Your Lordship's
> most obedient humble servant,
> The AUTHOR.

5

SUBSIDY

OR

SEPARATION

AMERICAN historians often argue about the conservatism or radicalism of the American Revolution: how revolutionary was it? The examination of social class distinctions, economic interests, and political participation produce no simple generalizations applicable equally to all thirteen colonies. But in one respect that Revolution was clearly revolutionary. An infant nation without the stability of tradition, without the strength of great armies, decided to sever all legal ties between church and state, creating a social structure for which the Western world at that time had no precedent. Separation of church and state was hardly the obvious thing to do: it was an almost unthinkable thing to do. How then did this particular revolution come about?

Several factors militated against the establishment of any single denomination. The two great contenders numerically were Congregationalism, which dominated New England, and Anglicanism, which dominated much of the remaining area. But the Church of England, as noted in the previous chapter, had aroused grave suspicions and often bitter resentments in the latter part of the eighteenth century. Indeed it suffered severely in the Revolutionary period, as many of its clergy—unsympathetic to the "causeless, unprovoked, and unnatural rebellion" —left the warring colonies for England. Congregationalism, on the other hand, was a regional church, having no real base outside of Connecticut and Massachusetts. The establishment in these two colonies, moreover, had managed to alienate many other religious groups by petty harassment, not-so-petty persecution, disenfranchisement, discriminatory taxation, and exile.

If neither Anglicans nor Congregationalists were obvious choices for a national church, were there other possibilities? No. Baptists and Quakers on principle opposed any alliance of church and state; Lutherans, Roman Catholics, and German and Dutch Reformed were too scanty in number to be serious contenders; Presbyterians were busy debating doctrine and tactics among themselves. Beyond these denominational positions stood the deism* of many leaders of the young republic, a deism that looked on institutional religion not in order to support it but rather to limit or weaken its operation. Jefferson's sentiments ("I believe there would never have been an infidel if there had never been a priest") were widely shared among the men in positions of influence and power. No single church body, therefore, bid fair to win the contest for national support. In fact, there was no contest.

Another real possibility, however, did present itself: establish *all* the churches, support and defend Christianity itself. (So

---

* Reacting against the scholasticism of revealed (biblical) religion and against the dogmatism of sectarian (denominational) religion, deism arose in the freshly harrowed ground of the European Enlightenment. A type of natural religion, deism saw God as an impersonal but orderly Creator whose nature is best revealed in Nature itself, whose will finds its fullest expression in the stable, observable laws of the universe. This God indulges in no "special providences," is moved by no special pleas. One may certainly revere or even adore Him, but it would be quite inappropriate to endeavor to use Him. In the opinion of the deist, churches and scriptures, dogmas and priests more often conceal than reveal this universal and benevolent Being. See also Chap. 7.

far as Judaism is concerned, America's Jewish population in 1790 was less than one-twentieth of one per cent.) This issue was most seriously joined at the state level, not the national one; but that state—Virginia—was crucial in directing the nation's course. And since such patriotic stalwarts as Patrick Henry and George Washington at times favored a plan of "general establishment," its defeat cannot be considered a foregone conclusion.

The bill "establishing a provision for teachers of the Christian religion," reprinted below, was one of several attempts to find a median position between a complete separation of church and state on the one hand and the legal support of a single denomination on the other. Such Virginia counties as Essex, Amelia, and Accomac formally petitioned the state's legislators "to take into their legislative patronage and protection, the concerns of our holy religion, a thorough knowledge and conscientious practice of which is the best security for the permanent peace and prosperity of civil government" (Amelia County, November 18, 1785). Six years earlier, James Henry of Accomac had presented the bill (October 25, 1779) given below. From that time until its final defeat in 1786, the issue of separation or subsidy hung in the balance.

Patrick Henry (1736–1799) and James Madison (1751–1836) were the principal antagonists. In October of 1785, Henry sponsored a bill before the Virginia General Assembly which is identical in sentiment with the 1779 proposal—both usually referred to as "general assessment" bills. But more than mere state support was called for: a kind of state-approved religious behavior could now be sanctioned. It makes an enormous difference to the social order whether the author of the statement, "That the Christian Religion is the true Religion," be a church or a state.

James Madison, fully cognizant of that difference, responded to Patrick Henry by presenting to the Assembly in 1786 a document of enduring national significance. Cogently and calmly argued, Madison's *Memorial and Remonstrance* loses little of its eloquence or force two centuries later. To go Patrick Henry's way, Madison declares, is to erect a "Beacon on our Coast, warning [the magnanimous sufferer] to seek some other haven where liberty and philanthropy . . . may offer a more certain repose from his troubles." But that beacon was never erected. Instead, Madison's *Memorial* together with Jefferson's *"Bill for Establishing Religious Freedom,"* both passed in Virginia in 1786, became beacons to a Constitutional Convention gathering in Philadelphia in May, 1787.

A

[The text is taken from H. J. Eckenrode, *Separation of Church and State in Virginia* (Richmond: Virginia State Library, 1910), pp. 58–61.]

A Bill Establishing a Provision for Teachers of the Christian Religion

For the encouragement of Religion and virtue, and for removing all restraints on the mind in its inquiries after truth, Be it enacted by the General Assembly, that all persons and Religious Societies who acknowledge that there is one God, and a future State of rewards and punishments, and that God ought to be publickly worshiped, shall be freely tolerated.

The Christian Religion shall in all times coming be deemed and held to be the established Religion of this Commonwealth; and all Denominations of Christians demeaning themselves peaceably and faithfully, shall enjoy equal privileges, civil and Religious.

To accomplish this desirable purpose without injury to the property of those Societies of Christians already incorporated by Law for the purpose of Religious Worship, and to put it fully into the power of every other Society of Christians, either already formed or to be hereafter formed to obtain the like incorporation, Be it further enacted, that the respective Societies of the Church of England already formed in this Commonwealth, shall be continued Corporate, and hold the Religious property now in their possession for ever.

Whenever _____ free male Persons not under twenty one Years of Age, professing the Christian Religion, shall agree to unite themselves in a Society for the purpose of Religious Worship, they shall be constituted a Church, and esteemed and regarded in Law as of the established Religion of this Commonwealth, and on their petition to the General Assembly shall be entitled to be incorporated and shall enjoy equal Privileges with any other Society of Christians, and all that associate with them for the purpose of Religious Worship, shall be esteemed as belonging to the Society so called.

Every Society so formed shall give themselves a name or denomination by which they shall be called and known in Law. And it is further enacted, that previous to the establishment and incorporation of the respective Societies of every denomination as aforesaid, and in order to entitle them thereto, each Society so petitioning shall agree to and subscribe in a Book the following five Articles, without which no agreement or Union of men upon pretence of Religious Worship shall entitle them to be incorporated and esteemed as a Church of the Established Religion of this Commonwealth.

First, That there is one Eternal God and a future State of Rewards and punishments.

Secondly, That God is publickly to be Worshiped.

Thirdly, That the Christian Religion is the true Religion.

Fourthly, That the Holy Scriptures of the old and new Testament are of divine inspiration, and are the only rule of Faith.

Fifthly, That it is the duty of every Man, when thereunto called by those who Govern, to bear witness to truth.

And that the People may forever enjoy the right of electing their own Teachers, Pastors, or Clergy; and at the same time that the State may have Security for the due discharge of the Pastoral office by those who shall be admitted to be Clergymen, Teachers,

or Pastors, no person shall officiate as minister of any established
Church who shall not have been chosen by a majority of the
Society to which he shall be minister, or by the persons appointed by the said majority to choose and procure a minister
for them, nor until the Minister so chosen shall have made and
subscribed the following declaration, over and above the aforesaid five articles, to be made in some Court of Record in this
Commonwealth, viz:

That he is determined by God's Grace out of the Holy Scriptures to instruct the people committed to his charge, and to teach
nothing (as required of necessity to eternal Salvation) but that
which he shall be persuaded may be concluded and proved from
the Scriptures; that he will use both publick and private admoni-
tions with prudence and discretion, as need shall require, and
occasion shall be given; that he will be diligent in prayers and
in reading the Holy Scriptures, and in such studies as lead to the
knowledge of the same; that he will be diligent to frame and
fashion himself and his Family according to the doctrines of
Christ, and to make both himself and them, as much as in him
lieth, wholesome examples and patterns to the flock of Christ;
and that he will maintain and set forward, as much as he can,
peace and love among all people, and especially among those
that are or shall be committed to his charge.

No person shall disturb or molest any Religious Assembly nor
shall use any reproachful, reviling or abusive language against
any Church under the penalty of _____, a second offence to
be deemed a breach of good behaviour.

No person whatsoever shall speak anything in their Religious
Assemblies disrespectfully or Seditiously of the Government of
this State.

And that permanent encouragement may be given for providing a sufficient number of ministers and teachers to be pro-
cured and continued to every part of this Commonwealth,

Be it further enacted, that the sum of _____ pounds of Tobacco, or such rate in Money as shall be yearly settled for each
County by the Court thereof, according to the Current price,

shall be paid annually for each Tithable by the person enlisting the same, for and towards the Support of Religious Teachers and places of Worship in manner following: Within _____ Months after the passing of this Act every freeholder, House-keeper, & person possessing Tithables, shall enroll his or her name with the Clerk of the County of which he or she shall be an Inhabitant, at the same time expressing to the Support of what Society or denomination of Christian he or she would choose to contribute; which inrollment shall be binding upon each such person, until he or she shall in like manner cause his or her name to be inrolled in any other Society.

The Clerk of each County Court shall annually before the day of _____ deliver to the Trustees of each Religious Society, a list of the several names inrolled in his office as members of such Society; with the number of Tithables belonging to each, according to the List taken and returned that Year. Whereupon such Trustees respectively shall meet and determine how the Assessment aforesaid upon such Tithables shall be laid out for the support of their teacher or places of worship, according to the true intent of this Act; and having entered such disposition in a Book to be kept for that purpose, shall deliver a Copy thereof to the Sheriff, together with the List of Tithables so received from the Clerk, and such Sheriff shall on or before the _____ day of _____ then next following, Collect, Levy or Distrain for the amount of such Assessment, which he shall account for and pay to the several persons to whom he shall have been directed to pay it by the Trustees of each respective Society, deducting Insolvents and Six per Centum for Collection.

If any Person shall fail to enlist his Tithables, the Sheriff shall nevertheless Collect or distrain for the Assessment aforesaid in like manner as if he or she had done so, and pay the same to that Religious Society of which he or she shall be inrolled as a member. And should any person liable to this Assessment fail to procure himself to be inrolled according to this Act, or to make his Election at the Time of paying his assessment to the Sheriff, the Sheriff shall nevertheless levy in like manner the Assessment aforesaid for his or her Tithables, and lay an Account upon Oath of all Tobacco or Monies so Collected before his Court in the months of _____ annually; or if no Court be then held, at the next Court which shall be held thereafter, who shall apportion the same between the several Religious Societies in the parish in which such person or persons shall reside, according to the amount of the Assessment for each, to be paid to the Order of such Trustees for the purposes of this Act. And every Sheriff shall annually before the _____ day of _____ enter into Bond, with sufficient Security to be approved by the County Court for the faithful Collection and disbursement of all Tobacco or Monies received in consequence of this Act; and the Trustees of any Religious Society, or any Creditor to whom money may by them be Ordered to be paid, on motion in the County Court, having given him ten days previous notice thereof, may have Judgment against any delinquent Sheriff and his Securities, his or their Executors or administrators, for what shall appear to be due from him to such Society or Creditor, or may bring suit on the Bond given him by the Sheriff; and the Bond shall not be discharged by any Judgment had thereon, but shall remain as a Security against him, and may be put in suit as often as any breach shall happen, until the whole penalty shall have been Levied.

And if any Society or Church so established, shall refuse to appoint some person to receive their Quota of the Assessment from the Sheriff, the money shall remain in his hands for one Year; and if then no person properly appointed shall apply for such money, the same shall by the County Court be equally apportioned between the several Religious Societies in the parish in which such person or persons shall reside, in proportion to the amount of the Assessment for each Society.

The Clerks of the respective County Courts shall be entitled to the same fees for making out and delivering the Lists of Tithables required by this Act as they are entitled to for like Services in other cases.

And be it farther enacted, that so much of an Act of Assembly passed in the Year 1748, intituled "An Act for the Support of the Clergy, and for the Regular Collecting and paying the parish Levies," as respects the Levying, Collecting and payment of the Salaries of the Clergy of the Church of England which has been suspended by several Acts of the General Assembly; and also so much of an Act intituled "ministers to be inducted," as requires Ordination by a Bishop in England, be and the same are hereby Repealed.

B

[The text is taken from Saul K. Padover, ed., *The Complete Madison: His Basic Writings* (New York: Harper & Brothers, 1953), pp. 299–306.]

A Memorial and Remonstrance

We, the subscribers, citizens of the said Commonwealth, having taken into serious consideration, a Bill printed by order of the last Session of General Assembly, entitled "A Bill establishing a provision for Teachers of the Christian Religion," and conceiving that the same, if finally armed with the sanctions of a law, will be a dangerous abuse of power, are bound as faithful members of a free State, to remonstrate against it, and to declare the reasons by which we are determined. We remonstrate against the said Bill,

1. Because we hold it for a "fundamental and undeniable truth," that Religion or the duty which we owe to our Creator and the manner of discharging it, can be directed only by reasons and conviction, not by force or violence. The Religion then of every man must be left to the conviction and conscience of every man; and it is the right of every man to exercise it as these may dictate. This right is in its nature an unalienable right. It is unalienable; because the opinions of men, depending only on the evidence contemplated by their own minds, cannot follow the dictates of

other men: It is unalienable also; because what is here a right towards men, is a duty towards the Creator. It is the duty of every man to render to the Creator such homage, and such only, as he believes to be acceptable to him. This duty is precedent both in order of time and degree of obligation, to the claims of Civil Society. Before any man can be considered as a member of Civil Society, he must be considered as a subject of the Governor of the Universe: And if a member of Civil Society, who enters into any subordinate Association, must always do it with a reservation of his duty to the general authority; much more must every man who becomes a member of any particular Civil Society, do it with a saving of his allegiance to the Universal Sovereign. We maintain therefore that in matters of Religion, no man's right is abridged by the institution of Civil Society, and that Religion is wholly exempt from its cognizance. True it is, that no other rule exists, by which any question which may divide a Society, can be ultimately determined, but the will of the majority; but it is also true, that the majority may trespass on the rights of the minority.

2. Because if religion be exempt from the authority of the Society at large, still less can it be subject to that of the Legislative Body. The latter are but the creatures and vicegerents of the former. Their jurisdiction is both derivative and limited: it is limited with regard to the co-ordinate departments, more necessarily is it limited with regard to the constituents. The preservation of a free government requires not merely, that the metes and bounds which separate each department of power may be invariably maintained; but more especially, that neither of them be suffered to overleap the great Barrier which defends the rights of the people. The Rulers who are guilty of such an encroachment, exceed the commission from which they derive their authority, and are Tyrants. The People who submit to it are governed by laws made neither by themselves, nor by an authority derived from them, and are slaves.

3. Because, it is proper to take alarm at the first experiment on our liberties. We hold this prudent jealousy to be the first

duty of citizens, and one of [the] noblest characteristics of the late Revolution. The freemen of America did not wait till usurped power had strengthened itself by exercise, and entangled the question in precedents. They saw all the consequences in the principle, and they avoided the consequences by denying the principle. We revere this lesson too much, soon to forget it. Who does not see that the same authority which can establish Christianity, in exclusion of all other Religions, may establish with the same ease any particular sect of Christians, in exclusion of all other Sects? That the same authority which can force a citizen to contribute three pence only of his property for the support of any one establishment, may force him to conform to any other establishment in all cases whatsoever?

4. Because, the bill violates that equality which ought to be the basis of every law, and which is more indispensable, in proportion as the validity or expediency of any law is more liable to be impeached. If "all men are by nature equally free and independent," all men are to be considered as entering into Society on equal conditions; as relinquishing no more, and therefore retaining no less, one than another, of their natural rights. Above all are they to be considered as retaining an "*equal* title to the free exercise of Religion according to the dictates of conscience." Whilst we assert for ourselves a freedom to embrace, to profess and to observe the Religion which we believe to be of divine origin, we cannot deny an equal freedom to those whose minds have not yet yielded to the evidence which has convinced us. If this freedom be abused, it is an offence against God, not against man: To God, therefore, not to men, must an account of it be rendered. As the Bill violates equality by subjecting some to peculiar burdens; so it violates the same principle, by granting to others peculiar exemptions. Are the Quakers and Menonists the only sects who think a compulsive support of their religions unnecessary and unwarantable? Can their piety alone be intrusted with the care of public worship? Ought their Religions to be endowed above all others, with extraordinary privileges, by which proselytes may be enticed from all others? We think too favor-

ably of the justice and good sense of these denominations, to believe that they either covet pre-eminencies over their fellow citizens, or that they will be seduced by them, from the common opposition to the measure.

5. Because the bill implies either that the Civil Magistrate is a competent Judge of Religious truth; or that he may employ Religion as an engine of Civil policy. The first is an arrogant pretension falsified by the contradictory opinions of Rulers in all ages, and throughout the world: The second an unhallowed perversion of the means of salvation.

6. Because the establishment proposed by the Bill is not requisite for the support of the Christian Religion. To say that it is, is a contradiction to the Christian Religion itself; for every page of it disavows a dependence on the powers of this world: it is a contradiction to fact; for it is known that this Religion both existed and flourished, not only without the support of human laws, but in spite of every opposition from them; and not only during the period of miraculous aid, but long after it had been left to its own evidence, and the ordinary care of Providence: Nay, it is a contradiction in terms; for a Religion not invented by human policy, must have pre-existed and been supported, before it was established by human policy. It is moreover to weaken in those who profess this Religion a pious confidence in its innate excellence, and the patronage of its Author; and to foster in those who still reject it, a suspicion that its friends are too conscious of its fallacies, to trust it to its own merits.

7. Because experience witnesseth that ecclesiastical establishments, instead of maintaining the purity and efficacy of Religion, have had a contrary operation. During almost fifteen centuries, has the legal establishment of Christianity been on trial. What have been its fruits? More or less in all places, pride and indolence in the Clergy; ignorance and servility in the laity; in both, superstition, bigotry and persecution. Enquire of the Teachers of Christianity for the ages in which it appeared in its greatest lustre; those of every sect, point to the ages prior to its incorporation with Civil policy. Propose a restoration of this

primitive state in which its Teachers depend on the voluntary rewards of their flocks; many of them predict its downfall. On which side ought their testimony to have greatest weight, when for or when against their interest?

8. Because the establishment in question is not necessary for the support of Civil Government. If it be urged as necessary for the support of Civil Government only as it is a means of supporting Religion, and it be not necessary for the latter purpose, it cannot be necessary for the former. If Religion be not within [the] cognizance of Civil Government, how can its legal establishment be said to be necessary to Civil Government? What influence in fact have ecclesiastical establishments had on Civil Society? In some instances they have been seen to erect a spiritual tyranny on the ruins of Civil authority; in many instances they have been seen upholding the thrones of political tyranny; in no instance have they been seen the guardians of the liberties of the people. Rulers who wished to subvert the public liberty, may have found an established clergy convenient auxiliaries.'A just government, instituted to secure & perpetuate it, needs them not. Such a government will be best supported by protecting every citizen in the enjoyment of his Religion with the same equal hand which protects his person and his property; by neither invading the equal rights of any Sect, nor suffering any Sect to invade those of another.

9. Because the proposed establishment is a departure from that generous policy, which, offering an asylum to the persecuted and oppressed of every Nation and Religion, promised a lustre to our country, and an accession to the number of its citizens. What a melancholy mark is the Bill of sudden degeneracy? Instead of holding forth an asylum to the persecuted, it is itself a signal of persecution. It degrades from the equal rank of Citizens all those whose opinions in Religion do not bend to those of the Legislative authority. Distant as it may be, in its present form, from the Inquisition it differs from it only in degree. The one is the first step, the other the last in the career of intolerance. The magnanimous sufferer under this cruel scourge in foreign

Regions, must view the Bill as a Beacon on our Coast, warning him to seek some other haven, where liberty and philanthropy in their due extent may offer a more certain repose from his troubles.

10. Because, it will have a like tendency to banish our Citizens. The allurements presented by other situations are every day thinning their number. To superadd a fresh motive to emigration, by revoking the liberty which they now enjoy, would be the same species of folly which has dishonoured and depopulated flourishing kingdoms.

11. Because, it will destroy that moderation and harmony which the forebearance of our laws to intermeddle with Religion, has produced amongst its several sects. Torrents of blood have been spilt in the old world, by vain attempts of the secular arm to extinguish Religious discord, by proscribing all difference in Religious opinions. Time has at length revealed the true remedy. Every relaxation of narrow and rigorous policy, wherever it has been tried, has been found to assuage the disease. The American theatre has exhibited proofs, that equal and compleat liberty, if it does not wholly eradicate it, sufficiently destroys its malignant influence on the health and prosperity of the State. If with the salutary effects of this system under our own eyes, we begin to contract the bonds of Religious freedom, we know no name that will too severely reproach our folly. At least let warning be taken at the first fruits of the threatened innovation. The very appearance of the Bill has transformed that "Christian forbearance, love and charity," which of late mutually prevailed, into animosities and jealousies, which may not soon be appeased. What mischiefs may not be dreaded should this enemy to the public quiet be armed with the force of a law?

12. Because, the policy of the bill is adverse to the diffusion of the light of Christianity. The first wish of those who enjoy this precious gift, ought to be that it may be imparted to the whole race of mankind. Compare the number of those who have as yet received it with the number still remaining under the dominion of false Religions; and how small is the former! Does the policy

of the Bill tend to lessen the disproportion? No; it at once discourages those who are strangers to the light of [revelation] from coming into the Region of it; and countenances, by example the nations who continue in darkness, in shutting out those who might convey it to them. Instead of levelling as far as possible, every obstacle to the victorious progress of truth, the Bill with an ignoble and unchristian timidity would circumscribe it, with a wall of defence, against the encroachments of error.

13. Because attempts to enforce by legal sanctions, acts obnoxious to so great a proportion of Citizens, tend to enervate the laws in general, and to slacken the bands of Society. If it be difficult to execute any law which is not generally deemed necessary or salutary, what must be the case where it is deemed invalid and dangerous? and what may be the effect of so striking an example of impotency in the Government, on its general authority.

14. Because a measure of such singular magnitude and delicacy ought not to be imposed, without the clearest evidence that it is called for by a majority of citizens: and no satisfactory method is yet proposed by which the voice of the majority in this case may be determined, or its influence secured. "The people of the respective counties are indeed requested to signify their opinion respecting the adoption of the Bill to the next Session of Assembly." But the representation must be made equal, before the voice either of the Representatives or of the Counties, will be that of the people. Our hope is that neither of the former will, after due consideration, espouse the dangerous principle of the Bill. Should the event disappoint us, it will still leave us in full confidence, that a fair appeal to the latter will reverse the sentence against our liberties.

15. Because, finally, "the equal right of every citizen to the free exercise of his Religion according to the dictates of conscience" is held by the same tenure with all our other rights. If we recur to its origin, it is equally the gift of nature; if we weigh its importance, it cannot be less dear to us; if we consult the

Declaration of those rights which pertain to the good people of Virginia, as the "basis and foundation of Government," it is enumerated with equal solemnity, or rather studied emphasis. Either then, we must say, that the will of the Legislature is the only measure of their authority; and that in the plenitude of this authority, they may sweep away all our fundamental rights; or, that they are bound to leave this particular right untouched and sacred: Either we must say, that they may controul the freedom of the press, may abolish the trial by jury, may swallow up the Executive and Judiciary Powers of the State; nay that they may despoil us of our very right of suffrage, and erect themselves into an independent and hereditary assembly: or we must say, that they have no authority to enact into law the Bill under consideration. We the subscribers say, that the General Assemly of this Commonwealth have no such authority: And that no effort may be omitted on our part against so dangerous an usurpation, we oppose to it, this remonstrance; earnestly praying, as we are in duty bound, that the Supreme Lawgiver of the Universe, by illuminating those to whom it is addressed, may on the one hand, turn their councils from every act which would affront his holy prerogative, or violate the trust committed to them: and on the other, guide them into every measure which may be worthy of his [blessing, may re] dound to their own praise, and may establish more firmly the liberties, the prosperity, and the Happiness of the Commonwealth.

6

SALVATION
OR
SAVAGERY

NOT ALL of America's religious issues have happy endings. The contention over the Indian question is one of the unhappiest. For despite a good deal of heroism, sacrifice, and high idealism on the part of Christians in America, the Indian was deceived, dispossessed, and ultimately reduced to a ward of the state. It is possible to match a list of atrocities with a list of saints (David Brainerd, Pierre Jean De Smet, Narcissa Whitman, etc.), but the record will not balance.

More to the point was the central and often agonizing query: what *is* the Christian's responsibility to the Indian? If one's motives were more or less worthy, differences in strategy—and even more in consequences—continued to exist. Given the fact of America's nationhood, given the force of the westward push, given the sharp surge in white population, what Solomon-solution suggested itself? Did Christian brotherhood or even common humanitarianism have anything clear to say in this stark confrontation between peoples and cultures? If so, it was not said powerfully enough as hoary cultures disintegrated and proud peoples declined. Some one-half million Indians in 1800 were fifty years later reduced by half.

In the 1820's, two men—both churchmen—looked at what the white man and especially the missionary was doing for or to the American Indian. Both looked at the Indians through sympathetic eyes, but what they saw and what they argued for contrasted sharply. Jedidiah Morse (1761–1826), Yale 1783, is best known as America's first writer of geography textbooks, his *American Geography* (1789) going through many editions and dominating the field as Noah Webster's spelling book dominated its field. Also the father of Samuel F. B. Morse (of Morse code fame), Jedidiah was nonetheless professionally neither a geographer nor a communications expert. He was a Congregational minister, his principal parish being in Charlestown, Massachusetts.

In 1820, under a presidential commission, Morse toured the trans-Appalachian west "for the purpose of ascertaining for the use of the government the actual state of the Indian tribes in our country." His report, published in 1822, was made to the Secretary of War, there being no Department of Interior until 1849. Morse saw the civilizing and Christianizing of the Indians as not only possible but highly desirable. What the American Board of Commissioners for Foreign Missions had been doing was proper and effective; it needed now only the further sanction and support of government. Morse is not insensitive to tribal integrity, seeing further removal to western reservations as plausible only for "the smaller tribes, and remnants of tribes." In the growing willingness of the Indian to be instructed, civilized, and converted the Congregational clergymen saw "the hand of heaven" at work.

William Newham Blane (1799–1825) saw another hand. Author of a five-hundred-page treatise, this "English Gentleman" looked down from superior heights on much of what he witnessed on this side of the Atlantic. Indeed his tome falls largely under the heading of what Henry Tuckerman called the

"English Abuse of America" (*America and Her Commentators* [1864], Chap. VII). Though Tuckerman strangely does not mention Blane, he does denounce collectively—and heatedly— "the arrant cockneyism and provincial impertinence of many of these superficial and sensation writers, on a subject whose true and grand relations they were incapable of grasping. . . ."

In the year that Morse's report was published, Blane was touring the United States and Canada—as in fact much of England seemed to be doing in the 1820's and 30's. The title of this chapter suggests that if Morse was for "salvation," then Blane must be for "savagery." This is the case only if we remind ourselves of the "noble savage" sentiments of much eighteenth- and early nineteenth-century thought. The virtue, intelligence, and joy of primitive natural man are such that it is he who should be sending out the missionaries. The kindest, most Christian thing we can do is to teach Indians the "necessary arts and . . . the advantages of civilization"; but above all, we can stop sending into their midst "well meaning persons religiously mad."

A

[The text is taken from Jedidiah Morse, *A Report to the Secretary of War of the United States on Indian Affairs* . . . (New Haven: S. Converse, 1822), pp. 81–84.]

Report to the Secretary of War

When we look back in the pages of history four or five hundred years, and see what then was the state of our own Ancestors, and whence sprung the most polished and scientific nations of Europe, we should scarcely have supposed, that any man, acquainted with history, or making any pretensions to candor, would be found among the objectors to attempts to civilize our Indians, and thus to save them from perishing. Yet, painful as is the fact, objections have been made to the present course of procedure with Indians, and from men too, whose standing and office in society are such, as it would be deemed disrespectful to pass unnoticed. "The project," it has been said, "is visionary and impracticable. Indians can never be tamed; they are incapable of receiving, or of enjoying, the blessings proposed to be offered to them." Some, I will hope, for the honor of our country, that the number is small, have proceeded farther, and said, "Indians are not worth saving. They are perishing—let them perish. The sooner they are gone, the better." And to hasten such a catastrophe, a formal project has been actually devised, and put on paper, and the projector has had the effrontery to offer his infernal project for the adoption of the government! ! !*

A sufficient answer to such of these objections, as require notice (for truly some of them are so shocking, that one can hardly think of them, much less undertake to answer them) will be found, I conceive, in the facts collected into the Appendix of this work. It is too late to say that Indians cannot be civilized. The facts referred to, beyond all question, prove the contrary. The evidence of actual experiment in every case, is paramount to all objections founded in mere theory, or, as in the present case, in naked and unsupported assertions. The specimens of composition, and the account given, on unquestionable authority, of the acquisitions of Indian youths, of other kinds of knowledge, in the Cornwall, and other Indian schools, can hardly fail to convince all, who are willing to be convinced, that it *is* practicable to civilize, educate and save Indians. Without fear of contradiction, then, we assume this point as established. Indians are of the same nature and original, and of one blood, with ourselves; of intellectual powers as strong, and capable of cultivation, as ours. They, as well as ourselves, are made to be immortal. To look down upon them, therefore, as an inferior race, as untameable, and to profit by their ignorance and weakness; to take their property from them for a small part of its real value, and in other ways to oppress them; is undoubtedly wrong, and

* I have not seen the document here referred to, but the fact stated rests on substantial authority. [Jedidiah Morse]

highly displeasing to our common Creator, Lawgiver and final Judge.

Plan for civilizing the Indians.

The general plan, embracing all its ramifications, which I would respectfully submit to the consideration and adoption of the government, with the improvements hereafter mentioned, is that, substantially, which has been devised by the American Board of Commissioners for Foreign Missions, and is now in successful operation under the direction of this Board, and of other similar associations of different denominations, and has already received the sanction and patronage of the Government. This plan, "in the full tide of successful experiment," is now in a course of exhibition before the public, and is looked at with joy and admiration, by philanthropists on both sides of the Atlantic.

Removal and colonization of the Indians, now living within the settlements of the white people.

On the subject of the removal of the Indians, who now dwell within our settlements, there are different opinions among wise and good men. The point on which they divide is, whether it be best to let these Indians quietly remain on their present Reservations, and to use our endeavors to civilize them where they are; or for the Government to take their Reservations, and give them an equivalent in lands to be purchased of other tribes beyond our present settlements. The Indians themselves too, are divided in opinion on this subject; a part are for removing, and a part for remaining, as in the case of the Cherokees, Delawares, Senecas, Oneidas, Shawanees, and indeed most of the other tribes living among us. Difficulties in deciding this question present themselves, on which side soever it be viewed. To remove these Indians far away from their present homes, from "the bones of their fathers," into a wilderness, among strangers, possibly hostile, to live as their new neighbors live, by hunting, a state to which they have not lately been accustomed, and which is incompatible with civilization, can hardly be reconciled with the professed views and objects of the Government in civilizing them. This would not be deemed by the world a wise course, nor one which would very probably lead to the desired end. Should that part of the tribes only, remove, who are willing to go, and the remainder be permitted to stay—this division of already enfeebled remnants of tribes, would but still more weaken their strength, diminish their influence, and hasten their destruction. Nor would this partial removal satisfy those who are for removing the whole; nor those either, who are for retaining the whole. The latter wish them to remain for the benevolent purpose of educating them all where they now are, urging, that they are now among us, in view of examples of civilized life; and where necessary instruction can be conveniently, and with little expense, imparted to them. On the other hand there is much to be said in favor of the removal of the smaller tribes, and remnants of tribes—not, however, into the wilderness, to return again to the savage life, but to some suitable, prepared portion of our country, where, collected in one body, they may be made comfortable, and with advantage be educated together, as has already been mentioned, in the manner in which we educate our own children. Some such course as this, I apprehend, will satisfy a great majority of the reflecting part of those who interest themselves at all in this subject, and is, in my belief, the only practicable course which can be pursued, consistently with the professed object of the Government.

Revolution now in operation among the Indians.

There is evidently a great and important revolution in the state of our Indian population already commenced, and now rapidly going forward, affecting immediately the tribes among us and on our borders, and which will ultimately and speedily be felt by those at the remotest distance. The evidence of this revolution exists in the peculiar interest which is felt and manifested for the general improvement and welfare of Indians, and in the peculiar corresponding feelings and movements among the Indians themselves. The civil and religious communities are remarkably awake on this subject, and are making joint efforts for the improvement and happiness of Indians, such as were never made in any former period of our history. The Chiefs and sensible men among these tribes, to a great extent, feel that a change in their situation has become necessary, that they must quit the hunter, and adopt the agricultural state, or perish. Of this fact I myself am a witness. There is an increasing willingness, which in some instances rises to strong desire, on the part of the Indians, to accept the benevolent offers of instruction held out to them by the Government, and by Christian Associations. There is a most remarkable reciprocity of feelings on this subject, which plainly indicates, that the hand of heaven is in it; as no power short of this could ever have produced such a state of things. This is for our encouragement, and it is encouragement enough, to persevere. In such circumstances we cannot go back. Honor, justice, humanity, all that makes man respectable in the sight of God and men, imperiously require us to go forward, in full faith, till this work, so auspiciously commenced, shall be accomplished.

B

[The text is taken from William Newham Blane, *An Excursion Through the United States and Canada During the Years 1822–23 by an English Gentleman* (London: Baldwin, Cradock, and Joy, 1824), pp. 230–33, 427–28.]

Missionaries . . .

After leaving St. Louis, I returned fifty-four miles by the same road that I had before travelled, to the little Village of Carlyle, on the Kaskaskia. Having arrived there early on the second day and seen my horse taken care of, I went, for the want of something better to do, to hear a Sermon delivered by some Missionaries, who were going to the Wilderness for the purpose of converting the Indians.

The sermon, as may easily be supposed, was nearly incomprehensible. A conversation arose afterwards between the preachers and their auditors upon doctrinal points, when the Missionaries, who were thorough Calvinists, did not hesitate to declare, that only a certain portion of the human race, *viz.* the elect, would be saved. All the rest, or at least 999 out of every 1000 were of course to be damned.

I perhaps however may be allowed to doubt, whether the Missionaries were perfectly correct, in this their charitable and sensible exposition of the intentions of the Almighty; for I can myself hardly imagine, that the beneficent author of all things will "show his power," as they call it, by sending such an immense proportion of the human race, into fire and brimstone. I cannot see, why a man born in the centre of China, and who never even heard of Christianity, should of necessity be a "vessel of wrath," whom the great Creator for his own better glorification, is to plunge into everlasting torments. Doubtless however I am wrong; for the Missionaries, going on with the subject, affirmed, that there were many *children* in the number of the non-elect; that there are infants in hell not a span long,—an amiable and enlightened doctrine, which has been also maintained in the Presbyterian Church at Philadelphia.

A woman who, like myself, was among the listeners, and who had just lost her child, was so much afflicted at this, that she began to cry. She knew not (and indeed how could she know?) whether her child was really one of the elect; and the idea of the bare possibility of its being in fire and brimstone distressed her terribly, and cost her an abundance of tears.

The reader may perhaps think, that the present system should be reversed; and that the Indians should send Missionaries to convert these unfortunate expounders of the Bible, to a more reasonable faith.

At any rate, nothing can well be imagined more absurd, than

the plan at present pursued by those wishing to convert the Aborigines to Christianity. Instead of preaching morality, instead of teaching them the useful arts, and of pointing out the advantages of civilization, and thus preparing them to quit their wild life and to adopt our mild doctrines; the Missionaries begin at once by requiring the Indians to believe the most incomprehensible dogmas. In fact their object is not so much to make the Indians civilized beings and Christians—No, they must make them Methodists, Baptists, Presbyterians, or members of whatever other sect they themselves belong to. Consequently the Indians, shocked as may easily be supposed at this method of proceeding, and astounded at the dogmas which they are required to believe, consider the whole a trick, and despise it as such.

The Missionaries are also in general men of very inferior education; for of course few of those that can obtain any employment at home, will sally forth to preach in woods. Many of them are also not of the very strictest chastity. A gentleman travelling from New Orleans to Tennessee, when passing through the Indian territory, met a little boy who appeared to be too white for an Indian: "Pray my little fellow," said the traveller, "are you a full-blooded Indian?" "No, Sir," replied the boy. "I am half Indian, half Missionary."

The Indians believe in one great incomprehensible Spirit, the Creator and Governor of all things; and although they have no altars, images, or temples, yet we may perhaps be permitted to believe, that their sincere and simple adoration may not be altogether displeasing to the Almighty. Indeed I should have been strongly tempted to hope, that these Indians, following the light of nature and doing what they believe to be right, would not be in danger of eternal punishment: but alas! this pleasing hope is utterly annihilated by the 18th Article of our holy Religion.

"They," it tells us, "are to be had accursed, that presume to say, that every man shall be saved by the Law or Sect which he professeth, so that he be diligent to frame his life according to that law and the Light of nature."

Being therefore myself a staunch High Churchman, and extremely unwilling to be had accursed, I am obliged to believe, that all these poor Indians will be damned; which I am sorry for, as I have known some among them, not only held in universal estimation, but who were really endowed with the utmost nobleness of soul. Of a truth I have heard it said by some philosophers, children of Belial, that this article is worthy of the one preceding it, (on predestination,) and that neither of them is consistent with the goodness of the Almighty. But I abhor and detest such profane reasoners, who will no doubt, in the next world, keep company with the Indians. * * *

To confess the truth, nothing can be more irrational than the method pursued by the Missionaries. They should first of all have taught the Indians the most necessary arts, and have shown them the advantages of civilization. When the Indians had sufficiently abandoned their wild mode of life, the Missionaries might then have proceeded to give them a learned education, so that by dint of study they might be enabled to form a candid and accurate estimate of the historical and other Evidences of Christianity. But instead of acting according to this rational plan, the Missionary Societies have sent among the Indians a set of well meaning persons religiously mad. These men preach to the noble-minded sensible chiefs, about grace, and election, and predestination, and regeneration, &c. &c. words which convey rather confused ideas. Moreover the Missionaries disgust their auditors by telling them that all their fathers and famous warriors are gone to a certain place of torture, because they did not believe in a religion they never heard of.

Even if the Missionaries ever do make converts, which but seldom happens, they inflict a curse upon the Indian and not a blessing, by destroying his high sense of honour, his great motive for practising virtue.

The Indians are an uncommonly intelligent and shrewd people; but although they will readily give their assent to all good arguments upon morality, yet I regret to say, that they are very sceptical with regard to accounts of miracles, wonders, mysteries, &c. The generality of the Missionaries plunge at once "in medias res," without attempting to explain the historical evidences of our holy religion, of which evidences indeed I very much doubt whether they themselves know any thing. Hence the Indians naturally refuse their belief to the very strange stories, which are related to them out of the Bible.

Dr. Franklin tells us of the remark of an Indian Chief, when a Missionary had been explaining to him, how Adam and Eve, by eating the apple in Paradise, occasioned the eternal damnation of all their posterity.—The Chief got up, and replied, with the utmost gravity, "that it was certainly a very bad thing to eat apples, as it was much better to make them into cider."

7

REASON
OR
REVELATION

THE ALTERNATION between faith and reason is a religious issue
not of a nation but of mankind. Ages and epochs are marked
out by the emphasis given to one or another repository of truth.
Never, of course, do men live wholly by faith, eschewing the
pragmatic rationalism that enables much of the daily work to get
done. Nor on the other hand do men ever live wholly by reason,
abandoning the essential hope that sustains the day's work and
continues to sustain when that work is over. But men and even
civilizations do consciously turn more either toward reason or
toward faith.

American history has seen several major confrontations between faith and reason. For "faith" one may normally read
"revelation" or "Bible," though sometimes one may read creed,
intuition, mysticism, or "concluding unscientific postscript." For
"reason" one may read philosophy or science or experience
or simply rejection of a particular dogmatic structure. The
eighteenth-century Enlightenment and more specifically the

French Revolution confronted American religion with its first major challenge wherein reason appeared not as revelation's ally or complement but as its competitor or surrogate.

In the final decade of the eighteenth century Thomas Paine (1737–1809) popularized—perhaps vulgarized—much of the Enlightenment's impatient criticism of Christian revelation. Paine arrived in Philadelphia from England just in time to become chief propagandist and pamphleteer on behalf of the colonists' cause. His *Common Sense* published early in 1776 as well as the *Crisis Papers* that began later in the same year brought him instant popularity in patriot circles. In a time that tried men's souls, his prose inspired those souls to drastic, definitive action. For a few years in America, his acclaim was at a peak.

That pervasive popularity quickly narrowed, however, with the publication of *The Age of Reason* (1794, 1796). Writing in Paris where he had gone to defend and promote the French Revolution—as he had defended and promoted the American—Paine readily became identified with the excesses of that foreign revolution, its Reign of Terror, its anticlericalism, its Jacobinism, its infidelity. Nothing in this scandalous book suggested that Paine was less than an extremist, less than a dedicated opponent of all organized religion. A man who would write that "The most detestable wickedness, the most horrid cruelties, and the greatest miseries that have afflicted the human race have had their origin in this thing called revelation"—a man who would write *that* deserved to be answered.

New England Federalists were especially alarmed by the French Revolution and its overt challenge to the New England way. Timothy Dwight (1752–1817) led the counterattacking forces against all those terrors—political, social and religious— for which "Jacobinism" became the useful, frightful epithet. President of Yale from 1795 to 1817, "Pope Dwight" exercised a leadership far beyond the limits of the college green. A grandson of New England's towering theological giant, Jonathan Edwards, Dwight was more significant as defender than as creator of social and intellectual patterns.

In his sermon cited below, Timothy Dwight shares little common ground with Thomas Paine. The split between natural, unaided reason and divine, explicit revelation has become a gaping chasm, with little possibility of erecting any bridge of understanding across it. As the gap widened throughout the nineteenth century, each side shouted at the other in voices more strident, in phrases more irrelevant. Reading Paine and Dwight, it is difficult to believe that they could be speaking to the same audience or even the same generation. And that is in fact the problem. The two intellectual worlds grow farther and farther apart as the nation moves from adolescence into maturity.

A

[The text is taken from W. M. Van der Weyde, ed., *The Life and Works of Thomas Paine* (New Rochelle, N. Y.: Thomas Paine National Historical Association, 1925), Vol. VIII (*The Age of Reason*), pp. 267–72, 275–77.]

The Age of Reason

In the former part of "The Age of Reason" I have spoken of the three frauds, *mystery, miracle* and *prophecy*; and as I have seen nothing in any of the answers to that work that in the least affects what I have there said upon those subjects, I shall not encumber this Second Part with additions that are not necessary.

I have spoken also in the same work upon what is called *revelation,* and have shown the absurd misapplication of that term to the books of the Old Testament and the New; for certainly revelation is out of the question in reciting anything of which man has been the actor or the witness.

That which a man has done or seen needs no revelation to tell him he has done it or seen it, for he knows it already; nor to enable him to tell it or to write it. It is ignorance or imposition to apply the term revelation in such cases; yet the Bible and Testament are classed under this fraudulent description of being all *revelation*.

Revelation then, so far as the term has relation between God and man, can only be applied to something which God reveals of His *will* to man; but though the power of the Almighty to make such a communication is necessarily admitted, because to that power all things are possible, yet the thing so revealed (if anything ever was revealed, and which, by the bye, it is impossible to prove) is revelation to the person only to whom it is made.

His account of it to another person is not revelation; and whoever puts faith in that account, puts it in the man from whom the account comes; and that man may have been deceived, or may have dreamed it, or he may be an impostor and may lie.

There is no possible criterion whereby to judge of the truth of what he tells, for even the morality of it would be no proof of revelation. In all such cases the proper answer would be, "When it is revealed to me, I will believe it to be a revelation; but it is not, and cannot be incumbent upon me to believe it to be revelation before; neither is it proper that I should take the word of man as the Word of God, and put man in the place of God."

This is the manner in which I have spoken of revelation in the former part of "The Age of Reason"; and which, while it reverentially admits revelation as a possible thing, because, as before said, to the Almighty all things are possible, it prevents the imposition of one man upon another, and precludes the wicked use of pretended revelation.

But though, speaking for myself, I thus admit the possibility of revelation, I totally disbelieve that the Almighty ever did communicate anything to man, by any mode of speech, in any language, or by any kind of vision, or appearance, or by any means which our senses are capable of receiving, otherwise than by the universal display of Himself in the works of the creation, and by that repugnance we feel in ourselves to bad actions, and the disposition to do good ones.

The most detestable wickedness, the most horrid cruelties, and the greatest miseries that have afflicted the human race have had their origin in this thing called revelation, or revealed religion. It has been the most dishonorable belief against the character of the Divinity, the most destructive to morality and the peace and happiness of man that ever was propagated since man began to exist.

It is better, far better, that we admitted, if it were possible, a thousand devils to roam at large, and to preach publicly the doctrine of devils, if there were any such, than that we permitted one such impostor and monster as Moses, Joshua, Samuel and the Bible prophets, to come with the pretended word of God in his mouth and have credit among us.

Whence arose all the horrid assassinations of whole nations of men, women and infants, with which the Bible is filled, and the bloody persecutions and tortures unto death, and religious wars, that since that time have laid Europe in blood and ashes— whence rose they but from this impious thing called revealed religion, and this monstrous belief that God has spoken to man? The lies of the Bible have been the cause of the one, and the lies of the Testament of the other.

Some Christians pretend that Christianity was not established by the sword; but of what period of time do they speak? It was impossible that twelve men could begin with the sword; they had not the power; but no sooner were the professors of Christianity sufficiently powerful to employ the sword than they did so, and the stake and fagot, too; and Mahomet could not do it sooner. By the same spirit that Peter cut off the ear of the high priest's servant (if the story be true), he would have cut off his head, and the head of his master, had he been able.

Besides this, Christianity founds itself originally upon the Bible, and the Bible was established altogether by the sword, and that in the worst use of it—not to terrify, but to extirpate. The Jews made no converts; they butchered all. The Bible is the sire of the Testament, and both are called the *Word of God*. The Christians read both books; the ministers preach from both books; and this thing called Christianity is made up of both. It is then false to say that Christianity was not established by the sword.

The only sect that has not persecuted are the Quakers, and

the only reason that can be given for it is that they are rather Deists than Christians. They do not believe much about Jesus Christ, and they call the Scriptures a dead letter. Had they called them by a worse name, they had been nearer the truth.

It is incumbent on every man who reverences the character of the Creator, and who wishes to lessen the catalogue of artificial miseries, and remove the cause that has sown persecutions thick among mankind, to expel all ideas of revealed religion, as a dangerous heresy and an impious fraud.

What is that we have learned from this pretended thing called revealed religion? Nothing that is useful to man, and everything that is dishonorable to his Maker. What is it the Bible teaches us?—rapine, cruelty, and murder. What is it the Testament teaches us?—to believe that the Almighty committed debauchery with a woman engaged to be married, and the belief of this debauchery is called faith.

As to the fragments of morality that are irregularly and thinly scattered in these books, they make no part of this pretended thing, revealed religion. They are the natural dictates of conscience, and the bonds by which society is held together, and without which it cannot exist, and are nearly the same in all religions and in all societies. * * *

If we consider the nature of our condition here, we must see there is no occasion for such a thing as *revealed religion*. What is it we want to know? Does not the creation, the universe we behold, preach to us the existence of an Almighty Power that governs and regulates the whole? And is not the evidence that this creation holds out to our senses infinitely stronger than anything we can read in a book that any impostor might make and call the Word of God? As for morality, the knowledge of it exists in every man's conscience.

Here we are. The existence of an Almighty Power is sufficiently demonstrated to us, though we cannot conceive, as it is impossible we should, the nature and manner of its existence. We cannot conceive how we came here ourselves, and yet we know for a fact that we are here.

We must know also that the Power that called us into being, can, if He pleases, and when He pleases, call us to account for the manner in which we have lived here; and, therefore, without seeking any other motive for the belief, it is rational to believe that He will, for we know beforehand that He can. The probability or even possibility of the thing is all that we ought to know; for if we knew it as a fact, we should be the mere slaves of terror; our belief would have no merit, and our best actions no virtue.

Deism, then, teaches us, without the possibility of being deceived, all that is necessary or proper to be known. The creation is the Bible of the Deist. He there reads, in the handwriting of the Creator himself, the certainty of His existence and the immutability of His power, and all other Bibles and Testaments are to him forgeries.

The probability that we may be called to account hereafter will, to a reflecting mind, have the influence of belief; for it is not our belief or our disbelief that can make or unmake the fact. As this is the state we are in, and which it is proper we should be in, as free agents, it is the fool only, and not the philosopher, or even the prudent man, that would live as if there were no God.

But the belief of a God is so weakened by being mixed with the strange fable of the Christian creed, and with the wild adventures related in the Bible, and [with] the obscurity and obscene nonsense of the Testament, that the mind of man is bewildered as in a fog. Viewing all these things in a confused mass, he confounds fact with fable; and as he cannot believe all, he feels a disposition to reject all.

But the belief of a God is a belief distinct from all other things, and ought not to be confounded with any. The notion of a Trinity of Gods has enfeebled the belief of one God. A multiplication of beliefs acts as a division of belief; and in proportion as anything is divided it is weakened.

Religion, by such means, becomes a thing of form, instead of fact—of notion, instead of principles; morality is banished to make room for an imaginary thing called faith, and this faith has

its origin in a supposed debauchery; a man is preached instead
of a God; an execution is an object for gratitude; the preachers
daub themselves with blood, like a troop of assassins, and pretend to admire the brilliancy it gives them; they preach a hum-
drum sermon on the merits of the execution; then praise Jesus
Christ for being executed, and condemn the Jews for doing it.
A man, by hearing all this nonsense lumped and preached together, confounds the God of the Creation with the imagined
God of the Christians, and lives as if there were none.

B

[The text is taken from Timothy Dwight, *Theology Explained and
Defended in a Series of Sermons* (New York: G. & C. & H. Carrill,
1830), Vol. IV, pp. 75–80.]

Hearing the Word of God

Luke 8:18 "Take heed, therefore, how ye hear."

The direction in the Text is, I apprehend, a direction given to
all men, who are in possession of the Gospel. It is delivered in
the most general terms; and may, therefore, be regarded as
extending to every mode of hearing, which is useful. There are
modes of hearing, which, unless I am deceived, are eventually
useful to sinners; and in which the Gospel becomes to sinners
the power of God unto salvation. I shall consider these modes,
as included in it; modes in which I should wish a sinful child of
my own, and for the same reason should wish others also, to hear
the Gospel. Such, as have heard in these modes, have in great
multitudes, as I verily believe, been profited, in a degree which
no man can estimate.

The persons, who in this sense would take heed how they hear
the Gospel; by which I intend the Scriptures at large; ought,
while they hear, to remember the following things.

1. That the Gospel is the Word of God.

To prevent any misapprehension, I wish it to be kept steadily in view, that no attention, or reverence, is here claimed to Preaching, any farther than the Gospel is preached. To the mere opinions, and declarations, of a Preacher, as such, no other respect is due, than that, which by common consent is rendered to the opinions and declarations of all men, of similar understanding and worth. The best opinions of men are merely useful, wholesome advice. The Scriptures are a Law; possessed of Divine authority, and obligation. So far as the doctrines, precepts, and ordinances, of the Scriptures are preached, they claim the reverence, which they themselves have challenged.

The solemn remembrance, that the Scriptures are the Word of God, involves a variety of interesting considerations.

In this character, particularly, they come home to us as the Word of Him, by whom we were created, and by whom we are preserved, and governed. From this Great and Glorious Being, all that we have, and all that we hope for, is, and must be, derived. We are his property; and are rightfully disposed of, and rightfully required to dispose of ourselves, according to his pleasure. In the Scriptures alone is this pleasure made known to us. In them alone, therefore, we learn the proper destination of our faculties, our services, and ourselves. The Law, by which we are here required to do his pleasure, is invested with all possible authority, and obligation; and demands our reverence, and obedience, in a manner supremely impressive.

As the Word of God, also, the Scriptures are dictated by his Wisdom, Goodness, and Truth. They are the Word of Him, who cannot mistake, deceive, nor injure. Consequently they contain all things, necessary for life and godliness; whatever we need to know, and whatever we ought to do, for the attainment of his approbation. On their entire wisdom and integrity, their fitness to promote the great purpose for which they were written, and their conduciveness to it in ourselves, we are wholly to rely. Not a doubt can be reasonably entertained concerning the truth of the doctrines, the soundness of the precepts, or the sincerity of the promises. Nor are we any more to distrust the certainty of the threatenings, or the reality of those awful dangers, which they disclose. We are bound on the one hand not to question the truth, and on the other, not to dispute the wisdom and goodness, of that, which is revealed. All things, which this sacred Book contains, are to be received as they are. Our own opinions are implicitly to bow before them: and we are ever to be ready to believe, that what we think the foolishness of God is wiser than men; than all the substituted opinions of ourselves or others. Let God be true, ought to be our invariable language, but every man who opposes his declarations, a liar.

Against this great and awful Being we have rebelled. Hence, although he is our Creator, Preserver, and Benefactor, he still regards our moral character with abhorrence. The Scriptures, therefore, are published to us as the Word of an offended God. Hence are derived all those denunciations of anger and punishment, found in them; which could have no place in the Will of God, as revealed to obedient creatures.

As the Word of God, the Scriptures announce to us, that, notwithstanding our rebellion, he is willing to be reconciled to us. We are, therefore, ever to remember, that they are the Word of the Father, and of the Redeemer, and of the Sanctifier, of mankind. In these venerable and amiable characters, God appears to us with infinite tenderness and endearment. His Word is thus presented to us as the pleasure of the best of all friends, and the most affectionate of all parents. In our ruined condition he beheld us with boundless mercy; and, unasked and undesired, undertook to rescue us from destruction. For this end, the Saviour came into the world, lived a life of humiliation, and died a death of anguish and infamy. For this end, the Spirit of Truth came into the world, to convince, renew, and purify, the hearts of mankind. Of these Three Persons in the One Jehovah, the Scriptures are the Word; willed by the Father, dictated by the Son, and inspired by the Holy Ghost.

As the Word of God, the Scriptures are the Word of Him, on whom we daily depend for life, and breath, and all things. Whatever we enjoy he gives: whatever we hope for must, if enjoyed at all, be also given by him. Without him, we are poor, and miserable, and in want of all things. With his favour, we shall be rich indeed, and have need of nothing.

The Scriptures are also the Word of Him, by whom we shall be judged, and rewarded. The day is hastening, when we shall be called to an account for all our conduct; and shall be compelled to rehearse it before him. If we have done well; if we have obeyed, worshipped, and glorified him, and served our generation according to his will; we shall be acquitted in this great trial, and received to everlasting glory. If we have done evil, and refused to do good; we shall be driven away to final and irremediable perdition.

Whenever we are assembled to hear the Gospel, we are to remember, that with reference to all these solemn things it is the Word of God.

2. That we are sinners, who infinitely need forgiveness and salvation.

As sinners, we are irreversibly condemned by that divine law, which we have broken, and by that just government, against which we have rebelled. The soul that sinneth shall die, was the original sentence of that law to mankind; the sentence of Him, who can neither deceive, nor change. The sentence will, therefore, be executed in its strict meaning on all, who disobey, and who do not become interested in the Redemption of Christ. Under such a sentence, infinitely dreadful, and unalterably certain, our danger is immensely great, and our ruin entire. From this sentence, therefore, we infinitely need a deliverance. Our all is at stake; and our souls are in a situation of the most terrible hazard. Hell, if we continue in this situation, is open before us, and destruction hath no covering.

It is impossible, that any beings should be in a state of more absolute and pressing necessity. Rational, immortal, and incapable of perishing by annhilation; we must be, and be for ever. But to exist for ever, and yet to be sinful and miserable only; is a doom, compared with which, all other characters and sufferings lose their deformity and wretchedness, and rise into happiness and distinction. When we are present in the house of God, we should recall with deep affection this intense and melancholy necessity; and feel the declarations of Scripture with a concern, suited to the inestimable importance of our situation.

3. That the Scriptures are the Book, in which alone the terms, and means, of salvation are published.

The Word Gospel, as you know, signifies good tidings, or joyful news. This name is given to the Scriptures generally, and to the New Testament particularly, because they contain the best of all tidings, ever published to this ruined world. Independently of the Gospel, all the race of Adam are under a sentence of condemnation, without a friend, and without a hope. To these forlorn and miserable beings, the infinitely merciful God has been pleased to make known a way of escape; a deliverance from destruction. This glorious communication is made to mankind in the Scriptures only. From no other source has man ever learned, that God is reconcileable on any terms; that sinners can be forgiven; that there is in the universe an Atonement for sin; or that any atonement will be accepted. From no other source have we been informed, that God will be pleased with any worship, which we can render; or, if he will, what that worship is. Without the Scriptures, we know not, that the connexion between God and man, between heaven and earth, can be renewed; or that the gates, which admit intelligent beings to the world of enjoyment, have been, or will ever be, opened to apostate creatures.

To beings, in circumstances of such necessity and danger, tidings even of partial deliverance must be delightful. But these are tidings of complete deliverance from sin, and of an entire escape from misery. To beings, left in absolute ignorance of reconciliation to God, and in absolute despair of future enjoyment; to whom the world of happiness was shut, and to whom the ages of eternity rolled onward no bright reversion; even the uncertain rumour of relief must, one would imagine, echo throughout every region of the globe, which they inhabited, and thrill with inexpressible emotions in every heart. But these are certain tidings from God Himself concerning this glorious possession; from the God, who cannot deceive; the God, whose promises endure for ever.

This great salvation is, however, proffered by God on his own terms only. In the same Scriptures are these terms found. From them alone can we learn on what conditions we may obtain life, and escape from death. The way of holiness, to which the Gospel alone directs us, is there made a highway; and wayfaring men, though fools, need not err therein.

In the Scriptures, also, are the means of this Divine, and immortal, attainment presented to our view. Here we are taught, that we become possessed of a title to everlasting life by Faith, Repentance, and Holiness. Here, also, is pointed out the way, in which these indispensable characteristics are communicated; viz. the Means of Grace, already mentioned in these discourses. Both the Means, and the terms, are eminently reasonable and desirable; in themselves real and superior good, and the way to greater good; easy of adoption and use, and, with the divine blessing, efficacious to the end, for which they are used; sanctioned with supreme authority by the testimony of God, and daily confirmed by their actual influence on multitudes of mankind.

When, therefore, we hear the Word of God, we are ever to remember, that we are taught things, in this respect infinitely interesting to us, and incapable of being derived from any other source.

4. That in order to be saved we must understand the Means, and the Terms, of salvation.

There is no other Word of God, but the Scriptures: and, beside God, there is no other being, who can inform us what we must do to be saved. Philosophers may investigate, and write, from generation to generation: this vast momentous subject has ever lain, and will ever lie, beyond their reach. Those who read, and understood, the instructions of the ancient philosophers, were never reformed by their doctrines. Those who read, and understand, the moral systems of Infidel philosophers, are never amended by them, but corrupted of course. The Scriptures, on the contrary, have been the means of renewing, and reforming, millions of the human race. But this sacred book was never of the least use to any man, by whom it was not in some good measure understood. To enable mankind at large to understand it, God instituted the Evangelical Ministry. All complicated objects of the intellect are far better known by sober reflection, and diligent research, than they can be by casual, or cursory, thinking. The Scriptures contain a system immensely complicated. They demand, therefore, the most patient, persevering study, and thorough investigation. Hence Ministers, consecrated originally to this employment, are commanded to give themselves wholly to the Ministry; particularly to reading and to meditation; that they may not be novices, nor furnish reasons to others for regarding their discourses with contempt. But all their labours will be to no purpose, unless those, who hear them, understand their discourses; however evangelically, and usefully, they may be written. Every hearer, therefore, should solemnly call to mind, in the house of God, that the means, and terms, of eternal life, then are published to him; that they are found no where, but in the Scriptures; and that the Scriptures can be of no benefit to him, unless he understands them. His highest interest, and indispensable duty, demand of him therefore, that he should hear, as for his life.

It ought to be added, that all these things are not only explained in the Scriptures, but enforced on the heart with supreme power and efficacy. Motives, of amazing import, are here presented, to persuade the sinner to repentance. Alarms compel; invitations allure; threatenings terrify; and promises encourage; of such a nature, and exhibited in such a manner, as boundless Wisdom and Goodness thought best fitted to affect the heart. But all these, also, are in vain, unless heard, understood, and realized, by the sinner.

8

FEELING
OR
FAITH

WHEN OPPOSED to reason, faith represents a kind of confidence or trust. Opposed to emotion, faith becomes *a faith,* a creed, an assent to propositions, an intellectual apprehension. And this issue of emotion versus doctrine (in biblical language, "zeal without knowledge") haunts America's churches from the seventeenth century to the present. As in the contention between reason or revelation, men do not live wholly by propositions or by glands. They form their parties, their sects, their orders and schools, however, according to the degrees of reliance placed either on "religious affections" or on religious propositions.

Removing the churches from all governmental patronage threw them wholly on their own resources for support and survival. Moreover, the open-market competition among denominations for membership and contributions inevitably led to experimentation with new techniques—the central question being: Does it work? That is, do we as a church secure more converts, gain more support, grow more rapidly than does some other church? Or, at least, do we grow rapidly enough to keep up with the needs of a booming, migrating national population. In the search for techniques and procedures, and for a fresher balance between feeling and faith, revivalism emerged as a popular though not universal favorite.

Charles G. Finney (1792–1875) deliberately and earnestly adopted "new measures" to meet the new national situation. President of Oberlin College from 1851 to 1866, Finney knew problems of recruitment in the West and on the frontier. But his restructured revivalism was far more than a frontier phenomenon: it proved to be remarkably and repeatedly successful in the urban centers of the East. Both in city and country Finney has continued to have many imitators down to the present—all believing that, while a true revival is a gift of God, men can nonetheless do much to prepare for and promote these showers of blessing.

Among Finney's new measures was the "anxious seat." Not a crucial innovation itself, the anxious seat easily became a focus for animosity and attack. For its use magnified the central uneasiness about revivalism—an uneasiness that had expressed itself from the first Great Awakening on: how much of all the excitement, contrition, and new resolve is mere emotional fluff? But for Finney "the delusion of the human heart" is a danger of at least equal magnitude. The person who is unwilling to take even the simple step to the anxious seat can no longer delude himself into thinking he is a Christian. Finney defends not only this evangelistic novelty, but novelty itself, for never in the history of the church has there "been an extensive reformation, except by new measures."

John Williamson Nevin (1803–1886), Presbyterian become German Reformed, made the "anxious bench" (his term) the scapegoat to bear all revivalism's sin. Nevin, a graduate of Union and of Princeton Theological Seminary, was like Finney also a college president: Franklin and Marshall in Lancaster, Pennsylvania. When he wrote the work excerpted below, however, he was professor of theology at Mercersburg Seminary, where with the noted church historian Philip Schaff (1819–1893) he made this small school a major center of creative theology.

The Anxious Bench is a sustained, 150-page attack on much of what Finney stood for and promoted. It provoked considerable stir and strong reaction "as was to be expected," Nevin calmly notes in his preface to the second edition. He wished to make clear he was not attacking "honest zeal in favor of serious religion," but seeking to distinguish clearly between "the system of the Anxious Bench, and the power of evangelical godliness working in its true form." With a German Reformed audience especially in mind, Nevin warned against Methodist infiltration, pointing out that "Wesley was a small man as compared with Melanchthon." Eying a problem that divided several American denominations into quarreling camps at this time, Nevin denounced the "revival machinery" and "solemn tricks" that offered a "justification by feeling rather than faith."

A

[The text is taken from Charles G. Finney, *Lectures on Revivals of Religion* (New York: Leavitt, Lord & Co., 1835; reprint, Cambridge, Mass.: Belknap Press of Harvard University Press, 1960), pp. 261–262, 267–76.]

Measures to Promote Revivals

In the present generation, many things have been introduced which have proved useful, but have been opposed on the ground *that they were innovations.* And as many are still unsettled in regard to them, I have thought it best to make some remarks concerning them. There are three things in particular, which have chiefly attracted remark, and therefore I shall speak of them. They are *Anxious Meetings, Protracted Meetings,* and the *Anxious Seat.* These are all opposed, and are called new measures.* * *

The Anxious Seat

By this I mean the appointment of some particular seat in the place of meeting, where the anxious may come and be addressed particularly, and be made subjects of prayer, and sometimes conversed with individually. Of late this measure has met with more opposition than any of the others. What is the great objection? I cannot see it. The *design* of the anxious seat is undoubtedly philosophical, and according to the laws of mind. It has two bearings:

1. When a person is seriously troubled in mind, every body knows that there is a powerful tendency to try to keep it private that he is so, and it is a great thing to get the individual willing to have the fact known to others. And as soon as you can get him willing to make known his feelings, you have accomplished a great deal. When a person is borne down with a sense of his condition, if you can get him willing to have it known, if you can get him to break away from the chains of pride, you have gained an important point towards his conversion. This is agreeable to the philosophy of the human mind. How many thousands are there who will bless God to eternity, that when pressed by the truth they were ever brought to take this step, by which they threw off the idea that it was a dreadful thing to have any body know that they were serious about their souls.

2. Another bearing of the anxious seat, is to detect deception and delusion, and thus prevent false hopes. It has been opposed on this ground, that it was calculated to create delusion and false hopes. But this objection is unreasonable. The truth is the other way. Suppose I were preaching on the subject of Temperance, and that I should first show the evils of intemperance, and bring up the drunkard and his family, and show the various evils produced, till every heart is beating with emotion. Then I portray the great danger of *moderate drinking,* and show how it leads to intoxication and ruin, and there is no safety but in TOTAL ABSTINENCE, till a hundred hearts are ready to say, "I will never drink another drop of ardent spirit in the world;

if I do, I shall expect to find a drunkard's grave." Now I stop
short, and let the pledge be circulated, and every one that is fully
resolved, is ready to sign it. But how many will begin to draw
back and hesitate, when you begin to call on them to *sign a
pledge* of total abstinence. One says to himself, "Shall I sign it,
or not? I thought my mind was made up, but this signing a
pledge *never* to drink again, I do not know about that." Thus
you see that when a person is called upon to give a pledge, if he
is found not to be decided, he makes it manifest that he was not
sincere. That is, he never came to that resolution on the subject, which could be relied on to control his future life. Just so
with the awakened sinner. Preach to him, and at the moment he
thinks he is willing to do anything, he thinks he is determined to
serve the Lord, but bring him to the test, call on him to do one
thing, to take one step, that shall identify him with the people
of God, or cross his pride—his pride comes up, and he refuses;
his delusion is brought out, and he finds himself a lost sinner
still; whereas, if you had not done it, he might have gone away
flattering himself that he was a Christian. If you say to him,
"There is the anxious seat, come out and avow your determination to be on the Lord's side," and if he is not willing to do so
small a thing as that, then he is not willing to do *any thing,* and
there he is, brought out before his own conscience. It uncovers
the delusion of the human heart, and prevents a great many
spurious conversions, by showing those who might otherwise
imagine themselves willing to do any thing for Christ, that in fact
they are willing to do *nothing*.

The church has always felt it necessary to have something of
the kind to answer this very purpose. In the days of the apostles
baptism answered this purpose. The gospel was preached to the
people, and then all those who were willing to be on the side of
Christ were called on to be *baptized*. It held the precise place
that the anxious seat does now, as a public manifestation of their
determination to be Christians. And in modern times, those who
have been violently opposed to the anxious seat, have been
obliged to adopt some substitute, or they could not get along in

promoting a revival. Some have adopted the expedient of inviting the people who were anxious for their souls, to stay for conversation after the rest of the congregation had retired. But what is the difference? This is as much setting up a test as the other. Others, who would be much ashamed to employ the anxious seat, have asked those who have any feeling on the subject, to sit still in their seats when the rest retire. Others have called the anxious to retire into the lecture room. The object of all these is the same, and the principle is the same, to bring people out from the refuge of false shame. One man I heard of, who was very far gone in his opposition to new measures, in one of his meetings requested all those who were willing to submit to God, or desired to be made subjects of prayer, to signify it by leaning forward and putting their heads down upon the pew before them. Who does not see that this was a mere evasion of the anxious seat, and that it was designed to answer the purpose in its place, and he adopted this because he felt that something of the kind was important?

Now what objection is there against taking a particular seat, or rising up, or going into the lecture-room? They all mean the same thing, when properly conducted. And they are not novelties in principle at all. The thing has always been done in substance. In Joshua's day, he called on the people to decide what they would do, and they spoke right out, in the meeting, "We will serve the Lord; the Lord our God will we serve, and his voice will we obey."

Remarks.

1. If we examine the history of the church we shall find that there never has been an extensive reformation, except by new measures. Whenever the churches get settled down into a *form* of doing things, they soon get to rely upon the outward doing of it, and so retain the form of religion while they lose the substance. And then it has always been found impossible to arouse them so as to bring about a reformation of the evils, and

produce a revival of religion, by simply pursuing that established form. Perhaps it is not too much to say, that it is impossible for God himself to bring about reformations but by new measures. At least, it is a fact that God has *always chosen* this way, as the wisest and best that he could devise or adopt. And although it has always been the case, that the very measures which God has chosen to employ, and which he has blessed in reviving his work, have been opposed as new measures, and have been denounced, yet he has continued to act upon the same principle. When he has found that a certain mode has lost its influence by having become a form, he brings up some new measure, which will BREAK IN upon their lazy habits, and WAKE UP a slumbering church. And great good has resulted.

2. The same distinctions, in substance, that now exist, have always existed, in all seasons of reformation and revival of religion. There have always been those who particularly adhered to their forms and notions, and precise way of doing things, as if they had a "Thus saith the Lord" for every one of them. They have called those that differed from them, who were trying to roll the ark of salvation forward, Methodists, New Lights, Radicals, New School, New Divinity, and various other opprobrious names. And the declensions that have followed have been uniformly owing to two causes, which should be by no means overlooked by the church.

(1.) The Old School, or Old Measure party, have persevered in their opposition, and eagerly seized hold of any real or apparent indiscretion in the friends of the work.

In such cases, the churches have gradually lost their confidence in the opposition to new measures, and the cry of "New Divinity," and "Innovation" has ceased to alarm them. They see that the blessing of God is with those that are thus accused of new measures and innovation, and the continued opposition of the Old School, together with the continued success of the New School, have destroyed their confidence in the opposition, and they get tired of hearing the incessant cry of "New Lights," and "New Divinity," and "New Measures." Thus the scale has turned, and the churches have pronounced a verdict in favor of the New School, and of condemnation against the Old School.

(2.) But now, mark me: right here in this state of things, the devil has, again and again, taken the advantage, and individuals have risen up, and being sustained by the confidence of the churches in the New Measure party, and finding them sick of opposition, and ready to do *any thing* that would promote the interests of Christ's kingdom, they have driven headlong themselves, and in many instances have carried the churches into the *very vortex* of those difficulties, which have been predicted by their opposers. Thus, when the battle had been fought, and the victory gained, the rash zeal of some well-meaning but headlong individuals, has brought about a reaction, that has spread a pall over the churches for years. This was the case, as is well known, in the days of President [Jonathan] Edwards. Here is a rock, upon which a light-house is now built, and upon which if the church now run aground, both parties are entirely without excuse. It is now well known, or ought to be known, that the declension which followed the revivals in those days, together with the declensions which have repeatedly occurred, were owing to the combined influence of the continued and pertinacious opposition of the Old School, and the ultimate bad spirit and recklessness of some individuals of the New School.

And here the note of alarm should be distinctly sounded to both parties, lest the devil should prevail against us, at the very point, and under the very circumstances, where he has so often prevailed. Shall the church never learn wisdom from experience? How often, O, how often must these scenes be acted over, before the millennium shall come! When will it once be, that the church may be revived, and religion prevail, without exciting such opposition *in the church,* as eventually to bring about a reaction?

3. The present cry against new measures is highly ridiculous, when we consider the quarter from which it comes, and all the circumstances in the case. It is truly astonishing that grave ministers should really feel alarmed at the new measures of the present day, as if new measures were something new under the

sun, and as if the present form and manner of doing things had descended from the apostles, and were established by a "Thus saith the Lord": when the truth is, that every step of the church's advance from the gross darkness of Popery, has been through the introduction of one new measure after another. We now look with astonishment, and are inclined to look almost with contempt, upon the cry of "Innovation," that has preceded our day; and as we review the fears that multitudes in the church have entertained in by-gone days, with respect to innovation, we find it difficult to account for what appear to us the groundless and absurd, at least, if not ridiculous objections and difficulties which they made. But, my hearers, is it not wonderful, that at this late day, after the church has had so much experience in these matters, that grave and pious men should seriously feel alarmed at the introduction of the simple, the philosophical, and greatly prospered measures of the last ten years? As if new measures were something not to be tolerated, of highly disastrous tendency, and that should wake the notes and echoes of alarm in every nook and corner of the church.

4. We see why it is that those who have been making the ado about new measures *have not been successful in promoting revivals.*

They have been taken up with the *evils,* real or imaginary, which have attended this great and blessed work of God. That there have been evils, no one will pretend to deny. But I do believe, that no revival ever existed since the world began, of so great power and extent as the one that has prevailed for the last ten years, which has not been attended with as great or greater evils. Still, a large portion of the church have been frightening themselves and others, by giving constant attention to the *evils* of revivals. One of the professors in a Presbyterian Theological Seminary, felt it his duty to write a series of letters to Presbyterians, which were extensively circulated, the object of which seemed to be to sound the note of alarm throughout all the borders of the church, in regard to the evils attending revivals. While men are taken up with the evils instead of the excellences of a blessed work of God, how can it be expected that they will be useful in promoting it? I would say all this in great kindness, but still it is a point upon which I must not be silent.

5. Without new measures it is impossible that the church should succeed in gaining the attention of the world to religion. There are so many exciting subjects constantly brought before the public mind, such a running to and fro, so many that cry "Lo here," and "Lo there," that the church cannot maintain her ground, cannot command attention, without very exciting preaching, and sufficient novelty in measures, to get the public ear. The measures of politicians, of infidels, and heretics, the scrambling after wealth, the increase of luxury, and the ten thousand exciting and counter-acting influences, that bear upon the church and upon the world, will gain their attention and turn all men away from the sanctuary and from the altars of the Lord, unless we increase in wisdom and piety, and wisely adopt such new measures as are calculated to get the attention, of men to the gospel of Christ. I have already said, in the course of these lectures, that novelties should be introduced no faster than they are really called for. They should be introduced with the greatest wisdom, and caution, and prayerfulness, and in manner calculated to excite as little opposition as possible. But new measures we *must have*. And may God prevent the Church from settling down in *any* set of forms, and getting the present or any other edition of her measures *stereotyped*.

6. It is evident that we must have more exciting preaching, to meet the character and wants of the age. Ministers are generally beginning to find this out. And some of them complain of it, and suppose it to be owing to new measures, as they call them. They say that such ministers as our fathers would have been glad to hear, now cannot be heard, cannot get a settlement, nor collect an audience. And they think that new measures have perverted the taste of the people. But this is not the difficulty. The character of the age is changed, and these men have not conformed to it, but retain the same stiff, dry, prosing style of preaching that answered half a century ago.

Look at the Methodists. Many of their ministers are unlearned, in the common sense of the term, many of them taken right from the shop or the farm, and yet they have gathered congregations, and pushed their way, and won souls every where. Wherever the Methodists have gone, their plain, pointed and simple, but warm and animated mode of preaching has always gathered congregations. Few Presbyterian ministers have gathered so large assemblies, or won so many souls. Now are we to be told that we must pursue the same old, formal mode of doing things, amidst all these changes? As well might the North River be rolled back, as the world converted under such preaching.. Those who adopt a different style of preaching, as the Methodists have done, will run away from us. The world will escape from under the influence of this old fashioned or rather new fashioned ministry. It is impossible that the public mind should be held by such preaching. We must have exciting, powerful preaching, or the devil will have the people, except what the Methodists can save. It is impossible that our ministers should continue to do good, unless we have innovations in regard to the style of preaching. Many ministers are finding it out already, that a Methodist preacher, without the advantages of a liberal education will draw a congregation around him which a Presbyterian minister, with perhaps ten times as much learning, cannot equal, because he has not the earnest manner of the other, and does not pour out fire upon his hearers when he preaches.

7. We see the importance of having *young ministers obtain right views of revivals.* In a multitude of cases, I have seen that great pains are taken to frighten our young men, who are preparing for the ministry, about the evils of revivals, new measures, and the like. Young men in some theological seminaries are taught to look upon new measures as if they were the very inventions of the devil. How can such men have revivals? So when they come out, they look about, and watch, and start, as if the devil was there. Some young men in Princeton, a few years ago, came out with an essay upon the "evils of revivals." I should like to know, now, how many of those young men have *enjoyed*

revivals among their people, since they have been in the ministry; and if any have, I should like to know whether they have not repented of that piece about the evils of revivals.

If I had a voice so loud as to be heard at Princeton, I would speak to those young men on this subject. It is high time to talk plainly on this point. The church is groaning in all her borders for the want of suitable ministers. Good men are laboring and are willing to labor night and day to assist in educating young men for the ministry, to promote revivals of religion; and when they come out of the seminary, some of them are as shy of all the measures that God blesses as they are of popery itself.

Shall it be so always? Must we educate young men for the ministry, and have them come out frightened to death about new measures, as if there had never been any such thing as new measures. They ought to know that new measures are no new thing in the church. Let them GO ALONG, and keep at work themselves, and not be frightened about new measures. I have been pained to see that some men, in giving accounts of revivals, have evidently felt themselves obliged to be particular in detailing the measures used, to avoid the inference that *new* measures were introduced; evidently feeling that even the church would undervalue the revival unless it appeared to have been promoted without new measures. Besides, this caution in detailing the measures to demonstrate that there was nothing *new,* looks like admitting that new measures are wrong because they are new, and that a revival is more valuable because it was not promoted by new measures. In this way, I apprehend that much evil has been done, already, and if the practice is to continue, it must come to this, that a revival must be judged of, by the fact that it occurred in connection with new or old measures. I never will countenance such a spirit, nor condescend to guard an account of a revival against the imputation of new or old measures. I believe new measures are *right,* that is, that it is no objection to a measure that it is new or old.

Let a minister enter fully into his work, and pour his heart to God for a blessing, and whenever he sees the want of any measure to bring the truth more powerfully before the minds of the people, let him adopt it and not be afraid, and God will not withhold his blessing. If ministers will not go forward, and will not preach the gospel with power and earnestness, and will not turn out of their tracks to do any thing *new* for the purpose of saving souls, they will grieve the Holy Spirit away, and God will visit them with his curse, and raise up other ministers to do work in the world.

8. *It is the right and duty of ministers to adopt new measures* for promoting revivals. In some places the church have opposed their minister when he has attempted to employ those measures which God has blessed for a revival, and have gone so far as to give up their prayer meetings, and give up laboring to save souls, and stand aloof from every thing, because their minister has adopted what they call new measures. No matter how reasonable the measures are in themselves, nor how seasonable, nor how much God may bless them. It is enough that they are called new measures, and they will not have any thing to do with new measures, nor tolerate them among the people. And thus they fall out by the way, and grieve away the Spirit of God, and put a stop to the revival, when the world around them is going to hell.

FINALLY.—This zealous adherence to particular forms and modes of doing things, which has led the church to resist innovations *in measures, savors strongly of fanaticism.* And what is not a little singular, is that fanatics of this stamp are always the first to cry out "fanaticism." What is that but fanaticism in the Roman Catholic Church, that causes them to adhere with such pertinacity to their particular modes, and forms, and ceremonies, and fooleries? They act as if all these things were established by divine authority; as if there were a "Thus saith the Lord" for every one of them. Now we justly style this a spirit of fanaticism, and esteem it worthy of rebuke. But it is just as absolutely fanatical, for the Presbyterian church, or any other church, to be sticklish for her particular forms, and to act as if *they* were established by divine authority. The fact is, that God has established, in no church, any particular *form,* or manner of worship, for promoting the interest of religion. The scriptures are entirely silent on these subjects, under the gospel dispensation, and the church is left to exercise her own discretion in relation to all such matters. And I hope it will not be thought unkind, when I say again, that to me it appears, that the unkind, angry zeal for a certain mode and manner of doing things, and the overbearing, exterminating cry against new measures, SAVORS STRONGLY OF FANATICISM.

The only thing insisted upon under the gospel of dispensation, in regard to measures, is that there should be *decency* and *order.* "Let all things be done decently and in order." We are required to guard against all confusion and disorderly conduct. But what is decency and order? Will it be pretended that an anxious meeting, or a protracted meeting, or an anxious seat, is inconsistent with decency and order? I should most sincerely deprecate, and most firmly resist whatever was indecent and disorderly in the worship of God's house. But I do not suppose that by "order" we are to understand any particular set mode, in which any church may have been accustomed to perform their service.

B

[The text is taken from John Williamson Nevin, *The Anxious Bench* (Chambersburg, Pa.: German Reformed Church, 1844), pp. 15-17, 19-31, 79-84.]

The Anxious Bench

It is true indeed, that throughout a large portion of the country the Anxious Bench, after having enjoyed a brief reputation, has fallen into discredit. It has been tried, and found wanting; and it might have been trusted that this experiment would be sufficient to drive it completely out of use. But unfortunately this has not been the case. Over a wide section of the land, we find it still holding its ground, without any regard to the disgrace with which it has been overtaken in the North and East. Peculiar circumstances have conspired to promote its credit, on this field.

It is within the range particularly of the German Churches, that a new life may be said to have been communicated latterly to the system of New Measures. No field is more interesting at this time, than that which is comprehended within these limits. A vast moral change is going forward upon it, involving consequences that no man can properly calculate. From various causes, a new feeling is at work everywhere on the subject of religion. As usual, the old struggles to maintain itself in opposition to the new, and a strong tendency to become extreme is created on both sides. The general mind unhappily has not been furnished thus far with proper protection and guidance, in the way of full religious teaching; and the result is that in these interesting circumstances it has become exposed more or less, at almost every point, to those wild fanatical influences, which in this country are sure to come in like a desolating flood wherever they can find room. Upstart sects have set themselves to take possession if possible of the entire field in this way, on the principle that the old organizations are corrupt and deserve to be destroyed. Their reliance of course in this work of reformation, is placed largely on New Measures! Thus a whole Babel of extravagance has been let loose upon the community, far and wide, in the name of religion, one sect vieing with another in the measure of its irregularities. In these circumstances, it has not been easy for the friends of earnest piety always in the regular churches, to abide by the ancient landmarks of truth and order. The temptation has been strong to fall in, at least to some extent, with the tide of fanaticism, as the only way of making war successfully on the dead formality that stared them in the face in one direction, and the only way of counteracting the proselyting zeal of these noisy sects in the other.* * * An inquiry into the merits of the Anxious Bench, and the system to which it belongs, is not only seasonable and fit in the circumstances of time, but loudly called on every side. It is no small question, that is involved in the case. The bearing of it upon the interests of religion in the German Churches, is of fundamental and vital importance. A crisis has evidently been reached in the history of these Churches; and one of the most serious points involved in it, is precisely this question of New Measures. Let this system prevail and rule with permanent sway, and the result of the religious movement which is now in progress, will be something widely different from what it would have been under other auspices. The old regular organizations, if they continue to exist at all, will not be the same Churches. Their entire complexion and history, in time to come, will be shaped by the course of things with regard to this point. In this view, the march of New Measures at the present time, may well challenge our anxious and solemn regard. It is an interest of no common magnitude, portentous in its aspect, and pregnant with consequences of vast account. The system is moving forward in full strength, and putting forth its pretensions in the boldest style on all sides. Surely we have a right, and may well feel it a duty, in such a case, to institute an examination into its merits.

Nor is it any reason for silence in the case, that we may have suffered as yet comparatively little in our own denomination, from the use of New Measures. We may congratulate ourselves that we have been thus favored, and that the impression seems to be steadily growing that they ought not to be encouraged in our communion. Still, linked together as the German Churches are throughout the land, we have reason to be jealous here of influences, that must in the nature of the case act upon us from without. In such circumstances there is occasion, and at the same time room, for consideration. It might answer little purpose to interpose remonstrance or inquiry, if the rage for New Measures were fairly let loose, as a sweeping wind, within our borders. It were idle to bespeak attention from the rolling whirlwind. But with the whirlwind in full view, we may be exhorted reasonably to consider and stand back from its destructive path. We are not yet committed to the cause of New Measures, in any respect. We are still free to reject or embrace them, as the interests of the Church, on calm reflection, may be found to require. In such circumstances precisely, may it be counted in all respects proper to subject the system to a serious examination.

It has been sometimes intimated, that it is not safe to oppose and condemn the use of New Measures, because of their connections and purpose. Their relation to the cause of revivals, is supposed to invest them with a sort of sacred character, which the friends of religion should at least respect, even if they may not be able in all cases, to approve. The system has taken hold of the "horns of the altar," and it seems to some like sacrilege to fall upon it there, or to force it away from the purposes of justice to any other place. It is a serious thing, we are told, to find fault with any movement, that claims to be animated by the Spirit of God. By so doing, we render it questionable whether we have ourselves any proper sympathy with revivals, and furnish occasion to the world also to blaspheme and oppose everything of the kind. But this is tyrannical enough, to take for granted the main point in dispute, and then employ it as a consideration to repress inquiry or to silence objection. If New Measures can be shown to proceed from the Holy Ghost, or to be identified in any view with the cause of revivals, they may well demand our reverence and respect. If they can be shown even to be of *adiaphorous* character with regard to religion, harmless at least if not positively helpful to the Spirit's work, they may then put in a reasonable plea to be tolerated in silence, if not absolutely approved. But neither the one nor the other of these positions can be successfully maintained. It is a mere trick unworthy of the gospel, for any one to confound with the sacred idea of a revival, things that do not belong to it in truth at all, for the purpose of compelling a judgment in their favor. The very design of the inquiry now proposed, is to show that the Anxious Bench, and the system to which it belongs, have no claim to be considered either salutary or safe, in the service of religion. It is believed, that instead of promoting the cause of true vital godliness, they are adopted to hinder its progress. The whole system is considered to be full of peril, for the most precious interests of the

Church. And why then should there be any reserve, in treating the subject with such freedom as it may seem to require? We may well feel indeed that the subject is solemn. All that relates to the interests of revivals, and the welfare of souls, is solemn; and it becomes us to approach it in a serious way. But this is no reason, why we should close our eyes against the truth, or refuse to call things by their proper names. This would be to trifle with sacred things truly.

And it should be borne in mind, that the danger against which we need to be warned in this case, is not confined by any means to one side. It is a serious thing to profane the worship of God, by offering upon his altar strange fire. Those who recommend and practice New Measures, should see well to it, that they be not themselves chargeable with the very sin, which they are too prone to charge upon such as withstand their views. It is surely not a case, in which men can be justified in taking up a judgment lightly, and with little or no reflection. Mighty interests are concerned in the question, whether such means should be employed in the service of God's sanctuary or not. A great responsibility is involved in urging the system upon a congregation, or in trying to give it currency and authority in a religious community. If it should be found after all, to be *not* the wisdom and power of God unto salvation, but the fruitful source of error and confusion in religion, an occasion of reproach to the gospel and of ruin to the souls of men, it would be a heavy account surely, to answer for any part taken in its favor.

It is truly strange, how onesided the patrons of this system show themselves, as a general thing, in their views and feelings with regard to the point now presented. They affect an extraordinary interest in the cause of revivals, and seem to have a pious dread of sinning against it in any way. But the danger of doing so, is all, to their view, in one direction. The idea of opposing the work of God, is terrible. Whatever claims to be his work, then, must be respected and reverenced. No matter what irregularities are attached to it, so long as it stands before us in the holy garb of a revival, it is counted unsafe to call it to

account. The maxim, *Prove all things,* must be discarded, as
well as the caution, *Believe not every spirit.* No room must be
allowed to criticism, where the object proposed is to rescue souls
from hell. To stand upon points of order in such a case, is to
clog the chariot wheels of salvation. Meanwhile the disastrous
consequences of false excitement, in the name of religion, are
entirely overlooked. No account is made comparatively, of the
danger of bringing both the truth and power of God into discredit, by countenancing pretensions to the name of a revival
where the thing itself is not present. The danger itself is by no
means imaginary. Spurious excitements are natural and common. Gross irregularity and extravagance, carried often to the
point of downright profanity, are actually at work, in connection with such excitements, on all sides. The whole interest
of revivals is endangered, by the assumption impudently put
forward, that these revolting excesses belong to the system.
False and ruinous views of religion, are widely disseminated.
Thousands of souls are deceived into a false hope. Vast obstruc-
tions are thrown in the way of true godliness. But of all this, no
account is made by those who are so sensitively jealous of
danger on the other side. The only alternative they seem to see,
is *Action* or *No action.* But the difference between *right* action
and *wrong* action, one would think, is full as important, to say
the least, as the difference between action and no action.* * *

It has been already stated, that the Anxious Bench is made the
direct object of regard in this tract, rather than New Measures
in general, for the very purpose of cutting off occasion, as much
as may be, from those who seek occasion, for confounding in
this way things that are entirely distinct. The particular is made
to stand for the general, in the way of specimen or type, so
as to exclude all that is not of the same complexion and spirit.
If any choose notwithstanding to take the idea of New Measures
in a wider sense, they have a right to please themselves in so
doing, if they see proper; but they can have no right surely to
obtrude their own arbitrary view on the present discussion.
There is a broad difference between New Measures in the one

sense, and New Measures in the other sense. It is overbearing impudence to pretend, that a protracted meeting, or a meeting for social prayer, is of the same character with the anxious bench, or the various devices for theatrical effect with which this is so frequently linked. Such meetings lie in the very conception of Christian worship, and are as old as the Church. The assertion sometimes heard, that the idea of protracted meetings, now so familiar and so generally approved, is one of recent origin, for which we are indebted to the system of New Measures, serves only to expose the ignorance of those by whom it is made. It is no less an abuse of terms, as well as of common sense, to include in this system tract societies, the cause of missions, and the benevolent agencies in general, by which the Church is endeavoring to diffuse the knowledge of the truth throughout the world. All these things are natural, direct utterances of the spirit of Christianity itself, and have no affinity whatever with the order of action represented by the Anxious Bench. The same thing may be said of revivals. They are as old as the gospel itself. Special effusions of the Spirit, the Church has a right to expect in every age, in proportion as she is found faithful to God's covenant; and where such effusions take place, an extraordinary use of the ordinary means of grace will appear, as a matter of course. But still a revival is one thing, and a Phrygian dance another; even though the Phrygian dance should be baptized into Christian Montanism. Life implies action, but all action is not life. It is sheer impudence to say, that new measures and revival measures are the same thing.

And there is good reason to believe, that the confusion which is said to prevail with regard to the whole subject, is much less in fact than is sometimes represented. As a general thing, people know very well that there is no affinity or connection, between the system represented by the Anxious Bench, and such evangelical interests as have now been mentioned. Even in those sections, where it has been found convenient to stretch the idea of New Measures over this hallowed territory, there is a better knowledge of the true state of the case probably than is often supposed.

But allowing the confusion to be as complete, among the German Churches, as it is represented, shall no effort be made to correct it, and put things in their proper light? Admit that the best practices, and most important interests, are in the eyes of many identified with the system of New Measures, in the proper sense, so that to assault the latter is considered an assault at the same time upon the former; still is that a reason for sparing and sheltering the system, under its own bad form? Is there no help for the German Churches, in this predicament? Must they have revivals, in the way of the Anxious Bench, or no revivals at all? Must it be with them Finneyism, Methodism, Winebrennerism,* or open war with serious religion, and the spirit of missions, under every form? Is the necessary alternative, in their case, quackery or death? Rather, in these circumstances, it becomes a solemn duty to take the difficulty by the horns, and reduce it to its proper posture. We owe it to the German Churches, not to suffer things so different, in a case of such vast moment, to be so deplorably confounded. The case is one that calls loudly for light, and it is high time that light should be extended to it without reserve. If it be a reigning error, to involve light and darkness in this way, under a common term, in the same sweeping censure, that is not a reason surely why we should try to uphold the darkness for the sake of the light, but a sacred requisition upon us rather, to insist on a clear, full discrimination of the one element from the other. If Finneyism and Winebrennerism, the anxious bench, revival machinery, solemn tricks for effect, decision displays at the bidding of the preacher, genuflections and prostrations in the aisle or around the altar, noise and disorder, extravagance and rant, mechanical conversions, justification by feeling rather than faith, and encouragement ministered to all fanatical impressions; if these things, and things in the same line indefinitely, have no

---

* John Winebrenner (1797–1860) began his professional career as a minister of the German Reformed Church. Attracted to the revivalistic approach, he turned from a more sober tradition to establish his own sect in Harrisburg, Pennsylvania, in 1830. This religious body which eventually took the name of the General Eldership of the Churches of God in North America continues to the present day.—ED.

connection in fact with true serious religion and the cause of revivals, but tend only to bring them into discredit, let the fact be openly proclaimed. Only in this way, may it be hoped that the reproach put upon revivals and other evangelical interests by some, under cover of their pretended connection with this system of New Measures in the true sense, will be in due time fairly rolled away.

The fact, that a crisis has come in the history of the German Churches, and that they are waking to the consciousness of a new life with regard to religion, only makes it the more important that this subject should *not* be suffered to rest in vague confusion. It is a popish maxim, by which ignorance is made to be the mother of devotion. We say rather, Let there be light. The cause of the Reformation was more endangered by its own carricature, in the wild fanaticism of the Annabaptists, than by all the opposition of Rome. Luther saved it, not by truckling compromise, but by boldly facing and unmasking the false spirit, so that all the world might see, that *Lutheran* Christianity was one thing, and wild Phrygian Montanism, with its pretended inspiration, quite another. So in the present crisis, the salvation of the old German Churches in this country is to be accomplished, not by encouraging them to "believe every spirit," but by engaging them, if possible, to "try the spirits, whether they be of God." Let things that are wrong be called by their right names, and separated from things that are right.

A heavy responsbility, in this case, rests upon the friends of New Measures. The circulation of spurious coin, in the name of money, brings the genuine currency into discredit. So also the surest way to create and cherish prejudice against true piety, is to identify it with counterfeit pretences to its name. Popery, in popish countries, is the fruitful source of infidelity. So in the case before us, it is sufficiently clear, that the zeal which the sticklers for the system of the Anxious Bench display, in pressing their irregularities on the Church as a necessary part of the life and power of Christianity, is doing more at present than any other cause, to promote the unhappy prejudice that is found to prevail, in certain quarters, against this interest in its true form. Many are led honestly to confound the one order of things with the other; and still more, no doubt, willingly accept the opportunity thus furnished, to strengthen themselves in their opposition to evangelical interests, under a plausible plea, against their own better knowledge. In either case, we see the mischievous force of the false issue, which the question of New Measures has been made to involve. The Anxious Bench, and its kindred extravagances, may be held justly responsible for a vast amount of evil, in this view. As a carricature always wrongs the original it is made falsely to represent, so has this spurious system, officiously usurping a name and place not properly its own, contributed in no small degree to bring serious religion itself into discredit, obscuring its true form, and inviting towards it prejudices that might otherwise have had no place. It has much to answer for, in the occasion it has given, and is giving still, for the name of God to be blasphemed, and the sacred cause of revivals to be vilified and opposed. * * *

The mourner strives of course to *feel* faith. The spiritual helpers standing round are actively concerned, to see him brought triumphantly through. Excitement rules the hour. No room is found either for instruction or reflection. A sea of feeling, blind, dark and tempestuous, rolls on all sides. Is it strange, that souls thus conditioned and surrounded, should become the victims of spiritual delusion? All high wrought excitement must, in its very nature, break, when it reaches a certain point. How natural that this relaxation, carrying with it the sense of relief as compared with the tension that had place before, should be mistaken on such an occasion for the peace of religion, that mysterious something which it is the object of all this process to fetch into the mind. And how natural that the wearied subject of such experience, should be hurried into a wild fit of joy by this imagination, and stand prepared, if need be, to clap his hands and shout hallelujah, over his fancied deliverance. Or even without this mimic sensation, how natural that the mourner, at a certain point, should allow himself to be persuaded by his own wishes, or by the authority of the minister perhaps, and other friends, telling him how easy it is to believe and urging him at last to consider the thing done; so as to take to himself the comfort of the new birth, as it were in spite of his own experience, and be counted among the converted. Altogether the danger of delusion and mistake, where this style of advancing the cause of religion prevails, must be acknowledged to be very great. The measure of the danger will vary of course, with the extent to which the characteristic spirit of the system is allowed to work. A Winebrennerian camp meeting, surrendering itself to the full sway of this spirit, will carry with it a more disastrous operation, than the simple Anxious Bench in a respectable and orderly Church. But in any form, the system is full of peril, as opening the way to spurious conversions, and encouraging sinners to rest in hopes that are vain and false.

There need be no reserve, in speaking or writing on this subject. Neither charity nor delicacy require us to be silent, where the truth of religion is itself so seriously concerned. To countenance the supposition, that the souls which are so plentifully "carried through" what is called the process of conversion under this system, are generally converted in fact, would be to wrong the Gospel. "Let God be true, though every man should be a liar." Of all the hundreds that are reported, from year to year, as brought into the kingdom, among the Methodists, United Brethren, Winebrennerians, and others who work in the same style, under the pressure of artificial excitement, how small a proportion give evidence subsequently that they have been truly regenerated. The Church at large does not feel bound at all to accept as genuine and worthy of confidence, the many cases of conversion they are able to number, as wrought with noise and tumult at camp meetings and on other occasions. It is taken for granted that a large part of them will not stand. And so it turns out, in fact. In many cases, the fruits of a great revival are reduced almost to nothing, before the end of a single year. So the system unfolds its own nakedness, in a practical way. And this nakedness comes to view, in some measure, wherever much account is made of the Anxious Bench. There may be no meth-odistical extravagance, no falling down or rolling in the dust, no shouting, jumping or clapping; only the excitement and dis-order necessarily belonging to the measure itself; still it is found that conversions made in this way do not as a general thing wear well. No one, whose judgment has been taught by proper obser-vation, will allow himself to confide in the results of a revival, however loudly trumpeted, in which the Anxious Bench is known to have played a prominent part. He may trust charitably that out of the fifty or a hundred converts thus hurried into the Church, some will be found "holding fast the beginning of their confidence firm unto the end"; but he will stand prepared to hear of a great falling away, in the case of the accession as a whole, in the course of no considerable time. Of some such re-vivals scarce a monument is to be found, at the end of a few months, unless it be in the spiritual atrophy they have left behind. And it often happens that churches instead of growing and gathering strength by these triumphs of grace as they are called, seem actually to loose ground in proportion to their fre-quency and power. If any weight is to be attached to observa-tions, which are on all sides within the reach of those who choose to inquire, it must be evident that as this system is in all respects *suited* to produce spurious conversions, so it is continually pro-ducing them in fact, to a terrible extent. For the evil is not to be measured of course simply by the actual amount of open de-fection, that may take place among those who are thus brought to "embrace religion." So many and so strong are the considera-tions that must operate upon a supposed convert, to hold fast at least the form of godliness, after it has been once assumed, though wholly ignorant of its power, that we may well be sur-prised to find the actual falling away, in the case of such in-gatherings, so very considerable as now represented. As it is, it becomes certain, in the very nature of the case, that this apostacy forms only a *part* of the false profession from which it springs. While some fall back openly to the world, others remain in the Church, with a name to live while they are dead. This presumption is abundantly confirmed by observation. Very many thus introduced into the Church show too plainly, by their un- hallowed tempers, and the general worldliness of their walk and conversation, that they have never known what religion means. They have had their "experience," centering in the Anxious Bench, on which they continue to build their profession and its hopes; but farther than this they give no signs of life. They have no part nor lot in the Christian salvation.

Notoriously, no conversions are more precarious and insecure than those of the Anxious Bench. They take place under such circumstances precisely, as should make them the object of earnest jealousy and distrust. The most ample evidence of their vanity, is presented on every side. And yet the patrons of the system are generally ready to endorse them, as though they carried the broad seal of heaven on their face. Of conversions in any other form, they can be sufficiently jealous. They think it well for the Church to use great caution, in the case of those who have been led quietly, under the ordinary means of grace to indulge the Christian hope. They shrink perhaps from the use of the Catechism altogether, lest they might seem to aim at a religion of merely human manufacture. But let the power of the Anxious Bench appear, and strange to tell, their caution is at once given to the winds. *This* they proclaim to be the finger of God. Here the work of religion is presumed at once to authen- ticate itself. With very little instruction, and almost no examina- tion, all who can persuade themselves that they are converted, are at once hailed as brethren and sisters in Christ Jesus, and with as little delay as possible gathered into the full communion of the Church. And this is held to be building on the true founda- tion gold, silver and precious stones, while such as try to make christians in a different way are regarded as working mainly, al- most as a matter of course, with wood, hay, and stubble. Won- derful infatuation! Stupendous inconsistency.

9

NATURE

OR

SUPERNATURE

THROUGH the seventeenth and eighteenth centuries, most theology in America was Calvinist in its orientation. And Calvinism sought above all to keep clear the distinctions between the finite and the infinite, between the sinful and the holy, between man and God. The breakdown of Calvinism and especially of that supersaturated solution known as Puritanism led to new, sometimes exotic growth in the young nation's theological thicket.

A rationalistic, rather arid Unitarian schism was one such product. An intuitional, rather sentimental Transcendentalism was another. A comprehensive, rather eclectic theological method and theory of language was a third. Beyond all of these was the surrender of the theological enterprise itself, accompanied by redoubled effort in good works and voluntary societies. In much of this, the sharp lines separating natural and supernatural began to blur. If man's reason was divine, what further need for supernatural revelation? If man's heart was in tune with nature and nature was part of God, what salvation was required? If progress could be presumed and man's perfectibility counted on, if lion and lamb do lie down together, what then shall separate the sacred from the profane?

Ralph Waldo Emerson (1803–1882) and Horace Bushnell (1802–1876) are not polar opposites as they address these questions. Each is too conscious of the richness and ambiguity of language to permit himself a rigid defense of dogmatic positions. Each is given to paradox and metaphor, and each is fleeing an uncritical, restrictive orthodoxy. Yet the tendencies of their thoughts do diverge, the path from Emerson moving ever farther from the Christian tradition to a self-help, New Thought orientation, the path from Bushnell returning in new guises and new phrases to restatements of basic Christian doctrines.

Emerson graduated from Harvard in 1821, taught school briefly, then entered Harvard Divinity School in 1825 to prepare himself for a career in the ministry. In 1829 he assumed a pastorate in Boston, but left it three years later in a dispute about the Lord's Supper. His career then became that of essayist, poet, and lecturer—the last having the most profound immediate effect, the first the most enduring one. At the center of a coterie at once highly parochial (Boston, Brook Farm, Concord) and yet international (Coleridge, Carlyle, Wordsworth), Emerson became the hallmark of American self-reliance, the canonical guide to the new divinity in man.

Emerson's essay on nature is a rhapsody to the world "out there" but also to the world "in here"—the responding, communing human heart. When we approach nature, "we come to our own . . . ever an old friend." If men were better than they are, it would not be necessary to go to nature for spiritual succor. But "man is fallen; nature is erect. . . ." The proper study of mankind is not man but "the fall of snowflakes," "the blowing of sleet," "the waving rye-field," "the reflections of trees and flowers in glassy lakes," and "the musical steaming odorous south wind." Through such a study "we feel that the soul of the workman streams through us. . . ."

Horace Bushnell, reversing Emerson's course, turned from another career (law) to the ministry. Accepting in 1833 the leadership of a church in Hartford, Connecticut, he remained a Congregational clergyman all his life—though plaguing ill-health forced him to an early retirement from pastoral duties. Bushnell found no easy comfort in the intellectual world either. If Congregationalists had taken creeds too literally as they defended them, Unitarians had taken those creeds just as literally in their counterattack. If the orthodox had been too uncritical in their preaching of "saving grace," the liberals had been too hasty in dismissing all notion of vicarious atonement. If Calvinists had too low a view of man, deists and romanticists had too high a view. If revivalists put too much emphasis on sudden, dramatic change, antirevivalists provided no theory of change at all. In sum, spiritual truths are not narrow, partisan, or linguistically exact, but rather universal, comprehensive, and metaphorically expressed. The gospel, said Bushnell, is "a gift to the imagination."

In the volume from which the extracts below are taken, Bushnell's disagreement with Emerson is most clearly seen with reference to man's sin. Said Bushnell, the "popular literature" of our time—namely Emerson and Carlyle—gives sin a kind of glory, "placing both it and virtue upon the common footing of a natural use and necessity." Such treatment of the reality of sin denies human responsibility and dismisses Christianity's supernatural truth. More against a cold rationalism than against Emerson, Bushnell also protests the view of his day which shuts God out of the world, reduces Him to the role of passive observer of the cosmic processes. This, Bushnell noted, is supposedly the only reasonable or scientific view possible, but that is nonsense. The presence of the supernatural—God's government of the world—is "the only worthy and exalted conception."

A

[The text is taken from Ralph Waldo Emerson, *Essays, Second Series* (Philadelphia: David McKay, 1891), pp. 183–86, 197–99, 209–12.]

Nature

There are days which occur in this climate, at almost any season of the year, wherein the world reaches its perfection, when the air, the heavenly bodies, and the earth, make a harmony, as if nature would indulge her offspring; when, in these bleak upper sides of the planet, nothing is to desire that we have heard of the happiest latitudes, and we bask in the shining hours of Florida and Cuba; when everything that has life gives sign of satisfaction, and the cattle that lie on the ground seem to have great and tranquil thoughts. These halcyons may be looked for with a little more assurance in that pure October weather, which we distinguish by the name of the Indian Summer. The day, immeasurably long, sleeps over the broad hills and warm wide fields. To have lived through all its sunny hours, seems longevity enough. The solitary places do not seem quite lonely. At the gates of the forest, the surprised man of the world is forced to leave his city estimates of great and small, wise and foolish. The knapsack of custom falls off his back with the first step he makes into these precincts. Here is sanctity which shames our religions, and reality which discredits our heroes. Here we find nature to be the circumstance which dwarfs every other circumstance, and judges like a god all men that come to her. We have crept out of our close and crowded houses into the night and morning, and we see what majestic beauties daily wrap us in their bosom. How willingly we would escape the barriers which render them comparatively impotent, escape the sophistication and second thought, and suffer nature to intrance us. The tempered light of the woods is like a perpetual morning, and is stimulating and heroic. The anciently reported spells of these places creep on us. The stems

of pines, hemlocks, and oaks, almost gleam like iron on the excited eye. The incommunicable trees begin to persuade us to live
with them, and quit our life of solemn trifles. Here no history,
or church, or state, is interpolated on the divine sky and the immortal year. How easily we might walk onward into the opening
landscape, absorbed by new pictures, and by thoughts fast suc-
ceeding each other, until by degrees the recollection of home was
crowded out of the mind, all memory obliterated by the tyranny
of the present, and we were led in triumph by nature.

These enchantments are medicinal, they sober and heal us.
These are plain pleasures, kindly and native to us. We come to
our own, and make friends with matter, which the ambitious
chatter of the schools would persuade us to despise. We never
can part with it; the mind loves its old home: as water to our
thirst, so is the rock, the ground, to our eyes, and hands, and
feet. It is firm water: it is cold flame: what health, what affinity!
Ever an old friend, ever like a dear friend and brother, when we
chat affectedly with strangers, comes in this honest face, and
takes a grave liberty with us, and shames us out of our nonsense.
Cities give not the human senses room enough. We go out daily
and nightly to feed the eyes on the horizon, and require so much
scope, just as we need water for our bath. There are all degrees
of natural influence, from these quarantine powers of nature, up
to her dearest and gravest ministrations to the imagination and
the soul. There is the bucket of cold water from the spring, the
wood-fire to which the chilled traveller rushes for safety,—and
there is the sublime moral of autumn and of noon. We nestle in
nature, and draw our living as parasites from her roots and
grains, and we receive glances from the heavenly bodies, which
call us to solitude, and foretell the remotest future. * * *

Things are so strictly related, that according to the skill of the
eye, from any one object the parts and properties of any other
may be predicted. If we had eyes to see it, a bit of stone from
the city wall would certify us of the necessity that man must exist,
as readily as the city. That identity makes us all one, and reduces
to nothing great intervals on our customary scale. We talk of

deviations from natural life, as if artificial life were not also natural. The smoothest curled courtier in the boudoirs of a palace has an animal nature, rude and aboriginal as a white bear, omnipotent to its own ends, and is directly related, there amid essences and billetsdoux, to Himmaleh mountain-chains, and the axis of the globe. If we consider how much we are nature's, we need not be superstitious about towns, as if that terrific or benefic force did not find us there also, and fashion cities. Nature who made the mason, made the house. We may easily hear too much of rural influences. The cool disengaged air of natural objects, makes them enviable to us, chafed and irritable creatures with red faces, and we think we shall be as grand as they, if we camp out and eat roots; but let us be men instead of wood-chucks, and the oak and the elm shall gladly serve us, though we sit in chairs of ivory on carpets of silk.

This guiding identity runs through all the surprises and contrasts of the piece, and characterizes every law. Man carries the world in his head, the whole astronomy and chemistry suspended in a thought. Because the history of nature is characterized in his brain, therefore is he the prophet and discoverer of her secrets. Every known fact in natural science was divined by the presentiment of somebody, before it was actually verified. A man does not tie his shoe without recognising laws which bind the farthest regions of nature: moon, plant, gas, crystal, are concrete geometry and numbers. Common sense knows its own, and recognises the fact at first sight in chemical experiment. The common sense of Franklin, Dalton, Davy, and Black, is the same common sense which made the arrangements which now it discovers. * * *

One look at the face of heaven and earth lays all petulance at rest, and soothes us to wiser convictions. To the intelligent, nature converts itself into a vast promise, and will not be rashly explained. Her secret is untold. Many and many an Oedipus arrives: he has the whole mystery teeming in his brain. Alas! the same sorcery has spoiled his skill; no syllable can he shape on his lips. Her mighty orbit vaults like the fresh rainbow into the deep, but no archangel's wing was yet strong enough to follow it, and report of the return of the curve. But it also appears, that our actions are seconded and disposed to greater conclusions than we designed. We are escorted on every hand through life by spiritual agents, and a beneficent purpose lies in wait for us. We cannot bandy words with nature, or deal with her as we deal with persons. If we measure our individual forces against hers, we may easily feel as if we were the sport of an insuperable destiny. But if, instead of identifying ourselves with the work, we feel that the soul of the workman streams through us, we shall find the peace of the morning dwelling first in our hearts, and the fathomless powers of gravity and chemistry and, over them, of life, pre-existing within us in their highest form.

The uneasiness which the thought of our helplessness in the chain of causes occasions us, results from looking too much at one condition of nature, namely, Motion. But the drag is never taken from the wheel. Wherever the impulse exceeds, the Rest or Identity insinuates its compensation. All over the wide fields of earth grows the prunella or self-heal. After every foolish day we sleep off the fumes and furies of its hours; and though we are always engaged with particulars, and often enslaved to them, we bring with us to every experiment the innate universal laws. These, while they exist in the mind as ideas, stand around us in nature forever embodied, a present sanity to expose and cure the insanity of men. Our servitude to particulars betrays into a hundred foolish expectations. We anticipate a new era from the invention of a locomotive, or a balloon; the new engine brings with it the old checks. They say that by electro-magnetism, your salad shall be grown from the seed, whilst your fowl is roasting for dinner: it is a symbol of our modern aims and endeavors,—of our condensation and acceleration of objects: but nothing is gained: nature cannot be cheated: man's life is but seventy salads long, grow they swift or grow they slow. In these checks and impossibilities, however, we find our advantage, not less than in the impulses. Let the victory fall where it will, we are on that side. And the knowledge that we traverse the whole scale of being, from the centre to the poles of nature, and have some stake in every possibility, lends that sublime lustre to death, which philosophy and religion have too outwardly and literally striven to express in the popular doctrine of the immortality of the soul. The reality is more excellent than the report. Here is no ruin, no discontinuity, no spent ball. The divine circulations never rest nor linger. Nature is the incarnation of a thought, and turns to a thought again, as ice becomes water and gas. The world is mind precipitated, and the volatile essence is forever escaping again into the state of free thought. Hence the virtue and pungency of the influence on the mind, of natural objects, whether inorganic or organized. Man imprisoned, man crystallized, man vegetative, speaks to man impersonated. That power which does not respect quantity, which makes the whole and the particle its equal channel, delegates its smile to the morning, and distils its essence into every drop of rain. Every moment instructs, and every object: for wisdom is infused into every form. It has been poured into us as blood; it convulsed us as pain; it slid into us as pleasure; it enveloped us in dull, melancholy days, or in days of cheerful labor; we did not guess its essence, until after a long time.

B

[The text is taken from Horace Bushnell, *Nature and the Super-natural, as Together constituting the One System of God* (London: Alexander Strahan & Co., 1867), pp. 93–98, 176–79, 364.]

Nature and the Supernatural

I begin then with the question, whether it is a real and proper fact that sin exists? In discussing this question, I abstain altogether from any close theologic definition of sin. Undoubtedly there is a something called *sin* in the Christian writings, which is not action or wrong-doing—something not included in the Pelagian definitions of sin, as commonly presented. But my argument requires me to look no farther at present than to this, which is the simplest conception of the subject, inquiring whether there is any such thing in the world as properly blamable action? Is there a transgression of right or of law—a positive disobedience to God—anything that rationally connects with remorse, or carries the sense of guilt as a genuine reality? Of course it is implied that the transgressor does what no mere thing, nothing in the line of cause and effect, can do—acts against God; or, what is nowise different, against the constituent harmony of things issued from the will of God. Hence the bad conscience, the sense of guilt or blame; that the wrong-doer recognizes in the act something from himself that is not from any mere principle of nature, not from God, contrary to God.

It appears in one view to be quite idle to raise this question. Why should we undertake the serious discussion of a question that every man has settled? Why argue for a fact that every man acknowledges? It would indeed be quite nugatory if all mankind could definitely see what they acknowledge. But they do not, and, what is more, many are abundantly ingenious to escape doing it. In fact, all the naturalism of our day begins just here, in the denial or disguised disallowance of this self-evident and everywhere visible fact, the existence of sin. Sometimes, where no such denial is intended or thought of, it is yet virtually made in the assumption of some theory or supposed principle of philosophy, which, legitimately carried out, conducts and will conduct other minds also to the formal denial, both of the fact of sin and of that responsibility which is its necessary precondition. We have thus a large class holding the condition of implicit naturalism, who asserts what amounts to a denial of responsibility, and so of the possibility of sin, without denying formally the fact, or conceiving that any truth of Christianity as a supernatural religion is brought in question. Of these we may cite, as a prominent instance and example, the phrenologists, who are many of them disciples and earnest advocates of the Christian doctrine. Still it is not difficult to see that, if human actions are nothing but results brought to pass or determined by the ratios of so many quantities of brain at given points under the skull, then are

they no more fit subjects of reward or blame than the motions of
the stars, determined also by their quantities of matter. Therefore some phrenologists add the conception of a higher nature
than the pulpy quantities; a person, a free-will power, presiding
over them and only using them as its incentives and instruments,
but never mechanically determined by them. This takes phre-
nology out of the conditions of naturalism, and, for just the same
reason, and in the same breath, renders sin a possibility; otherwise the science, however fondly accepted as the ally of Christianity (a sorry kind of ally at the best) is only a tacit and
implict form of naturalism, that virtually excludes the faith of
Christianity.

On the other hand, we have met with advocates of naturalism,
who have not been quite able to deny the existence of sin, or who
even assert the fact in ways of doubtful significance. Thus Mr.
Parker, in his *Discourses of Religion,* having it for his main
object to disprove the credibility of miracles and of everything
supernatural in Christianity, still admits in words the existence
of sin. He even accounts it one of the merits of Calvinistic and
Lutheran orthodoxy that it "shows (we quote his own language)
the hatefulness of sin and the terrible evils it brings upon the
world"; and, what is yet more decisive, he represents it as being
one of the faults of the moderate school of Protestants, that "they
reflect too little on the evil that comes from violating the law
of God." And yet the whole matter of supernaturalism, which he
is discussing, hinges on precisely this and nothing else, viz., the
question whether there is any such thing as a real "violation of
the law of God," any "hatefulness in sin," any "terrible evils
brought on the world" by means of it. For to violate the law of
God is itself an act supernatural, out of the order of nature, and
against the order of nature, as truly even as a miracle, else it is
nothing. The very sin of the sin is that it is against God, and
everything that comes from God; the acting of a soul or power
against the constituent frame of nature and its internal harmony,
followed, therefore, as in due time we shall show, by real disorder of nature, which nothing but a supernatural agency of

redemption can ever effectually repair. Of this, the fundamental fact on which, in reality, the whole question he is discussing turns, he takes no manner of notice. Admitting the existence of sin, his speculations still go on their way, as if it were a fact of no significance in regard to his argument. If he had sounded the question of sin more deeply, ascertaining what it is and what it involves, he might well enough have spared himself the labour of his book. He either would never have written it at all, or else he would have denied the existence of sin altogether, as being only a necessary condition of the supernatural. * * *

But the advocates of naturalism are commonly more thorough and consistent; not consistent with each other, that is too much to be expected, but consistent with themselves, in trying each to find some way of disallowing sin, or so far explaining it away, as to reduce it within the terms of mere cause and effect in nature. Thus, for example, Fourier conceives that what we call sin, by a kind of misnomer, is predicable only of society, not of the individual man. Considered as creatures of God, all men, as truly as the first man before sin, have and continue always to have a right and perfect nature, in the same manner as the stars. He accordingly assumes it as the fundamental principle of the new science, that "man's attractions," like theirs, "are proportioned to his destinies"; so that, by means of his passions, he will even gravitate naturally toward the condition of order and well-being, with the same infallible certainty as they. It only happens that society is not fitly organized, and that produces all the mischief. There really is no sin, apart from the fact that men have not had the science to organize society rightly. He does not appear to notice the fact that if these human stars, called men, are all harmoniously tempered and set in a perfect balance of inward attractions, by them to be swayed under the laws of cause and effect, that fact *is* organization, the very harmony of the spheres itself. And then the assumption that society is not fitly organized, or badly disorganized, is simply absurd; not less absurd the hope that man is going to scheme it into organization himself. Doubtless society is badly enough organized, but we have no place for the fact, and can have none, till we look on men as powers, not under cause and effect; capable, in that manner, of sin, and liable to it; through the bad experiment of it, to be trained up into character, which is itself the completed organization of felicity. Under this view bad organization or disorganization is possible, because sin is possible; and will be a fact, as certainly as sin is a fact—otherwise neither possible nor a fact. * * *

The popular literature of our time, represented by such writers as Carlyle and Emerson, is in a similar vein; not always denying sin, for to lose it would be to lose the spice and spirit of half their representations of humanity; but contriving rather to exalt and glorify it, by placing both it and virtue upon the common footing of a natural use and necessity. Glorifying also themselves in the plausible audacity of their offence; for it is one of the frequent infirmities of literature that it courts effect by taking on the airs of licentiousness.

But this kind of originality has now come to its limit or point of reaction; for, when licentiousness becomes a theory, regularly asserted, and formally vindicated, it is then no better than truth. The poetry is gone, and it dies of its own flatness. * * *

It will further assist our conceptions and modify our impressions of this subject, if we inquire briefly into the office and probable use of what is called nature. That nature is not appointed as any final end of God, we have shown before. It is only ordained, as we then intimated, to be played upon by the powers; that is, by God Himself and all free agents under Him. Instead of being the veritable system or universe of God, as in our sensuality or scientific conceit we make it, we may call it more truly the ball or medial substance occupied by so many players; that is, by the spiritual universe under God as the Lord of Hosts. There could be no commerce of so many players in the game referred to, without some medium or medial instrument; and the instrument needed to be a constant, invariable substance, as regards shape, weight, size, elasticity, inertia, and all the natural properties pertaining to it. If the ball changed weight, colour, density, shape every moment, no skill could be acquired or evinced in the use of it; there would be no real test in the game, and no social commerce of play in the parties using it. Therefore it needed to be, so far, a constant quantity. So, demonstrably, there needs to be, between us and God, and between us and one another, some constant quantity, so that we can act upon each other, trace the effects of our practice and that of others, learn the mind of God, the misery and baseness of wrong, the worth of principles, and the blessedness of virtue, from what we experience; attaining thus to such a degree of wisdom, that we can set our life on a footing of success and divine approbation. What we call nature is this constant quantity interposed between us and God, and between us and each other—the great ball, in using which, our life battle is played. Or, considering the grand immensity of planetary worlds, careering through the fields of light, all these, we may say, rolling eternally onward in their rounds of order, bearing their wondrous furniture with them, such as science discovers, and weaving their interminable lines of causes, are the ball of exercise, in which, and by which, God is training and teaching the spiritual hosts of His empire. They are set in a system of immutable order and constancy for this reason; but with the design, beforehand, that all the free beings or powers shall play their activity on them and into them, and that He, too, by the free insertion of His, may turn them about by His counsel, and so make Himself and His counsel open to the commerce of His children.

So far, therefore, from discovering anything undignified or superstitious in the admission of a supernatural agency and government of God in the world, it is, in fact, the only worthy and exalted conception. It no more humbles the world or deranges the scientific order of it to let God act upon it, than to let man do the same; as we certainly know that he does, without any thought of overturning its laws. On the other hand, to imagine, in the way of dignifying the world, that God must let it alone and simply see it go, is only to confess that it was made for no such glorious intent as we have supposed. * * *

Besides, if it be maintained that nature is the proper universe of God, and that no conception is admissible of powers outside of nature acting upon it to vary the action it would otherwise have by itself, then follows the very shocking consequence that, since the creation, God has had and can hereafter have no work of liberty to do. Nature is His monument, and not His garment. Not only are miracles out of the question, but counsel and action also. He is under a scientific embargo, neither hearing nor helping His children, nor indeed giving any signs of recognition. And the reason is worse, if possible, and more chilling than the fact, viz., that if He should stir, He would move something that science requires to be let alone! A great many Christians are confused and chilled by a difficulty resembled to this feeling, when they go to God in worship or prayer, that nothing can reasonably be expected of Him, because reason allows Him to do nothing. It is as if He were one of those spent meteors to which the Indians offer sacrifice—a hard, cold rock of iron, which they worship for the noise it made a long time ago, when it fell from the sky, and not because it is likely ever to make even a noise again. * * *

It is also a matter of consequence to be anticipated in a just and full establishment of supernatural verities, that intellectual and moral philosophy are destined, in this way, to be finally Christianized; and so, that all science will, at last, be melted into unity with the religion of Christ. Our professors of philosophy leave it to the theologians to settle the question whether man is a sinner or not, and go on to assume that he is in the normal state of his being, acting precisely according to his nature; when, if the theologians chance to doubt any of their conclusions, the reply is, that they do not understand philosophy.

Now it is either true that man is a sinner, or it is not. If he is not a sinner, then he exists normally, and what he is in his action, he is in his nature, and a great many questions will be settled accordingly. On the other hand, if he is a sinner, acting against God, acting as he was not made to act, then he is, by the supposition, a disordered nature, a being in the state of unnature. Any philosophy therefore which does not recognize the fact, but deduces his nature from his present demonstrations, must be wholly at fault.

10

CIVILIZATION
OR
BARBARISM

WHAT would become of society in the rapidly growing American West was, to be sure, more a national issue than a religious one. Yet whether civilization or barbarism would win out was seen, in large measure, as a question of Christianity's success as a civilizing force. The state of "religion and morals" was a generally accepted index to the state of the society itself. Was the West to become the seat of the new Jerusalem, the fufillment of utopian dreams? Or, was it to become the ultimate testimony to democracy's inherent weaknesses, to Christianity's impotence as a creative, constructive force?

A first step by way of answering these sharp queries was to find out something about that West. Over both Americans in the East and foreigners abroad, the prospect of hacking a crude but honest civilization out of the wilderness cast a seductive spell. Names like Pleasant Hill, New Harmony, and Nauvoo suggest another sort of attraction and promise—by no means always fulfilled. But in the 1820's and 30's the West was host to large numbers of uninvited guests, some of whom came to scoff and some to pray. Few changed sides.

In the summer of 1812, at the request of the Missionary Societies of Massachusetts and Connecticut, John F. Schermerhorn and Samuel J. Mills began a careful, year-long inspection tour "of that part of the United States which lies west of the Allegany Mountains, with regard to religion and morals" (published in Hartford, 1814). Their clear purpose was to determine the churches' responsibility for Western society as well as where and how that responsibility could best be met. In general, their report suggested much to be done: in Ohio, for example, "the people are loose in morals; the profanation of the Lord's day, swearing and drunkenness together with horse-racing and gambling are very common." The report, not unbiased in its denominational preferences, helped bring about a tremendous voluntary effort to win the West: mission societies, Sunday-school unions, tract and education societies—and many more. One additional contribution from the East was Lyman Beecher.

Beecher (1775–1863), father of Henry Ward Beecher and Harriet B. Stowe, was ordained two years following his graduation from Yale in 1797. Serving a succession of churches in New York, Connecticut, and Massachusetts, Beecher decided in 1832 to cast his lot with the West. Cincinnati (pop. about 25,000) became his base, where he assumed the presidency of newly-founded Lane Theological Seminary. This school was intended to provide the kind of native (i.e., Western) leadership deemed necessary for the effective civilizing and Christianizing of the area. Unfortunately, the school was caught up in the furies of abolitionism, most of its students departing in 1834 to join in a freer Oberlin.

Lyman Beecher's *Plea for the West* breathes the utopian spirit. The West is a place to begin anew, to create an ideal Christian society, to show mankind just what ought to be done and how. All is on a grand scale in the West, wrote Beecher, and his own thoughts are no exception to this claim. Population will multiply twenty fold in a couple of generations (it didn't); the institutions of the East will be duplicated in the West (they weren't); the "government of force will cease . . . till the whole earth is free" (regrettably, it hasn't). But bold, energetic aspiration did do much for the West—an aspiration which was for many based on that marvelous Calvinist paradox: "The certainty of success calls us to immediate effort."

The sharply contrasting tone of the second selection demonstrates that aspiration lies in the heart of the beholder. William Faux, one of the nineteenth century's many beholders, was interested not in what greatness lay ahead but in what crudities, deceits, barbarisms, corruptions, and murders lay all around. "An English farmer," as he describes himself, Faux was not an exemplar of great literary taste or cultural achievement. He was an example, however, of those foreign observers whose purpose it was to denigrate America and discourage emigration. He executed that purpose with sufficient distinction to win an assessment in the *North American Review* as one of the many "paltry adventurers, who come over to this country to make their fortunes by speculation, and, being disappointed in the attempt to jump into riches without industry, without principle, without delay, return to England and pander to the taste for American calumny, in order to pay the expenses of the expedition, by the sale of their falsehoods." *

What won Faux a thirty-three-page attack in this major American journal was not so much his publication of *Memorable Days in America* (London, 1823) as that his diatribe was apparently given credence in respectable English circles. *North American Review* editors had little patience with British reviewers who found Faux's volume praiseworthy, or those who commented that "the want of an established church is a fatal error in the [U.S.] constitution; that this want of a national religion is the reason of the vicious and heartless conduct of the Americans; and that it has made the bulk of the people infidels and fanatics." * * Like Schermerhorn and Mills, Faux bemoans

* Vol. XIX (1824), pp. 92–93.
** *Ibid.*, p. 114.

the absence of moral sensitivity. But unlike the two Christian missionaries, the English farmer does not see America's churches as a central or even relevant force in determining the way a society—or perhaps a nation—may go.

A

[The text is taken from Lyman Beecher, *A Plea for the West* (2d ed.; Cincinnati: Truman & Smith, 1835), pp. 35–43.]

A Plea for the West

When I first entered the West, its vastness overpowered me with the impression of its uncontrollable greatness, in which all human effort must be lost. But when I perceived the active intercourse between the great cities, like the rapid circulation of a giant's blood; and heard merchants speak of just stepping up to Pittsburgh—only six hundred miles—and back in a few days; and others just from New-Orleans, or St. Louis, or the Far West; and others going thither; and when I heard my ministerial brethren negotiating exchanges in the near neighborhood—only one hundred miles up or down the river—and going and returning on Saturday and Monday, and without trespassing on the Sabbath;—then did I perceive how God, who seeth the end from the beginning, had prepared the West to be mighty, and still wieldable, that the moral energy of his word and spirit might take it up as a very little thing.

This vast territory is occupied now by ten states and will soon be by twelve. Forty years since it contained only about one hundred and fifty thousand souls; while it now contains little short of five millions. At the close of this century, if no calamity intervenes, it will contain, probably, one hundred millions—a day which some of our children may live to see; and when fully peopled, may accommodate three hundred millions. It is half as large as all Europe, four times as large as the Atlantic states, and twenty times as large as New-England. Was there ever such a spectacle—such a field in which to plant the seeds of an immortal harvest!—so vast a ship, so richly laden with the world's treasures and riches, whose helm is offered to the guiding influence of early forming institutions!

The certainty of success calls us to immediate effort. If we knew not what to do, if all was effort and expense in untried experiments, there might be some pretext for the paralysis of amazement and inaction. But we know what to do: the means are obvious, and well tried, and certain. The sun and the rain of heaven are not more sure to call forth a bounteous vegetation, than Bibles, and Sabbaths, and schools, and seminaries, are to diffuse intellectual light and warmth for the bounteous fruits of righteousness and peace. The corn and the acorn of the East are not more sure to vegetate at the West than the institutions which have blessed the East are to bless the West.

But these all-pervading orbs of illumination and centres of attraction must be established. Such is the gravitating tendency of society, that no spontaneous effort at arms-length will hold it up. It is by the constant energy and strong attraction of powerful institutions only that the needed intellectual and moral power can be applied: and the present is the age of founding them. If this work be done, and well done, our country is safe, and the world's hope is secure. The government of force will cease, and that of intelligence and virtue will take its place; and nation after nation cheered by our example, will follow in our footsteps, till the whole earth is free. There is no danger that our agriculture and arts will not prosper: the danger is, that our intelligence and virtue will falter and fall back into a dark minded, vicious populace—a poor, uneducated reckless mass of infuriated animalism, to rush on resistless as the tornado, or to burn as if set on fire of hell.

Until Europe, by universal education, is delivered from such masses of feudal ignorance and servitude, she sits upon a volcano, and despotism and revolution will arbitrate her destiny.

Consider, too, how quickly and how cheaply the guarantee of a perpetual and boundless prosperity can be secured. The

West needs but a momentary aid, when almost as soon as received, should it be needed, she will repay and quadruple both principle and interest. Lend a hand to get up her institutions, to give ubiquity to her schools and Sabbaths and sanctuaries, while her forests are falling and her ocean floods of population rolling in, and afterwards we will not come here to ask for aid; for there is a wealth and chivalrous munificence there, which, when it has first performed the necessary work of self-preservation, will pour with you a noble tide of rival benevolence into that river which is "to make glad the city of our God."

All at the West, is on a great scale, and the minds and the views of the people correspond with these relative proportions. Already, where churches are formed, they give more liberally than churches of the same relative condition at the East; and I have no doubt the time is at the door, when the abundance of her means and enterprise will take the lead in those glorious enterprises which are to emancipate the world.

It is not parsimony which renders momentary aid necessary to the West: it is want of time and of assimilation for the consciousness and wielding of her powers. And how cheaply can the aid be rendered for rearing immediately the first generation of her institutions; cheaper than we could rear the barracks to accommodate an army for the defence of our liberty, for a single campaign; cheaper than the taxations of crime and its punishment during the same period, in the absence of literary and evangelical influence.

Consider, also, that the mighty resources of the West are worse than useless, without the supervening influence of the government of God.

To balance the temptation of such unrivaled abundance, the capacity of the West for self-destruction, without religious and moral culture, will be as terrific as her capacity for self-preservation, with it, will be glorious. But all the moral energies of the government of God over men, are indissolubly associated with "the ministry of reconciliation." The Sabbath, and the preaching of the gospel, are Heaven's consecrated instrumentality for the efficacious administration of the government of mind in a happy, social state. By these only does the Sun of Righteousness arise with healing in his beams; and ignorance, and vice, and super-stition encamp around evangelical institutions, to rush in when-ever their light and power is extinct.

The great experiment is now making, and from its extent and rapid filling up is making in the West, whether the perpetuity of our republican institutions can be reconciled with universal suf-frage. Without the education of the head and heart of the nation, they cannot be; and the question to be decided is, can the nation, or the vast balance power of it be so imbued with intelligence and virtue, as to bring out, in laws and their administration, a perpetual self-preserving energy? We know that the work is a vast one, and of great difficulty; and yet we believe it can be done.

B

[The text is taken from Reuben Gold Thwaites, ed., *Early Western Travels 1748–1846* (Cleveland: Arthur H. Clarke Co., 1904–7), Vol. XI, pp. 301–304.]

Memorable Days in America

Once for all, from an inquiring Englishman in the United States. To the Editor of the Stamford News.

Ingle's Refuge, Banks of Ohio, State of Indiana, 25th December, 1819.

SIR,

To my esteemed friends and countrymen, living within the wide circuit of your paper, and expecting many long promised epistles, say that the task is impracticable, and therefore justly abandoned. What they need, *truth,* is always difficult to attain; and a correct impression of things, made by weight of unwill-ing, or long concealed evidence, examined and cross-examined, will, perhaps, be found in my journal, calculated to undeceive, disappoint, and, as usual, offend, nearly all those of whom, and for whom I have written.

It is, I regret to say, too true, that the writings of emigrants, however respectable, present a partial or unfaithful portraiture; "shewing things as they should be, not as they are."* Such authority, then, is questionable and deceptive. Each individual destined never to return, wants, and tempts, his friends to follow; the motive, perhaps, is innocent, or venial, but the consequences are evil and disastrous.

My peregrinations, visits, and visitations, to many points and intersections of the compass, and to all ranks of native and adopted citizens, on this continent, are little short of eight thousand miles. Of those visited, and added to the number of my acquaintance, exclusive of excellencies, honourables, generals, majors, captains, judges, and squires, are our two distinguished expatriates, [Morris] Birkbeck and [George] Flower, with whom I have spent days more interesting than fall to the lot of travellers in common. Of their success or failure, satisfaction or disappointment, I, at present, say nothing. By me, they were met with feelings of respect, and quitted with regret.

My inquiries have been, as promised, directed to one grand object; that of ascertaining, by first-rate means, the past and present condition, and future probable prospects, of British emigrants, and the consequent good or evil of emigration, in the

* At least one of Faux's fellow Englishmen took seriously the challenge to tell things "as they are." This was Thomas Brothers, another of England's nineteenth-century visitors to America. Brothers was not enchanted by what he saw; indeed, he was frightened. For it seemed to him that democracy was well on its inevitable way to mobocracy, where the country would be run by "a few unprincipled and lawless men." To warn his fellow countrymen, Thomas Brothers thoughtfully added to his volume an appendix of "Miscellaneous Murders, Riots, and Other Outrages in 1834, 1835, 1836, 1837, and 1838." The cases cited were but a few examples "of many thousands which the author could produce of the same character, and all from newspapers published and edited by Americans." This—and more—may be consulted in Thomas Brothers, *The United States of North America As They Are; Not As They Are Generally Described: Being a Cure for Radicalism* (London: Longman, Orme, Brown, Green & Longmans, 1840).—Ed.

hope of clearly defining and exposing its character, so that it may no longer remain a doubtful or desperate enterprise, a journey in the dark, alternately praised or blamed, but a cause, attaching to it *certain* consequences, which, for some persons to embrace, or shun, is become a visible, tangible, matter of duty.

To my countrymen disposed to emigrate, but who can, by encreased exertion, keep their unequalled comforts and honour unimpaired, I would say, in a voice which should be heard from shore to shore, "Stay where you are; for neither America, nor the world, have any thing to offer you in exchange!" But to those of *decreasing* means, and *increasing* families, uprooted, withering, and seeking a transplantation *somewhere,* full of hard, dirty-handed industry, and with means sufficient for location here, I would say, "Haste away; you have no other refuge from poverty, which, in England, is crime, punishable with neglect, and contempt everlasting!" But, if you come, come one and all of you, male and female, in your working jackets, with axes, ploughshares, and pruninghooks in your hands, prepared long to suffer many privations, expecting to be your own servants,— no man's masters; to find liberty and independence, any thing but soft indulgence; and America, a land only of everlasting, well-rewarded labour. Thus, morally and physically qualified, the dark, lonely wilds and interminable forests, which now surround me, shall bow before you, yielding to your cultivation every common good thing, but not satisfaction, which is not of earthly growth! For you, even *you,* escaped from prisons and pauperism, will, sometimes, "hang your harps on the willow, and weep," when you remember distant England. Very few emigrants, whatsoever may have been their disgusts and evils in the old country, or their successes in the new, can forget their "dear native land." The recollection is, indeed, an impediment to their prosperity; distance only enhances her value, and, as a much-loved, ungrateful mistress, her charms only are remembered and cherished. This seems an indestructible feeling; the incurable mania of the British exile.

I am now living on wild bucks and bears, mixed up, and

barbarizing with men almost as wild as they: men, systematically unprincipled, and in whom the moral sense seems to have no existence: this is the lot of all coming here. The climate is not good in any season, and though better here than east of the mountains, is yet unfriendly to industry every where. Summer, amidst breezy shades, champaigne and brandy; and winter, with two down beds, one over you and one under you, and a hickory fire continually, are just tolerable! The autumn is pleasant enough, but too generally pestilential.

Having to commence in the morning, a journey of one thousand miles, on horseback, on my way to England, through the Cities of Washington and Charleston, and the worst roads and weather in the universe, the mercury being now three degrees below zero; riding, and not writing, presses on the attention of, Sir,

Your obedient servant,
W. FAUX

11

FREEDOM

OR

SLAVERY

THAT BLOODIEST issue in all America's history also divided church families and rived Christian doctrine. Second only to Christianity's doctrine of God was its doctrine of man. Man is a child of God, of a God who is no respecter of persons, of a God in whom there is no East or West, no Scythian or Greek, neither slave nor free. But what does all that mean in a specific historical setting? in a given social and economic context? with respect to a peculiar institution which even the Bible apparently accepts? In the search for answers, Christian denounced Christian, brother fought brother. Baptists, Methodists, and Presbyterians found themselves split asunder, north and south, white and black. Both sides read the same Bible, said Lincoln, "and pray to the same God; and each invokes His aid against the other. . . . The prayers of both could not be answered. . . ."

A generation before 1860 the lines of geographical division were not sharply drawn. Emancipation societies were vigorous in the South, and radical abolitionists were attacked in the North.

Nor were theological "liberals" uniformly proslavery, with "conservatives" assuming an opposing stance. Evangelical religion, under Charles Finney's leadership, recruited large numbers into the antislavery ranks. For a time men discussed the philosophical merits of the institution, its practical abuses, its future enlargement or gradual withering away. For a time, these discussions continued; then time ran out.

William Ellery Channing (1780–1842), of Harvard's class of 1798, spent most of his professional career as pastor of the Federal Street Church in Boston. Immensely influential both as speaker and writer, Channing gradually assumed the leadership of New England's Unitarian separation from Calvinist Congregationalism. Unitarianism, despite its name, quarreled with Calvinism more over the nature of man than over the nature of God. A doctrine of total depravity, Channing argued, undermines moral responsibility and human freedom. Man's nature is essentially good, his rational and moral faculties essentially unimpaired. Man therefore has rights—not granted by an indulgent society, but rights inherent in his very nature. "Man's rights belong to him as a moral being, as capable of perceiving moral distinctions, as a subject of moral obligations."

In his addresses on *Slavery,* published in 1835, Channing displays the broad nature of his learning, the careful structure of his argumentation. His eight chapters examine slavery from every major angle: man as a property, man as a creature with sacred rights, slavery as an intrinsic evil ("An institution so founded in wrong, so imbued with injustice, cannot be made a good"), slavery as removable, and finally "a few reflections on the duties belonging to the times." Chapter Five, from which the major portion below is taken, considers the scriptural arguments on behalf of slavery. This portion is chosen not because it was for Channing the keystone of his case but because for so many of his opponents the case for public defense rested precisely there.

So it did for James Henley Thornwell (1812–1862), Presbyterian clergyman and president of South Carolina College from 1851 to 1855. Presbyterians, as noted above, separated into northern and southern branches during the war years—not to be reunited even a century later. Thornwell's leadership was lost to the newly formed Presbyterian Church, U.S., by an early death. But his considerable genius was lost even earlier than that by being diverted "into the desert of proslavery controversy."*

Pro- and anti-slavery sentiments cannot be divided precisely along theological lines—as previously noted. But it did not help the abolitionist cause in the South that several notorious radicals on the slavery question were also radical theologically. Or, as Thornwell's editors say: Christians "cannot always be blinded to scriptural truth by theories of human rights and humanitarian schemes, conceived in the womb of a rationalist philosophy." So it was reason versus revelation all over again, except that in this case the conclusions had been reached before the arguments began. The sermon abbreviated below was delivered May 26, 1850 in Charleston, South Carolina, at the dedication of a new church erected for Negro Presbyterians. In it Thornwell frequently alludes to "Dr. Channing," quoting him in order to demonstrate his irrelevance, his imprecision, his heresy. Slavery, the South Carolinian concludes, is "one of the schools in which immortal spirits are trained for their final destiny. If it is attended with severer hardships, these hardships are compensated by fewer duties, and the very violence of its temptations give dignity and lustre to its virtues."

A

[The text is taken from *The Works of William E. Channing, D.D.* (Boston: American Unitarian Association, 1903), pp. 688–91, 723–724, 739–40.]

Slavery

The first question to be proposed by a rational being is, not what is profitable, but what is right. Duty must be primary,

---

* E. A. Smith, *The Presbyterian Ministry in American Culture* (Philadelphia: Westminster Press, 1962), p. 171.

prominent, most conspicuous among the objects of human thought and pursuit. If we cast it down from its supremacy, if we inquire first for our interests, and then for our duties, we shall certainly err. We can never see the right clearly and fully but by making it our first concern. No judgment can be just or wise but that which is built on the conviction of the paramount worth and importance of duty. This is the fundamental truth, the supreme law of reason; and the mind which does not start from this, in its inquiries into human affairs, is doomed to great, perhaps fatal, error.* * *

Of late our country has been convulsed by the question of slavery; and the people, in proportion as they have felt vehemently, have thought superficially, or hardly thought at all; and we see the results in a singular want of well-defined principles, in a strange vagueness and inconsistency of opinion, and in the proneness to excess which belongs to unsettled minds. The multitude have been called, now to contemplate the horrors of slavery, and now to shudder at the ruin and bloodshed which must follow emancipation. The word massacre has resounded through the land, striking terror into strong as well as tender hearts, and awakening indignation against whatever may seem to threaten such a consummation. The consequence is that not a few dread all discussion of the subject, and, if not reconciled to the continuance of slavery, at least believe that they have no duty to perform, no testimony to bear, no influence to exert, no sentiments to cherish and spread, in relation to this evil. What is still worse, opinions either favoring or extenuating it are heard with little or no disapprobation. Concessions are made to it which would once have shocked the community; whilst to assail it is pronounced unwise and perilous. No stronger reason for a calm exposition of its true character can be given than this very state of the public mind. A community can suffer no greater calamity than the loss of its principles. Lofty and pure sentiment is the life and hope of a people. There was never such an obligation to discuss slavery as at this moment, when recent events have done much to unsettle and obscure men's minds in regard to it. This result is to be ascribed in part to the injudicious vehemence of those who have taken into their hands the cause of the slave. Such ought to remember, that to espouse a good cause is not enough. We must maintain it in a spirit answering to its dignity. Let no man touch the great interests of humanity who does not strive to sanctify himself for the work by cleansing his heart of all wrath and uncharitableness, who cannot hope that he is in a measure baptized into the spirit of universal love. Even sympathy with the injured and oppressed may do harm, by being partial, exclusive, and bitterly indignant. How far the declension of the spirit of freedom is to be ascribed to the cause now suggested, I do not say. The effect is plain, and whoever sees and laments the evil should strive to arrest it.* * *

But this subject has more than philosophical dignity. It has an important bearing on character. Our interest in it is one test by which our comprehension of the distinctive spirit of Christianity must be judged. Christianity is the manifestation and inculcation of universal love. The great teaching of Christianity is, that we must recognize and respect human nature in all its forms in the poorest, most ignorant, most fallen. We must look beneath "the flesh" to the "spirit." The spiritual principle in man is what entitles him to our brotherly regard. To be just to this is the great injunction of our religion. To overlook this, on account of condition or color, is to violate the great Christian law. We have reason to think that it is one design of God in appointing the vast diversities of human condition, to put to the test, and to bring out most distinctly, the principle of spiritual love. It is wisely ordered that human nature is not set before us in a few forms of beauty, magnificence, and outward glory. To be dazzled and attracted by these would be no sign of reverence for what is interior and spiritual in human nature. To lead us to discern and love this, we are brought into connection with fellow-creatures whose outward circumstances are repulsive. To recognize our own spiritual nature and God's image in these humble forms, to recognize as brethren those who want all

outward distinctions, is the chief way in which we are to manifest the spirit of him who came to raise the fallen and to save
the lost. We see then, the moral importance of the question of
slavery. According to our decision of it, we determine our comprehension of the Christian law. He who cannot see a brother, a
child of God, a man possessing all the rights of humanity,
under a skin darker than his own, wants the vision of a Christian. He worships the outward. The spirit is not yet revealed to
him. To look unmoved on the degradation and wrongs of a
fellow-creature, because burned by a fiercer sun, proves us
strangers to justice and love in those universal forms which
characterize Christianity. The greatest of all distinctions, the
only enduring one, is moral goodness, virtue, religion. Outward
distinctions cannot add to the dignity of this. The wealth of
worlds is "not sufficient for a burnt-offering" on its altar. A
being capable of this is invested by God with solemn claims on
his fellow-creatures. To exclude millions of such beings from
our sympathy, because of outward disadvantages, proves that,
in whatever else we surpass them, we are not their superiors in
Christian virtue.* * *

Attempts are often made to support slavery by the authority
of revelation. "Slavery," it is said, "is allowed in the Old Testament, and not condemned in the New. Paul commands slaves
to obey. He commands masters, not to release their slaves, but
to treat them justly. Therefore slavery is right, is sanctified by
God's word." In this age of the world, and amidst the light
which has been thrown on the true interpretation of the Scriptures, such reasoning hardly deserves notice. A few words only
will be offered in reply.

This reasoning proves too much. If usages, sanctioned in the
Old Testament and not forbidden in the New, are right, then
our moral code will undergo a sad deterioration. Polygamy was
allowed to the Israelites, was the practice of the holiest men,
and was common and licensed in the age of the Apostles. But
the Apostles nowhere condemn it, nor was the renunciation of it
made an essential condition of admission into the Christian

church. It is true that in one passage Christ has condemned it by implication. But is not slavery condemned by stronger implication, in the many passages which make the new religion to consist in serving one another, and in doing to others what we would that they should do to ourselves? Why may not Scripture be used to stock our houses with wives as well as with slaves?

Again. Paul is said to sanction slavery. Let us now ask, What was slavery in the age of Paul? It was the slavery, not so much of black as of white men, not merely of barbarians, but of Greeks, not merely of the ignorant and debased, but of the virtuous, educated, and refined. Piracy and conquest were the chief means of supplying the slave-market, and they heeded neither character nor condition. Sometimes the greater part of the population of a captured city was sold into bondage, sometimes the whole, as in the case of Jerusalem. Noble and royal families, the rich and great, the learned and powerful, the philosopher and poet, the wisest and best men, were condemned to the chain. Such was ancient slavery. . . .

Slavery, in the age of the Apostle, had so penetrated society, was so intimately interwoven with it and the materials of servile war were so abundant, that a religion preaching freedom to the slave would have shaken the social fabric to its foundation, and would have armed against itself the whole power of the state. Paul did not then assail the institution. He satisfied himself with spreading principles which, however slowly, could not but work its destruction.***

Let me offer another remark. The perversion of Scripture to the support of slavery is singularly inexcusable in this country. Paul not only commanded slaves to obey their masters. He delivered these precepts: "Let every soul be subject unto the higher powers. For there is no power but of God: the powers that be are ordained of God. Whosoever, therefore, resisteth the power, resisteth the ordinance of God: and they that resist shall receive to themselves damnation." This passage was written in the time of Nero. It teaches passive obedience to despotism more strongly than any text teaches the lawfulness of slavery.

Accordingly it has been quoted for ages by the supporters of arbitrary power, and made the stronghold of tyranny. Did our fathers acquiesce in the most obvious interpretation of this text? Because the first Christians were taught to obey despotic rule, did our fathers feel as if Christianity had stripped men of their rights? Did they argue that tyranny was to be excused because forcible opposition to it is in most cases wrong? Did they argue that absolute power ceases to be unjust because, as a general rule, it is the duty of subjects to obey? Did they infer that bad institutions ought to be perpetual because the subversion of them by force will almost always inflict greater evil than it removes? No; they were wiser interpreters of God's word. They believed that despotism was a wrong, notwithstanding the general obligation upon its subjects to obey: and that whenever a whole people should so feel the wrong as to demand its removal, the time for removing it had fully come. Such is the school in which we here have been brought up. To us, it is no mean proof of the divine original of Christianity, that it teaches human brotherhood and favors human rights; and yet, on the ground of two or three passages, which admit different constructions, we make Christianity the minister of slavery, the forger of chains for those whom it came to make free.

It is a plain rule of scriptural criticism, that particular texts should be interpreted according to the general tenor and spirit of Christianity. And what is the general, the perpetual teaching of Christianity in regard to social duty? "All things whatsoever ye would that men should do to you, do ye even so to them; for this is the law and the prophets." Now, does not every man feel that nothing, nothing could induce him to consent to be a slave? Does he not feel that, if reduced to this abject lot, his whole nature, his reason, conscience, affections, would cry out against it as the greatest of calamities and wrongs? Can he pretend, then, that, in holding others in bondage, he does to his neighbor what he would that his neighbor should do to him? Of what avail are a few texts, which were designed for local and temporary use, when urged against the vital, essential spirit, and the plainest precepts of our religion? * * *

The work which I proposed to myself is now completed. I ask and hope for it the Divine blessing, as far as it expresses truth, and breathes the spirit of justice and humanity. If I have written any thing under the influence of prejudice, passion, or unkindness to any human being, I ask forgiveness of God and man. I have spoken strongly, not to offend or give pain, but to produce in others deep convictions corresponding to my own. Nothing could have induced me to fix my thoughts on this painful subject, but a conviction, which pressed on me with increasing weight, that the times demanded a plain and free exposition of the truth. The few last months have increased my solicitude for the country. Public sentiment has seemed to me to be losing its healthfulness and vigor. I have seen symptoms of the decline of the old spirit of liberty. Servile opinions have seemed to gain ground among us. The faith of our fathers in free institutions has waxed faint, and is giving place to despair of human improvement. I have perceived a disposition to deride abstract rights, to speak of freedom as a dream, and of republican governments as built on sand. I have perceived a faintheartedness in the cause of human rights. The condemnation which has been passed on abolitionists has seemed to be settling into acquiescence in slavery. The sympathies of the community have been turned from the slave to the master. The impious doctrine, that human laws can repeal the divine, can convert unjust and oppressive power into a moral right, has more and more tinctured the style of conversation and the press. With these sad and solemn views of society, I could not be silent; and I thank God, amidst the consciousness of great weakness and imperfection, that I have been able to offer this humble tribute, this sincere though feeble testimony, this expression of heart-felt allegiance, to the cause of freedom, justice, and humanity.

Having stated the circumstances which have moved me to write, I ought to say that they do not discourage me. Were darker omens to gather round us, I should not despair. With a faith like his who came to prepare the way for the Great Deliverer, I feel and can say, "The kingdom of heaven," the reign of justice and disinterested love, "is at hand, and all flesh shall see the salvation of God." I know, and rejoice to know, that a power, mightier than the prejudices and oppression of ages, is working on earth for the world's redemption,—the power of Christian truth and goodness. It descended from heaven in the person of Christ. It was manifest in his life and death. From his cross it went forth conquering and to conquer. Its mission is "to preach deliverence to the captive, and to set at liberty them that are bound." It has opened many a prison-door. It is ordained to break every chain. I have faith in its triumphs. I do not, cannot despair.

B

[The text is taken from J. B. Adger and J. L. Girardeau, eds., *The Collected Writings of James Henley Thornwell D.D., Ll.D.* (Richmond: Presbyterian Committee of Publication, 1873), pp. 404–408, 414–16, 422–24.]

The Christian Doctrine of Slavery

* * * God has not permitted such a remarkable phenomenon as the unanimity of the civilized world, in its execration of Slavery, to take place without design. This great battle with the Abolitionists has not been fought in vain. The muster of such immense forces, the fury and bitterness of the conflict, the disparity in resources of the parties in the war, the conspicuousness, the unexampled conspicuousness of the event, have all been ordered for wise and beneficent results; and when the smoke shall have rolled away, it will be seen that a real progress has been made in the practical solution of the problems which produced the collision.

What disasters it will be necessary to pass through before the nations can be taught the lessons of Providence, what lights shall be extinguished, and what horrors experienced, no human sagacity can foresee. But that the world is now the theatre of

an extraordinary conflict of great principles, that the foundations of society are about to be explored to their depths, and the
sources of social and political prosperity laid bare—that the
questions in dispute involve all that is dear and precious to man
on earth, the most superficial observer cannot fail to perceive.
Experiment after experiment may be made, disaster succeed
disaster, in carrying out the principles of an atheistic philosophy,
until the nations, wearied and heart-sickened with changes without improvement, shall open their eyes to the real causes of
their calamities, and learn the lessons which wisdom shall evolve
from the events that have passed. Truth must triumph. God will
vindicate the appointments of His Providence: and if our institutions are indeed consistent with righteousness and truth, we
can calmly afford to bide our time; we can watch the storm
which is beating furiously against us, without terror or dismay;
we can receive the assault of the civilized world, trusting in
Him who has all the elements at His command, and can save as
easily by one as a thousand. If our principles are true, the world
must come to them; and we can quietly appeal from the verdict
of existing generations to the more impartial verdict of the men
who shall have seen the issue of the struggle in which we are
now involved. It is not the narrow question of Abolitionism or
Slavery—not simply whether we shall emancipate our negroes
or not; the real question is the relations of man to society, of
States to the individual, and of the individual to States—a
question as broad as the interests of the human race.

These are the mighty questions which are shaking thrones to
their centres, upheaving the masses like an earthquake, and
rocking the solid pillars of this Union. The parties in this conflict are not merely Abolitionists and Slaveholders; they are
Atheists, Socialists, Communists, Red Republicans, Jacobins on
the one side, and the friends of order and regulated freedom on
the other. In one word, the world is the battle ground, Christianity and Atheism the combatants, and the progress of humanity the stake. One party seems to regard society, with all its
complicated interests, its divisions and subdivisions, as the ma-

chinery of man, which, as it has been invented and arranged by
his ingenuity and skill, may be taken to pieces, reconstructed,
altered or repaired, as experience shall indicate defects or confusion in the original plan. The other party beholds in it the
ordinance of God; and contemplates "this little scene of human
life" as placed in the middle of a scheme, whose beginnings must
be traced to the unfathomable depths of the past, and whose
development and completion must be sought in the still more
unfathomable depths of the future—a scheme, as Butler expresses it, "not fixed, but progressive, every way incomprehensible"; in which, consequently, irregularity is the confession
of our ignorance, disorder the proof of our blindness, and with
which it is as awful temerity to tamper as to sport with the
name of God.

It is a great lesson, that, as the weakness of man can never
make that straight which God hath made crooked, true wisdom
consists in discharging the duties of every relation; and the true
secret of progress is in the improvement and elevation which are
gradually superinduced by this spirit.

The part, accordingly, which is assigned to us, in the tumult
of the age, is the maintenance of the principles upon which the
security of social order and the development of humanity depend, in their application to the distinctive institutions which
have provoked upon us the malediction of the world. The Apostle briefly sums up all that in incumbent, at the present crisis,
upon the slaveholders of the South in the words: Masters, give
unto your servants that which is just and equal, knowing that
ye also have a Master in heaven. It would be an useless waste of
time to spend many words in proving that the servants contemplated by the Apostle were slaves. Finding it impossible to deny
that Slavery, as an existing element of society, is actually sanctioned by Christ and His Apostles, those who would preserve
some show of consistency in their veneration of the Scriptures,
and their condemnation of us, resolve the conduct of the founders of Christianity into motives of prudence and considerations
of policy. While they admit that the letter of the Scriptures is

distinctly and unambiguously in our favour, they maintain that their spirit is against us; and, that our Saviour was content to leave the destruction of whatsoever was morally wrong in the social fabric to the slow progress of changes in individual opinions, wrought by the silent influence of religion, rather than endanger the stability of governments by sudden and disastrous revolutions. "The Apostle does not," says a learned commentator, "interfere with any established relations, however, as in the case of Slavery, morally and politically wrong, but only enjoins the discharge of the duties which the very persons themselves recognize." It is not for me to explain how the imputation of a defective morality can be reconciled with the great Protestant dogma, that the Bible is an adequate rule of faith and practice; or upon what principles slaveholders should be rejected from the fellowship of the Christian Church now, when Paul received them as brethren, and sanctioned the bondage in which they held their servants.

But it may be worth while to expose the confusion of ideas, from which this distinction betwixt the letter and the spirit of the Gospel has arisen, and which has been a source of serious perplexity both to the defenders and the enemies of Slavery. Many Christian men have been led, in reference to this subject, to lend their sanction to principles which, in all other applications, they would reject with abhorrence, because they have felt that the genuis and temper of Christianity were inconsistent with the genius and temper of Slavery; while others, driven to the opposite extreme, from a faithful study of the letter, have been led to deny the principles which lie at the foundation of all human progress, and to assume an attitude in regard to human rights and liberty, which, in their abstract forms, can be characterized as little less than monstrous.

That is a desperate cause which is either incompatible with the general tone and spirit of Christianity, or with the progress of true liberty, which is only another name for the social and political development of man. If it can be shown that Slavery contravenes the spirit of the Gospel, that as a social relation it is essentially unfavourable to the cultivation and growth of the graces of the Spirit, that it is unfriendly to the development of piety and to communion with God; or, that it retards the onward progress of man, that it hinders the march of society to its destined goal, and contradicts that supremacy of justice which is the soul of the State and the life-blood of freedom—if these propositions can be satisfactorily sustained, then it is self-condemned; religion and philanthropy alike require us to labour for its destruction, and every good man amongst us would feel bound to contribute to its removal; and even the voice of patriotism would demand that we should wipe from our country the foul reproach of standing in the way of the destined improvement of mankind.

The confusion upon this subject has arisen from a twofold misapprehension—one in relation to the nature of the Slavery tolerated in the letter of the Scriptures, and the other in relation to the spirit of Christianity itself.* * *

If, then, Slavery is not inconsistent with the existence of personal rights and of moral obligation, it may be asked, In what does its peculiarity consist? What is it that makes a man a slave? We answer, The obligation to labour for another, determined by the Providence of God, independently of the provisions of a contract. The right which the master has is a right, not to the *man,* but to his *labour;* the duty which the slave owes is the service which, in conformity with this right, the master exacts. The essential difference betwixt free labour and slave labour is, that one is rendered in consequence of a contract; the other is rendered in consequence of a command. The labourers in each case are equally moral, equally responsible, equally men. But they work upon different principles.

It is strange that Channing and [William] Whewell should have overlooked the essential distinction of this form of service, as it lies patent in the writings of philosophers who preceded them. The definition given by [William] Paley, a man preeminently marked by perspicuity of thought and vigour of expression, is exactly the same in spirit with our own. In the actual condition of society, the intervention of a contract is not always a matter of very great moment, since it is not always a security to freedom of choice. The Providence of God marks out for the slave the precise services, in the lawful commands of the master, which it is the Divine will that he should render. The painful necessities of his case are often as stringent upon the free labourer, and determine, with as stern a mandate, what contracts he shall make. Neither can he be said to select his employments. God allots to each his portion—places one immediately under command, and leaves the other not unfrequently a petitioner for a master.

Whatever control the master has over the person of the slave is subsidiary to this right to his labour; what he sells is not the man, but the property in his services. True he chastises the man, but the punishments inflicted for disobedience are no more inconsistent with personal responsibilities than the punishments inflicted by the law for breaches of contract. On the contrary, punishment in contradistinction from suffering always implies responsibility, and a right which cannot be enforced is a right, which society, as an organized community, has not yet acknowledged. The chastisements of slaves are accordingly no more entitled to awaken the indignation of loyal and faithful citizens—however pretended philanthropists may describe the horrors of the scourge and the lash—than the penalties of disgrace, imprisonment, or death, which all nations have inflicted upon crimes against the State. All that is necessary, in any case, is that the punishment should be *just*. Pain unrighteously inflicted is cruelty, whether that cruelty springs from the tyranny of a single master, or the tyranny of that greater master, the State. Whether adequate provisions shall be made to protect the slave from inhumanity and oppression, whether he shall be exempt from suffering except for disobedience and for crime, are questions to be decided by the law of the land; and in this matter the codes of different nations, and of the same nation at different times, have been various. Justice and religion require that such provisions should be made. It is no part of the essence

of Slavery, however, that the rights of the slave should be left to
the caprice or to the interest of the master; and in the Southern
States provisions are actually made—whether adequate or inadequate it is useless here to discuss—to protect him from want,
cruelty, and unlawful domination. Provisions are made which
recognize the doctrine of the Apostle, that he is a subject of
rights, and that justice must be rendered to his claims. When
Slavery is pronounced to be essentially sinful, the argument
cannot turn upon incidental circumstances of the system, upon
the defective arrangement of the details, the inadequate securities which the law awards against the infringement of acknowledged right; it must turn upon the nature of the relation itself,
and must boldly attempt to prove that he ceases to be a man,
who is under obligation, without the formalities of a contract,
to labour under the direction and for the benefit of another. If
such a position is inconsistent with the essential elements of
humanity, then Slavery is inhuman; if society, on the other hand,
has distinctly recognized the contrary as essential to good order,
as in the case of children, apprentices and criminals, then
Slavery is consistent with the rights of man, and the pathetic
declamation of Abolitionists falls to the ground.* * *

The fundamental mistake of those who affirm Slavery to be
essentially sinful is that the duties of all men are specifically
the same. Though they do not state the proposition in so many
words, and in its naked form would probably dissent from it,
yet a little attention to their reasoning puts it beyond doubt,
that this is the radical assumption upon which they proceed—
all men are bound to do specifically the same things. As there
are obviously duties of some men, in some relations, which
cannot be practised by a slave, they infer that the institution
strips him of his rights, and curtails the fair proportions of his
humanity. The argument, fully and legitimately carried out,
would condemn every arrangement of society, which did not
secure to all its members an absolute equality of position; it is
the very spirit of socialism and communism.

The doctrine of the Bible, on the other hand, is that the

specific duties—the things actually required to be done—are as various as the circumstances in which men are placed. Moral perfection does not depend upon the number or variety of single acts, but upon the general habitudes of the soul. He is upright whose temper of mind is in conformity with the law, and whose prevailing disposition would always prompt him, in all the relations of life, to do what is right. There may be many right things which he will never be required to perform, but he is entitled to the praise of excellence if he cultivates a spirit which would lead him to perform them, if circumstances should ever make them his duty. The heart may be in full and perfect sympathy with the whole spirit of the law, where the moral training has been confined to comparatively a narrow circle of actual duties. He may be full of benevolence who has never had the means or opportunity of bestowing costly alms upon the poor; he may cherish the gentleness of a lamb who has received no injuries to be forgiven, no wrongs to be forgotten; and he may possess the patience of a martyr, or the fortitude of a hero, whose virtue has never been tried by severe suffering or danger. The circumstances in which men are placed in this sublunary state are exceedingly diversified, but there is probably no external condition in which the actual discipline to which men are subjected may not terminate in the temper of universal holiness. Some are tried in one way, some in another; some are required to do one set of things, some another; but the spirit of true obedience is universally the same, and the result of an effectual probation is, in every case, a moral sympathy with the moral perfections of God. The lesson is the same, however different the text-books from which it has been taught.

Now, unless Slavery is incompatible with the habitudes of holiness, unless it is inconsistent with the spirit of philanthropy or the spirit of piety, unless it furnishes no opportunities for obedience to the law, it is not inconsistent with the pursuit or attainment of the highest excellence. It is no abridgment of moral freedom; the slave may come from the probation of *his* circumstances as fully stamped with the image of God, as those who have enjoyed an easier lot—he may be as completely in unison with the spirit of universal rectitude, as if he had been trained on "flowery beds of ease." Let him discharge his *whole* duty in the actual circumstances of his case, and he is entitled to the praise of a perfect and an upright man. The question with God is, not *what* he has done, but *how:* man looketh at the outward circumstances, but God looketh at the heart.

12

SCIENCE

OR

RELIGION

IF SOME religious issues do not have happy endings, others do not have endings at all. The "warfare" between science and religion continues on many fronts; on college campuses, at least, it shows no sign of abatement. In the seventeenth century the most notorious battles were in the field of astronomy, in the eighteenth century, mathematics became the challenge; biology took over in the nineteenth century, while in the twentieth religion found itself sparring with new physics, psychoanalysis, and the social sciences generally. It has been a long war.

Or is "warfare" much too strong a term for what is sometimes described as only a conflict of method and interest—like the difference between, say, a technician's handbook and a poet's journal? The term is borrowed, of course, from Andrew D. White's famous two-volume *History of the Warfare between Science and Theology,* published near the end of the nineteenth century. White stressed that the warfare was not with religion, but only with theology: that is, with religion hardened into dogma. Sharing the confidence of his age in the wondrous wisdom of science, White dismissed such warfare as silly and costly. Religion looks foolish obstructing the scientific pursuit of truth. Science loses its momentum and sometimes its integrity when confronted by conflicts with dogma. Writing on the heels of the unedifying controversy over evolution, White saw the solution as a relatively simple one: religion (i.e., theology) should get out of science's way.

A couple of generations later, less confidence in this simple solution is found, while "warfare" proves a still useful term. The poet and the technician may not be at war, though their language and their action markedly differ. But science and religion, each operating from its own base of influence or power, do train guns at each other, do restrict or minimize the opposing forces, do ridicule, harass, and persecute as conditions and opportunities permit. The warfare may be genteel or crude, but it is there. And it is not just a disagreement about propositions— which is why A. D. White's "theology" dodge won't do. It is a divergence in attitude: one wishing to manipulate, control, describe; the other to worship, involve, understand.

Lyman Abbott (1835–1922) does not represent "science" as against "religion"; rather, he represents that large company of theologians seeking to enlist scientific discoveries and hypotheses on the side of religious doctrines and discussions. A native of Massachusetts, Abbott labored in a church in Indiana during the Civil War, but turned his attention after the war to journalism. In 1876 he joined with Henry Ward Beecher in editing the *Christian Union* (later *Outlook*), and in 1890 succeeded Beecher as pastor of the Plymouth Congregational Church in Brooklyn. He was a prolific writer; one of his best-known books is *The Theology of an Evolutionist,* published in Boston in 1897.

It is his autobiographical work, however, which most clearly reconstructs Abbott's thinking at the time evolution became a burning issue for American churchmen. By the 1870's it had become necessary to take sides. For if Charles Darwin's laboriously and rather narrowly argued *Origin of Species* (1859) permitted churchmen to look the other way, his more shocking and openly relevant *Descent of Man* (1871) granted no such indulgence. Abbott, persuaded by the testimony of "the scientific experts" that evolution was true, proceeded to reinterpret his Christian theism to fit this new world view. Creation is a process, not a product. God's method is growth, man's method is manufacture. Jesus reveals to man what he, through evolution, may be ("What Jesus was, humanity is becoming"). And the Bible is not an infallible, static record of what God has done in the past; it is living, open-ended invitation to see how God can move now and in the years ahead.

Charles Hodge (1797–1878) was less ready to surrender his judgments to the "scientific experts"—who, he pointed out, did not agree with each other anyway. A Pennsylvanian, Presbyterian, and Princetonian, Hodge enjoyed a long and distinguished career teaching systematic theology at Princeton Seminary. Just as Lyman Abbot does not represent "science" against "religion," so Charles Hodge does not represent an obscurantist "religion" decrying and demeaning every advance made in the name of "science." But Hodge does represent those theologians who, believing in the legitimacy of their own pursuit of truth, were unwilling to grant either an infallibility or an omniscience to science. "Scientific men must come to recognize practically, and not merely in words, that there are other kinds of evidence of truth than the testimony of the senses."

In his 178-page treatise *What Is Darwinism?* Hodge shows a familiarity with the *scientific* aspects of evolution at least equal and probably superior to Abbott's. The contrast between the two men, however, is not so much in their respective levels of intelligence or grasp of data as in the extremely divergent religious implications they saw in Darwinism. If Abbott can agree with John Fiske that evolution is merely God's way of doing things, Hodge can only see evolution as making God look irrelevant and altogether unworthy of a rational man's worship. If there is no design in nature, if chance is king, then God no longer sits upon His throne. If science is our only revelation, then the Bible is

reduced to myth and pious fraud. But religion, which is not
mere feeling, has its sources too: "The Spirit of Truth shall guide
you in all truth."

A

[The text is taken from Lyman Abbott, *Reminiscences* (Boston and
New York: Houghton Mifflin & Co., 1915), pp. 456–62. Used by
permission.]

A Religious Revolution

* * * Darwin's volume "The Descent of Man," published in
1871, had put before the world his conclusion that man is
descended, or, as I prefer to say, ascended, from a prior animal race—a conclusion fatal to the theological doctrine of the
fall and involving, not only the origin of the race and the scientific accuracy of the Bible, but the origin, reality, and nature of
sin and of its cure.

The current theory which had been almost universally accepted in the church for centuries, except in some minor details,
may be briefly stated thus: God made man about six thousand
years ago; made him innocent and virtuous. Man broke God's
law, and, as a result, his descendants inherited a depraved
nature—that it, a tendency to sin. The world was therefore a
kind of vast reformatory, populated solely by men and women
possessed by evil predispositions. To suffer the penalty of their
sins and make pardon and a mended career possible Jesus Christ
had come into the world.

If there had been no fall, if there was no inherited depravity,
if the world was not a reformatory, what became of this whole
system of evangelical doctrine? And what became of the human
experience of which that doctrine was an intellectual expression? Was sin only an imperfect development? Was there no
essential difference between the rawness of a growing boy and

the deliberate wickednes of a hardened criminal? Was there no common inheritance of guilt which united humanity under a common condemnation? Was literature, as well as theology, all awry? Was there no truth in Hawthorne's affirmation: "It is a terrible thought that an individual wrong-doing melts into the great mass of human crime, and makes us—who dreamed only of our own little separate sin—makes us guilty of the whole"? And was there no forgiveness of sins? No remission of penalty and no substitute for penalty? No recuperation and no world disease which called eloquently for world recuperation? Was there, in short, no sin but immaturity, and no redemption but development? There are those who will read these questions thus naïvely confessed with an amused sense of intellectual superiority. But they are questions which in the decade following the publication of "The Descent of Man" Christian teachers everywhere were asking themselves and each other with great concern, and that concern I shared with them. There are many who are still asking these questions, having found to them no answer.

I believe that I am open-minded; my critics would say, too open-minded. There is no theory which concerns the well-being of humanity which I am not willing to investigate. When I was in college, a peripatetic lecturer obtained the use of one of our college rooms to give a lecture to prove that there was no such force in nature as gravitation. I was one of the students who went to hear him. The same spirit of curiosity has led me to read all sorts of teachers, from Mrs. Eddy to Herbert Spencer. The doctrine of evolution, as expounded by Darwin, I found accepted by a steadily increasing number of scientific men. I recognized that they were as honest as I, as eager to learn the truth, and much more intelligent than I was upon all scientific subjects. I set myself to the task of getting a sympathetic acquaintance with their point of view and seeing what was its bearing on Christian faith. For the latter purpose I went back of the Christian creeds to the Bible, on which those creeds were supposed to be founded. And I discovered, to my surprise, that, whether true or not, the doctrine of the fall had no such importance in the Bible as had been given to it in the theologies of the Church. It is mentioned in the third chapter of Genesis, and not again referred to in the Old Testament. Neither historian, poet, philosopher, nor prophet refers to it, unless such a general statement as, "God hath made man upright; but they have sought out many inventions" can be regarded as such a reference. Jesus never alludes to the fall; nor the Apostles in their apostolic preaching nor John in his Epistles. Paul refers to it, but only incidentally and parenthetically. In the one chapter which gives with some fullness his interpretation of sin—the seventh chapter of Romans—he treats temptation as a struggle between the flesh and the spirit and sin as a victory of the flesh over the spirit; a portrayal which accords with and is effectively interpreted by the evolutionary doctrine that man is gradually emerging from an animal nature into a spiritual manhood.

I was not long in coming to the conclusion that animal man was developed from a lower order of creation. This was the view of the scientific experts, and on questions on which I have no first-hand knowledge I accept the conclusions of those who have. Such scientific objections as the failure to discover a "missing link" I left the scientists to wrestle with. The objection that evolution could not be reconciled with Genesis gave me no concern, for I had long before decided that the Bible is no authority on scientific questions. To the sneer, "So you think your ancestor was a monkey, do you!" I replied, "I would as soon have a monkey as a mud man for an ancestor." This sentence, first uttered, I believe, in a commencement address before the Northwestern University in Chicago, brought upon me an avalanche of condemnation—but no reply. In truth, no reply was possible. For the question whether God made the animal man by a mechanical process in an hour or by a process of growth continuing through centuries is quite immaterial to one who believes that into man God breathes a divine life. For a considerable time I held that this inbreathing was a new and creative act. Darwin's "The Expression of the Emotions in Man and Animals" did nothing to convince me that spiritual man is a development from unspiritual qualities. Drummond's "Ascent of Man," with its emphasis on struggle for others as a factor in spiritual development, a factor of which Darwin took little or no account, led me to see that such a spiritual development is at least quite probable, and, without being dogmatic on that point, I became a radical evolutionist; by which I mean I accepted to the full John Fiske's aphorism: "Evolution is God's way of doing things."

This doctrine of evolution not only tallied with the conclusions I had previously reached respecting the authority of the Bible, but clarified it. If evolution is God's way of doing other things, why not God's way of giving to mankind a revelation of himself and his will?

In a lecture delivered at a Sunday-School convention at Chautauqua in 1876 I had told the Sunday-School teachers that the Bible is not a book but a library; that its formation took over a thousand years; that the books of which it is composed were written in different languages, by men of different temperaments, who were not only without conscious cooperation, but lived centuries apart; and that in studying and teaching it they must take account of the time in which, the people to which, and the temperament of the men by whom each book or teaching was uttered. My legal and historical studies had further prepared me for the view of the Bible which now modern scholarship generally accepts. I had learned from my historical studies that history is always composed of preexisting materials, and that these materials are often woven by the writer into his narrative. It was not unnatural to suppose that the Bible histories were composed in the same manner, and that there were incorporated in them, along with documents and well-attested legends, some popular tales and current folk-lore. . . . And I came, though only after several years of study, to my present understanding of the Bible: that it is not a book, fallible or infallible, *about* religion; it is a literature full *of* religion—that is, of the gradually developed experiences of men who had some perception of the

Infinite in nature and in human life, which they recorded for the benefit of their own and subsequent times. And it is valuable, not because it is a substitute for a living experience of a living God, but because it inspires us to look for our experience of God in our own times and in our own souls.* * *

B

[The text is taken from Charles Hodge, *What Is Darwinism?* (New York: Scribner, Armstrong & Co., 1874), pp. 141–43, 144–46, 151–52, 168–74.]

What Is Darwinism?

* * * So much, and it is very little, on the general question of the relation of science to religion. But what is to be thought of the special relation of Mr. Darwin's theory to the truths of natural and revealed religion? We have already seen that Darwinism includes the three elements, evolution, natural selection, and the denial of design in nature. These points, however, cannot now be considered separately.

It is conceded that a man may be an evolutionist and yet not be an atheist and may admit of design in nature. But we cannot see how the theory of evolution can be reconciled with the declarations of the Scriptures. Others may see it, and be able to reconcile their allegiance to science with their allegiance to the Bible. Professor [Thomas] Huxley, as we have seen, pronounces the thing impossible. As all error is antagonistic to truth, if the evolution theory be false, it must be opposed to the truths of religion so far as the two come into contact. Mr. [J. S.] Henslow, indeed, says Science and Religion are not antagonistic because they are different spheres of thought. This is often said by men who do not admit that there is any thought at all in religion; that it is merely a matter of feeling. The fact, however, is that religion is a system of knowledge, as well as a state of feeling. The truths on which all religion is founded are drawn within the domain of science, the nature of the first cause, its relation to the world, the nature of second causes, the origin of life, anthropology, including the origin, nature, and destiny of man. Religion has to fight for its life against a large class of scientific men. All attempts to prevent her exercising her right to be heard are unreasonable and vain.

It should be premised that this paper was written for the single purpose of answering the question, What is Darwinism? The discussion of the merits of the theory was not within the scope of the writer. What follows, therefore, is to be considered only in the light of a practical conclusion.

1. The first objection to the theory is its *prima facie* incredibility. That a single plant or animal should be developed from a mere cell, is such a wonder, that nothing but daily observation of the fact could induce any man to believe it. Let any one ask himself, suppose this fact was not thus familiar, what amount of speculation, of arguments from analogies, possibilities, and probabilities, could avail to produce conviction of its truth. . . .

Further, the variations by which the change of species is effected are so trifling as often to be imperceptible, and their accumulation of them so slow as to evade notice,—the time requisite to accomplish any marked change must be counted by millions, or milliards of years. Here is another demand on our credulity. The apex is reached when we are told that all these transmutations are effected by chance, that is, without purpose or intention. Taking all these things into consideration, we think it may, with moderation, be said, that a more absolutely incredible theory was never propounded for acceptance among men.

2. There is no pretence that the theory can be proved. Mr. Darwin does not pretend to prove it. He admits that all the facts in the case can be accounted for on the assumption of divine purpose and control. All that he claims for his theory is that it is possible. His mode of arguing is that if we suppose this and that, then it may have happened thus and so. Amiable and attractive as the man presents himself in his writings, it rouses

indignation, in one class at least of his readers, to see him by such a mode of arguing reaching conclusions which are subversive of the fundamental truths of religion.

3. Another fact cannot fail to attract attention. When the theory of evolution was propounded in 1844 in the "Vestiges of Creation," it was universally rejected; when proposed by Mr. Darwin, less than twenty years afterward, it was received with acclamation. Why is this? The facts are now what they were then. They were as well known then as they are now. The theory, so far as evolution is concerned, was then just what it is now. How then is it, that what was scientifically false in 1844 is scientifically true in 1864? When a drama is introduced in a theatre and universally condemned, and a little while afterward, with a little change in the scenery, it is received with rapturous applause, the natural conclusion is, that the change is in the audience and not in the drama.

There is only one cause for the fact referred to, that we can think of. The "Vestiges of Creation" did not expressly or effectually exclude design. Darwin does. This is a reason assigned by the most zealous advocates of his theory for their adoption of it.* * *

4. All the evidence we have in favor of the fixedness of species is, of course, evidence not only against Darwinism, but against evolution in all its forms. It would seem idle to discuss the question of the mutability of species, until satisfied what species is. This, unhappily, is a question which it is exceedingly difficult to answer. Not only do the definitions given by scientific men differ almost indefinitely, but there is endless diversity in classification. Think of four hundred and eighty species of humming-birds. Haeckel says that one naturalist makes ten, another forty, another two hundred, and another one, species of a certain fossil; and we have just heard that Agassiz had collected eight hundred species of the same fossil animal. Haeckel also says that there are no two zoologists or any two botanists who agree altogether in their classification. Mr. Darwin says, "No clear line of demarcation has yet been drawn between species

and sub-species, and varieties."* * * Mr. Darwin is not a Monist, for in admitting creation, he admits a dualism as between God and the world. Neither is he a Materialist, inasmuch as he assumes a supernatural origin for the infinitesimal modicum of life and intelligence in the primordial animalcule, from which without divine purpose or agency, all living things in the whole history of our earth have descended. All the innumerable varieties of plants, all the countless forms of animals, with all their instincts and faculties, all the varieties of men with their intellectual endowments, and their moral and religious nature, have, according to Darwin, been evolved by the agency of the blind, unconscious laws of nature. This infinitesimal spark of supernaturalism in Mr. Darwin's theory, would inevitably have gone out of itself, had it not been rudely and contemptuously trodden out by his bolder, and more logical successors.

The grand and fatal objection to Darwinism is this exclusion of design in the origin of species, or the production of living organisms. By design is meant the intelligent and voluntary selection of an end, and the intelligent and voluntary choice, application, and control of means appropriate to the accomplishment of that end. That design, therefore, implies intelligence, is involved in its very nature. No man can perceive this adaptation of means to the accomplishment of a preconceived end, without experiencing an irresistible conviction that it is the work of mind. No man does doubt it, and no man can doubt it. Darwin does not deny it. [Ernst] Haeckel does not deny it. No Darwinian denies it. What they do is to deny that there is any design in nature. It is merely apparent, as when the wind of the Bay of Biscay, as Huxley says, "selects the right kind of sand and spreads it in heaps upon the plains." But in thus denying design in nature, these writers array against themselves the intuitive perceptions and irresistible convictions of all mankind,—a barrier which no man has ever been able to surmount. Sir William Thomson, in the address already referred to, says: "I feel profoundly convinced that the argument of design has been greatly too much lost sight of in recent zoological speculations.

Reaction against the frivolities of teleology, such as are to be found, not rarely, in the notes of the learned commentators on 'Paley's Natural Theology,' has, I believe, had a temporary effect of turning attention from the solid irrefragable argument so well put forward in that excellent old book. But overpowering proof of intelligence and benevolent design lie all around us, and if ever perplexities, whether metaphysical or scientific, turn us away from them for a time, they come back upon us with irresistible force, showing to us through nature the influence of a free will, and teaching us that all living beings depend upon one everacting Creator and Ruler."

It is impossible for even Mr. Darwin, inconsistent as it is with his whole theory, to deny all design in the constitution of nature. What is his law of heredity? Why should like beget like? Take two germ cells, one of a plant, another of an animal; no man by microscope or by chemical analysis, or by the magic power of the spectroscope, can detect the slightest difference between them, yet the one infallibly develops into a plant and the other into an animal. Take the germ of a fish and of a bird, and they are equally indistinguishable; yet the one always under all conditions develops into a fish and the other into a bird. Why is this? There is no physical force, whether light, heat, electricity, or anything else, which makes the slightest approximation to accounting for that fact. To say, as Stuart Mill would say, that it is an ultimate fact, and needs no explanation, is to say that there may be an effect without an adequate cause. . . . [I]t may be asked, what would it avail to get rid of design in the vegetable and animal kingdom, while the whole universe is full of it? That this ordered Cosmos is not from necessity or chance, is almost a self-evident fact. Not one man in a million of those who ever heard of God, either does doubt or can doubt it. Besides how are the cosmical relations of light, heat, electricity, to the constituent parts of the universe, and especially, so far as this earth is concerned, to vegetable and animal life, to be accounted for? Is this all chance work? Is it by chance that light and heat cause plants to carry on their wonderful operations, transmuting the inorganic into the organic, dead matter into living and life sustaining matter? Is it without a purpose that water instead of contracting, expands at the freezing point?—a fact to which is due that the earth north of the tropic is habitable for man or beast. It is no answer to this question to say that a few other substances have the same peculiarity, when no good end, that we can see, is thereby accomplished. No man is so foolish as to deny that his eye was intended to enable him to see, because he cannot tell what the spleen was made for. It is, however, useless to dwell upon this subject. If a man denies that there is design in nature, he can with quite as good reason deny that there is any design in any or in all the works ever executed by man.

The conclusion of the whole matter is, that the denial of design in nature is virtually the denial of God. Mr. Darwin's theory does deny all design in nature, therefore, his theory is virtually atheistical; his theory, not he himself. He believes in a Creator. But when that Creator, millions on millions of ages ago, did something,—called matter and a living germ into existence,— and then abandoned the universe to itself to be controlled by chance and necessity, without any purpose on his part as to the result, or any intervention or guidance, then He is virtually consigned, so far as we are concerned, to non-existence.

13

SYSTEMS

OR

SOULS

IN AMERICA'S transition from a land of small farms to a nation of factories and cities, many a maladjustment lies. The complex of problems attending wholesale urbanization and rapid industrialization proved immune to all simple solutions—either in the nineteenth century or the twentieth. But the magnitude of those problems precluded their being ignored, even where they could not be solved. With what voice should the churches speak? How must they address themselves to questions of labor and capital, war and peace, poverty and wealth, race and equality, exploitation and justice? Or should they speak directly to these topics at all?

Churchmen agreed that Christianity had some relevance to the great public issues of the day. They did not agree, however, regarding the nature of that relevance. On the one hand clergymen argued that their divinely appointed task was to change the hearts of men; redeemed persons would then proceed to set economic, social, and political malfunctions aright. Others contended that the immediate, urgent need was to alter the systems, to change society so that it did not degrade and stifle the soul. The therapy must be administered to the social whole rather than to the social atom. From a later vantage point, it is easy to observe that these two strategies need not have been mutually exclusive or antagonistic. But so they generally were in the final decades of the nineteenth century, and so they have often continued to be well into the twentieth.

Washington Gladden (1836–1918) represents in persuasive fashion those American churchmen who believed that systems needed salvation. As pastor of a Columbus, Ohio church the last thirty-six years of his life, Gladden came to know industrial and urban problems first hand. He was called upon for direct mediation in labor-capital disputes, and spat upon when he complied. By his conscience he was also called upon to demonstrate Christianity's relevance to a nation's problems. Willing even to speak of *Social Salvation* (1902), Gladden along with his younger contemporary, Walter Rauschenbusch (1861–1918), was the steady voice and creative mind on behalf of the churches' social action.

In his volume on *Applied Christianity,* Washington Gladden recognizes that opinion is divided as to the churches' responsibility. "Preach the gospel faithfully, and it will make an end of all this strife," argue many. But, Gladden counters, you may change a man's heart while still leaving his head "sadly muddled." Christianity is law as well as gospel, and the former no less than the latter requires proclamation. "This Christian law, when it is faithfully preached, will make short work with the theories of materialistic political economy." Not content with vague homiletics, Gladden addressed himself to specific ills, to precise grievances, to appropriate responses. Christianity must be applied.

One year older than Gladden, Phillips Brooks (1835–1893) was a top pulpit orator of the nineteenth century, his fame enduring long after his death. A graduate of Harvard (1855), Brooks was four years later ordained a priest of the Protestant Episcopal Church. His most famous pulpit was that of Boston's Trinity Church, which he held for more than twenty years. In great demand as a speaker, he also assumed increasing denominational responsibilities, serving as Bishop of Massachusetts the last two years of his life. To many his name is most familiar as the author of "O Little Town of Bethlehem."

In the Boston address given below, Brooks sees the problems of the working man in terms that contrast starkly with Gladden's analysis. Like a refrain, the sins of "intemperance, sloth, and selfishness" are repeatedly cited as the major problems to be solved. Granted, conflicts between capital and labor do exist, but they will be ameliorated if the "working-men of our country can live worthier and nobler lives. . . ." Though the rich and the poor will always be with us, they can not only learn to adjust to each other, but also the poor man can become rich and the rich man can become poor. This mobility guarantees "that there can be no permanent or serious danger to the community in which these two classes will always be."

A

[The text is taken from Washington Gladden, *Applied Christianity: Moral Aspects of Social Questions* (Boston and New York: Houghton Mifflin & Co., 1889), pp. 161–67, 170–73.]

The Wage-Workers and the Churches

* * * Such, then, is the state of industrial society at the present time. The hundreds of thousands of unemployed laborers, vainly asking for work; the rapid increase of pauperism, indicated by the fact that during the last Winter, in the chief cities of this rich commonwealth, nearly one tenth of the population sought charitable aid from the infirmary director or the benevolent societies; the strikes and lock-outs reported every day in the newspapers; the sudden and alarming growth of the more violent types of socialism, are ominous signs of the times. Any one who keeps his ear close enough to the ground will hear mutterings of discontent and anger in unexpected quarters.

It is evident that the wage-workers, as a class, are discontented. They feel that they are not getting their fair share of the gains of advancing civilization.

It is evident that they are becoming more and more widely separated from their employers in the social scale.

It is evident that the old relations of friendliness between the two classes are giving place to alienation and enmity.

It is evident that the working people have the impression that the churches are mainly under the control of the capitalists and of those in sympathy with them.

If all these things are so, the reasons why the working people are inclined to withdraw from the churches ought also to be plain.

The fact of a great and growing discontent among the working classes, the fact of the increasing separation and alienation between wage-workers and their employers, are facts that cannot be disputed by any intelligent person. It may be doubted whether existing circumstances are bearing as severely upon the laborer as he imagines; it may be that he is better off than he thinks he is. But the question with which we are now concerned is, What does he think about it? He may be wrong in cherishing such unfriendly and resentful feelings toward his employer; but does he cherish them? He may be in error in thinking that the capitalist classes exercise a preponderating influence in the churches; but does he think so? If his state of mind is what it is assumed to be in this discussion, you have a reason for church neglect which is wide-spread and deep-seated; you have a disorder to cure which is constitutional and obstinate, and which will never be removed by the sprinkling of rosewater; you have a problem on your hands which calls for clear thinking and heroic endeavor.

The "masses" of our cities that we are trying to reach are

composed, to a large extent, of these wage-workers, and we shall never reach them over this barrier. The sooner the churches recognize this fact and adjust their theories and their methods to it, the sooner they will begin to see daylight shine through this dark problem of church neglect. So long as we ignore this fundamental difficulty, all our efforts to allure these neglecters will be in vain. A few of them will come in now and then in response to our urgent invitations; some of them, less thoughtful, or more hopeful, or more long-suffering than the rest, will continue to worship with us, finding in the promise of the life to come some help to bear the hardships of the life that now is; but the great multitude will turn upon us suspiciously or resentfully when they hear our invitations, saying: We want none of your free seats, we can do without your fine music and your pious commonplaces, we do not greatly care for your hand-shaking in the house of God and the perfunctory calls of your visitors at our houses. All we ask is justice. We want a chance to earn a decent living. We want a fair share of the wealth that our labor is helping to produce. We do not want to be left far behind when our neighbors, the employers, the traders, the professional people, are pushing on to plenty and prosperity. In the midst of all this overflowing bounty, we want something more than meagre subsistence. We are not quite sure whether you people of the churches want us to have it or not. Many of you, as we are bitterly aware, act as though you did not greatly care what became of us; and we hear from many of you hard and heartless comments on every effort we make to fight the fates that are bearing us down. It looks to us as though your sympathies were chiefly given to the people who are getting rich at our expense. Until our minds are clearer on this score, we shall never be drawn to your churches, charm you never so wisely.

What are you going to do with people who talk in this way? That is the one tremendous question which the Church of God is called to answer to-day. . . .

"The only cure of all this trouble," some one will confidently answer, "is the gospel. Preach the gospel faithfully, and it will

make an end of all this strife." This answer assumes that the
fault all lies with the people now in the churches. What effect
can the faithful preaching of the gospel have upon those who
do not and will not hear it? If the gospel thus preached reaches
these neglecting multitudes, it can only be through those who
now listen to it. And the very trouble we are considering is that
those who now frequent the churches find it difficult, and almost
impossible, to put themselves into friendly relations with the
neglecting multitudes.

What is meant by those who use this language is simply this:
that the strife between labor and capital arises from the natural
depravity of the human heart; and that, if men were soundly
converted, all these grounds of contention would be removed.
Unfortunately, this reasoning overlooks some important facts.
The gospel, considered simply as an evangelistic or converting
agency, will never put an end to this trouble. There are plenty
of people in our churches to-day, who give every evidence of
having been soundly converted, but who are conducting themselves continually in such a manner as to cause this trouble,
instead of curing it. When a man is converted, he has a purpose
to do right; and if you choose to go a little farther and say that he
has the disposition to do right, I will not stop to dispute you.
But he may have very crude ideas as to what right is; his heart
may be regenerated, but his head may still be sadly muddled.
And there are thousands of people in all our churches who mean
to do right by their working people, but whose ideas have been
so perverted by a false political economy that they are continually doing them grievous wrong.* * *

All good Christians believe, of course, that they ought to love
their neighbors as themselves; but there are many among them
who need help in answering the question, "Who is my neighbor?" The idea that the operatives in his factory, the brakemen
on his freight trains, the miners in his coal mines are his neighbors, is an idea that does not come home to many a good Christian. He has been told that the law that governs his relations
with them—the only law that can usefully govern his relations

with them—is the law of competition, the law of supply and demand. In all this vast industrial realm, as he has been taught, self-interest is the only motive power. In the family, in social life, to a certain extent also in civil life, the force of good-will must combined with the force of self-love; altruism must be coordinated with egoism; but in the industrial world, in the relations of employer and employed, this benevolent impulse must be suppressed. In this kingdom of industry they say that altruism is an interloper. In the family, in the neighborhood, in the state, if men were governed only by self-interest, we should have endless strife; in the industrial world, if we are governed by self-interest alone, we shall have peace and plenty. So he has been instructed. Over the entrance to the thronging avenues and the humming workshops of the industrial realm, an unmoral science has written, in iron letters: "ALL LOVE ABANDON, YE WHO ENTER HERE!" If beyond those portals is pandemonium, who can wonder? The first business of the Church of God is to preach that legend down, and to put in place of it: "YOUR WAGE-WORKER IS YOUR NEAREST NEIGHBOR."

In many respects the old relation of lord and villain, of master and slave, was a better relation than that now subsisting between the employer and the workman. There was many a master who tried to obey the Christian law; who remembered those in bonds as bound with them; who identified himself with his bondmen, loved them, cared for them, ministered unto them, and who was loved by them in return. We used to preach to the masters that their slaves were their brethren; and it was the right doctrine to preach. In one respect the Christian master did infringe upon the Christian law of brotherhood; he deprived his slave of his liberty. That was a great injury. We did right to upbraid him because of it. Doubtless the denial of liberty is a grave wrong—the gravest, perhaps, of wrongs—because liberty is the very condition of character. But while the Christian master deprived his slave of liberty, he gave him love. And now, when the slave gains his liberty, and becomes the hired man of his former master, is there no more love due from the one to the other?

Is the "cash nexus" the only bond between them now? Is there no responsibility of the stronger for the welfare of the weaker? When we pass from status to contract, do we leave Christ's law behind? Is the relation between the capitalist and the laborer either love without liberty, or liberty without love? Nay, but it is liberty and love,—the good fellowship of brethren, whose rights are equal, whose duties are reciprocal, whose interests are identical.

This is what the Church of God has to say about this business; and it is high time that the Church of God were saying it from hearts of flame with tongues of fire. We must make men believe that Christianity has a right to rule this kingdom of industry, as well as all the other kingdoms of this world; that her law is the only law on which any kind of society will rest in security and peace; that ways must be found of incorporating good-will as a regulative principle, as an integral element, into the very structure of industrial society.

B

[The text is taken from Phillips Brooks, *Essays and Addresses: Religious, Literary, and Social* (New York: E. P. Dutton & Co., 1894), pp. 369–74.]

Address at the Laying of Corner-Stone of the Wells Memorial Working-Men's Club and Institute, Boston, May 30, 1882

* * * What is the battle that is to be fought here? In the inspiring words of your president's address it has already been explained to us. The battle that is to be fought out in this building he made plain to us when he bade us think of those that are to be cultivated here, when he bade us remember that in sobriety, in intelligence, in industry, in skill, in thrift, there lay the great salvation of the working-men; when he told us that the enemies of the working-man were intemperance, the yielding to his lusts, the giving up of those things which are of infinite value for those which are of immediate value; unskilfulness, the willingness to do things in a poor, meager, and shambling way instead of doing them in the best and finest way in which they can be done, unthriftiness, the lavish hand that flings far and wide that which it were best to keep—these are the things that are the real enemies of the working-men to-day, and the enemy of the working-man in America is the enemy of America.

Just as truly is the enemy of American liberty the vices which beset our working-men as were those men who a quarter of a century ago lifted up their hands against the government. And far more insidious, far more difficult to conquer. With these enemies the great conflict is to be fought, not only in this but in every institution like this, and in the lives and homes of the working-men throughout our land. To us, holding these views, the laying of the corner-stone to-day, it seems to me, is the sounding of the bugle call that summons the army into existence that is to fight against our great modern enemies.

You, working-men of Boston, must set your faces against those great enemies of whom I have spoken—intemperance, slothfulness, unskilfulness, and the rest. It is because this building is to be used for the education and the training of the soldiers for this new army in this coming war that we rejoice in the laying of this cornerstone to-day.

There is another enemy, of lighter weight it sometimes seems, and yet which does certainly strike at the vitals of the working-man. The dark and heavy brooding care which rests upon their lives. The way in which cheerfulness seems to be driven out of their experiences, the way in which discontent becomes fastened in their minds—here is one of the enemies of the working-man againt which this club sets its face. With its great army of cheerfulness it sets itself against the dreadful attacks that this enemy, care and wretchedness, is always bringing upon our working-men. Against uncheerfulness, against unthriftiness, against wretchedness and poverty this club sets its face, and every appliance about which we have heard something this afternoon is but the detail of the way in which the soldiers are to be equipped in this great fight. . . . There are hard questions besetting all the workshops in the land, questions about the relations of poor man to the rich man, and of the rich man to the poor; questions about the relations of capital to labor and labor to capital. These things, which employ the best thoughts of our times, must find their ultimate settlement in the lives of the two great classes, and the way in which they are adjusted to one another in this life; and if the working-men of our country can live worthier and nobler lives they not merely will do something to conquer the enemies I have just been speaking of, but they will do something to help the solution of these great problems that seem to loom up with such danger in the future. They will do something to make more true the relations between the two great classes, the rich and the poor, though, thank God, there is no fixed barrier between them, because the poor man of to-day is the rich man of to-morrow, and the rich man sometimes becomes poor, so that there can be no permanent or serious danger to the community in which these two classes will always be.

This building would mean little if simply the working-men of Boston in the future years might come and have a good time here. It would mean little, surely, if they should rest content in the discussion of such questions as the tenure of the working-man's work. But we will not let our wishes or our hopes stop short of the belief that in this work, in this house, and in the occupations that belong to it, there must be some sort of light thrown upon the puzzling and bewildering questions of our social lives, of the relations of class to class, of the way in which men here in God's great world are to live and work together harmoniously, notwithstanding their different conditions.

If I be right in this view, and if the war which was thought to be finished seventeen years ago is not finished yet, but has come down to us, is still going on to-day, and we enter into our part of it in this new experience, which is inaugurated with this building, then this certainly is a memorable day. We learned in our war that ultimately the great power of victory must always rest, not in the mere equipment of the army, not in the mere advantage of position, not in the mere rapidity of the movements of the troops, but the ultimate salvation of the country must depend upon the character of the soldier himself. If that were true in that old war it is certainly true in this new war of which we are speaking now; we may be equipped as completely as we please, we may make our appliances as efficacious as our skill can make them, but unless the men who are actually to do the fighting with the enemies of the country—idleness, intemperance, selfishness, that prevails throughout our city—unless these men be noble, manful, consecrated men, all our appliances will fail.

It is because we believe that the men who have undertaken this work are such consecrated, manly, noble, lofty-minded, and religious men that we have vast hopes for a great future before us to-day. If the old times needed men of iron, the new times, with their new tasks, need finer men, men of finer temper, in whom subtler elements have been mixed, men who have been tried in hotter fires. If the old times needed men of iron, the new times need men of steel. If it was a hard thing to go and serve one's country in the fields of South Carolina and Virginia, it is a harder thing for the working-man to do his duty now, by himself, by his country, and by his city, and by his race, in the toils which are consecrated in this building whose corner-stone we have just laid. Therefore we ask God's blessing to-day, not simply upon the building, but upon the men who are to live within it. We ask that that God from whom alone can come true joy may come and make this place one of abundant happiness; that that God through whose power alone men can learn completely to control their appetites may come and make this house the house of temperance; that that God who is the true Teacher of His children may come and make men anxious to do their work in the most skilful and thorough way; that that God who is Father of us all may teach us how to live our daily lives, looking up and looking down, and helping all alike and smoothing the path of life for all.

The enemies that we have got to fight are before us on the field in this new battle—all Boston is full of them. Intemperance, sloth, selfishness, are here before us, and the great question with all such institutions as this is whether they can possibly overtake them, whether they can fight them before they have ravaged the field, and turn them back and drive them away.

Some of us can remember how from the Rappahannock up through Maryland, into the very heart of Pennsylvania, Meade chased the invading forces of Lee over the fields. We remember the two days of Gettysburg, how the Federal army on the first day just held its ground and how on the second day the tide of invasion was turned back! It was a critical time. We had been chasing the enemy, who had got the start, and the fight was with an enemy upon the soil where it had already secured its position; and when the tidings came that Lee was turned back into Maryland, the whole country lifted up its voice in cheers and thanksgiving.

So you will find that, however you may go forward in the good work, the enemy is on the soil before you, that intemperance and ignorance and unthriftiness and infidelity and irreligion and selfishness have possession of the field here in Boston now. God grant that you and those who come up afterwards may be the men fitted for the occasion, able to take your place here and to do the work that those men began twenty years ago upon the field of Gettysburg.

14

PROTESTANTISM

OR

PLURALISM

In the second half of the nineteenth century, the Protestant frame for American culture found itself pressed on all sides. Numerically, Roman Catholicism had become the largest religious institution in the country, while hundreds of thousands of others—Jews and Eastern Orthodox, for example—continued to crowd in upon the seaboard cities. Competing religions and competing irreligion created uneasiness in Protestant circles— an uneasiness not alone regarding denominational strength but about America's institutions and destiny as well.

For Protestantism had in part been victimized by its own success and the successes of "our country." Political speeches and executive proclamations, school curricula and social reforms, all seemed securely Christian, comfortably Protestant. The excesses of the nineteenth century nativist movements only dramatize a subtle and therefore easy identification of American liberty with Protestant loyalty. Where indeed was the line between church and world, between cult and culture? If newly-arrived Catholics found the line too forbidding, native-born

Protestants found it (if they looked) too faint. The resulting confusion of realms made it possible to find anarchy in heresy, tyranny in heterodoxy, and disloyalty in dissent.

Josiah Strong (1847–1916) was no thoughtless reactionary. Along with Washington Gladden and others, Strong had been among the first to recognize problems which urbanization and industrialization posed. He was also in the forefront of the ecumenical movement among Protestants, resigning as secretary of the Evangelical Alliance in 1898 only to help bring into being a more significant Federal Council of Churches a decade later. Like Lyman Beecher, Strong envisioned great things for a nation dedicated to civil liberty and kept true to its course by "spiritual Christianity." But writing two generations after Beecher, Josiah Strong saw in that vision some haunting spectres.

Most of the "perils" which frightened him threatened in one way or another the Anglo-Saxon Protestantism in which, he argued, not only America's but the world's hope lay. Immigration was such a peril, as was the city and as were the Mormons. But Roman Catholicism placed the country in double jeopardy as it struck at both the ethnic and the spiritual foundations of America's civilization. Witness "the irreconcilable hostility of the Roman hierarchy toward our public school system," a system whose preservation is essential to democracy. Witness the "irreconcilable difference between papal principles and the fundamental principles of our free institutions" which ask no allegiance outside the laws of the land. Witness the sharp rate of growth of Catholicism in the United States, the inevitable effect of which is to permit the Pope to possess the land and "make America Catholic." Finally, witness the "diametrically opposed principles of Romanism and of the Republic, thus forcing all Romanists in the United States to choose between two masters, both of whom they now profess to serve." As the nineteenth century drew to a close, Josiah Strong thus threw down the gauntlet specifically to America's Catholics but more diffusely to millions of others who did not ally themselves with an Anglo-Saxon Protestant heritage.

In the first decade of the twentieth century, James Cardinal Gibbons (1834–1921) picked it up. As the able administrator of Catholic affairs in America (from the archdiocesan headquarters in Baltimore), Cardinal Gibbons had of course long been aware of tensions—foreign and domestic—between policies and practices enunciated by the Vatican and those pursued in Washington. He had also become aware that Catholicism fared remarkably well in an atmosphere of civil and religious liberty; indeed, its state of health in America was more promising than in many European nations. Thus, with conviction and enthusiasm, the Cardinal (elevated to that eminence by Leo XIII in 1886) defended America's civil institutions even as he defended the workingmen and even as he devoted himself to the welfare of the immigrant millions.

In the pages of the respected *North American Review* (1909), Cardinal Gibbons responded to the kind of sentiments expressed by Josiah Strong and held by countless others. It was not the first such response, nor would it be the last, but it was an eloquent plea that Americans take American principles seriously. Do you Protestants interpret religious freedom "to apply only to yourselves; or are you willing to conceive that to others likewise is to be left the freedom to follow their consciences?" Again with Europe's quarrels fresh in mind, Gibbons urges that nothing be done "to introduce religious strife into the politics of America," for religious wars are the bloodiest of wars and religious passions the most difficult to control. All Americans must recognize that the Church and the Republic are not two contrary masters, but two complementary societies each enriching and securing the future of the other.

A

[The text is taken from Josiah Strong, *Our Country: Its Possible Future and Its Present Crisis* (New York: Baker & Taylor Co., 1891; reprint, Cambridge, Mass.: Belknap Press of Harvard University Press, 1963), pp. 73–82.]

Our Country

* * * We have made a brief comparison of some of the fundamental principles of Romanism with those of the Republic. And,

1. We have seen the supreme sovereignty of the Pope opposed to the sovereignty of the people.

2. We have seen that the commands of the Pope, instead of the constitution and laws of the land, demand the highest allegiance of Roman Catholics in the United States.

3. We have seen that the alien Romanist who seeks citizenship swears true obedience to the Pope instead of "renouncing forever all allegiance to any foreign prince, potentate, state or sovereignty," as required by our laws.

4. We have seen that Romanism teaches religious intolerance instead of religious liberty.

5. We have seen that Rome demands the censorship of ideas and of the press, instead of the freedom of the press and of speech.

6. We have seen that she approves the union of church and state instead of their entire separation.

7. We have seen that she is opposed to our public school system.

Manifestly there is an irreconcilable difference between papal principles and the fundamental principles of our free institutions. Popular government is self-government. A nation is capable of self-government only so far as the individuals who compose it are capable of self-government. To place one's conscience, therefore, in the keeping of another, and to disavow all personal responsibility in obeying the dictation of another, is as far as possible from *self*-government, and, therefore, wholly inconsistent with republican institutions, and, if sufficiently common, dangerous to their stability. It is the theory of absolutism in the state, that man exists for the state. It is the theory of absolutism in the church that man exists for the church. But in republican and Protestant America it is believed that church and state exist for the people and are to be administered by them. Our fundamental ideas of society, therefore, are as radically opposed to Vaticanism as to imperialism, and it is as inconsistent with our liberties for Americans to yield allegiance to the Pope as to the Czar. It is true the Third Plenary Council in Baltimore denied that there is any antagonism between the laws, institutions and spirit of the Roman church and those of our country, and in so doing illustrated the French proverb that "To deny is to confess." No Protestant church makes any such denials.

History fully justifies the teaching of philosophers that civil and political society tends to take the form of religious society. Absolutism in religion cannot fail in time to have an undermining influence on political equality. Already do we see its baneful influence in our large cities. It is for the most part the voters who accept absolutism in their faith who accept the dictation of their petty political popes, and suffer themselves to be led to the polls like so many sheep.

Says the eminent Professor [Emile] de Laveleye: "To-day we can prove to demonstration that which men of intellect in the eighteenth century were only beginning to perceive. The decisive influence which forms of worship bring to bear on political life and political economy had not hitherto been apparent. Now it breaks forth in the light, and is more and more closely seen in contemporary events." "Representative government is the natural government of Protestant populations. Despotic government is the congenial government of Catholic populations." * * *

Many of our Roman Catholic fellow citizens undoubtedly love

the country, and believe that in seeking to Romanize it they are
serving its highest interests, but when we remember, as has
been shown, that the fundamental principles of Romanism are
opposed to those of the Republic, that the difference between
them does not admit of adjustment, but is diametric and utter,
it becomes evident that it would be impossible to "make America
Catholic," (which the archbishop of St. Paul declared at the
late Baltimore Congress to be the mission of Roman Catholics in
this country) without bringing the principles of that church
into active conflict with those of our government, thus compelling
Roman Catholics to choose between them, and in that event,
every Romanist who remained obedient to the Pope, that is,
who continued to be a Romanist, would necessarily become disloyal to our free institutions.

It is said, and truly, that there are two types of Roman
Catholics in the United States. They may be distinguished as
those who are "more Catholic than Roman," and those who are
more Roman than Catholic. The former have felt the influence
of modern thought, have been liberalized, and come into a large
measure of sympathy with American institutions. Many are disposed to think that men of this class will control the Roman
church in this country and already talk of an "American Catholic
Church." But there is no such thing as an American or
Mexican or Spanish Catholic Church. It is the Roman Catholic
Church in America, Mexico and Spain, having one and the same
head, whose word is law, as absolute and as unquestioned among
Roman Catholics here as in Spain or Mexico. "The archbishops
and bishops of the United States, in Third Plenary Council
assembled," in their Pastoral Letter "to their clergy and faithful
people," declare: "We glory that we are, and, with God's
blessing, shall continue to be, not the American Church, nor
the Church in the United States, nor a Church in any other
sense, exclusive or limited, but an integral part of the one, holy,
Catholic and Apostolic Church of Jesus Christ."

The Roman Catholics of the United States have repudiated
none of the utterances of Leo XIII. or of Pius IX., nor have

they declared their political independence of the Vatican. On the contrary, the most liberal leaders of the church here vehemently affirm their enthusiastic loyalty to the Pope. The Pastoral Letter issued by the Third Plenary Council of Baltimore (December 7, 1884), and signed by Cardinal Gibbons, "In his own name and in the name of all the Fathers," says: "Nor are there in the world more devoted adherents of the Catholic Church, the See of Peter, and the Vicar of Christ, than the Catholics of the United States." Says a writer on the recent Roman Catholic Congress at Baltimore· "It was well that Masonic pseudo-Catholics, compromisers of the papal authority, persecutors of the clergy, anti-Jesuits, social revolutionalists, legal robbers of church property, lay educationists, anti-clericals, should learn once for all, that the Catholic laymen of America are proud of being pro-papal without compromise; that they are proud of the Jesuits from whose chaste loins the church in the United States drew its vigorous life." This writer is not quoted as a representative of ,moderate Romanism, but, as one who very justly expresses the sentiment of loyalty to the Pope, which characterized the Baltimore Congress, and which, so far as we can judge, was shared by all alike.

It is undoubtedly safe to say that there is not a member of the hierarchy in America, who does not accept the infallibility of the Pope and who has not sworn to obey him. Now this dogma of papal infallibility as defined by the Vatican Council and interpreted by Pius IX. and Leo XIII. carries with it logically all of the fundamental principles of Romanism which have been discussed. Infallibility is necessarily intolerant. It can no more compromise with a conflicting opinion than could a mathematical demonstration. Truth cannot make concessions to error. Infallibility represents absolute truth. It is as absolute as God himself, and can no more enter into compromise than God can compromise with sin. And if infallibility is as intolerant as the truth, it is also as authoritative. Truth may be rejected, but even on the scaffold it is king, and has the right and always must have the right to rule absolutely, to control utterly every reasoning being. If I believed the Pope to be the infallible vicar of Christ, I would surrender myself to him as unreservedly as to God himself. How can a true Roman Catholic do otherwise? A man may have breathed the air of the nineteenth century and of free America enough to be out of sympathy with the absolutism and intolerance of Romanism, but if he accepts the Pope's right to dictate his beliefs and acts, of what avail are his liberal sympathies? He is simply the instrument of the absolute and intolerant papal will. His sympathies can assert themselves and control his life only as he breaks with the Pope, that is, ceases to be a Roman Catholic. I fear we have little ground to expect that many would thus break with the Pope, were a distinct issue raised. Everyone born a Roman Catholic is suckled on authority. His training affects every fiber of his mental constitution. He has been taught that he must not judge for himself, nor trust to his own convictions. If he finds his sympathies, his judgment and convictions in conflict with a papal decree, it is the perfectly natural result of his training for him to distrust himself. His will, accustomed all his life to yield to authority without question, is not equal to the conflict that would follow disobedience. . . .

Moreover it should be borne in mind that the more moderate Roman Catholics in the United States are generally those who in childhood had the benefit of our public schools, and their intelligence and liberality are due chiefly to the training there received. In the public schools they learned to think and were largely Americanized by associating with American children. But their children are being subjected to very different influences in the parochial schools. They are there given a training calculated to make them narrow and bigoted; and, being separated as much as possible from all Protestant children, they grow up suspicious of Protestants, and so thoroughly sectarianized and Romanized as to be well protected against the broadening and Americanizing influences of our civilization in after life.

We have seen the fundamental principles of our free institutions laid side by side with some of those of Romanism, expressed in the words of the highest possible authorities in the

Roman Catholic Church; and thus presented they have declared for themselves the inherent contradiction which exists between them.

B

[The text is taken from James Cardinal Gibbons, "The Church and the Republic," *North American Review,* Vol. 189 (March, 1909), pp. 321–26; reprinted in Gibbons' *A Retrospect of Fifty Years* (Baltimore and New York: John Murphy Co., 1916), Vol. I, pp. 210–21.]

The Church and the Republic

Sixteen millions of Catholics live their lives on our land with undisturbed belief in the perfect harmony existing between their religion and their duties as American citizens. It never occurs to their minds to question the truth of a belief which all their experience confirms. Love of religion and love of country burn together in their hearts.

They love their Church as the divine spiritual society set up by Jesus Christ, through which they are brought into a closer communion with God, learn His revealed truth and His holy law, receive the help they need to lead Christian lives, and are inspired with the hope of eternal happiness. They love their country with the spontaneous and ardent love of all patriots, because it is their country, and the source to them of untold blessings. They prefer its form of government before any other. They admire its institutions and the spirit of its laws. They accept the Constitution without reserve, with no desire, as Catholics, to see it changed in any feature. They can, with a clear conscience, swear to uphold it.

With an appreciation, the greater because their fathers or they themselves have known persecution—in the British Isles, in Germany, in Poland and elsewhere—they prize both the liberty they enjoy as citizens, and the liberty assured to the Church.

The separation of Church and State in this country seems to them the natural, inevitable and best conceivable plan, the one that would work best among us, both for the good of religion and of the State. Any change in their relations they would contemplate with dread. They are well aware, indeed, that the Church here enjoys a larger liberty and a more secure position than in any country today where Church and State are united. They have a deep distrust and a strong dislike of the intermeddling of the State with the concerns of religion; and such a restriction as the Church was obliged to endure in France, binding the Pope to choose Catholic bishops only from among the candidates presented to him by unbelieving government officials, seems to them—not fully appreciating the difficulties of the situation—a scandal and a shame. They most assuredly desire never to see a like system introduced into the government of the Church in America. No establishment or religion is being dreamed of here, of course, by anyone; but, were it to be attempted, it would meet with united opposition from the Catholic people, priests and prelates.

Catholics feel at home among their countrymen. They are conscious of an unstained record of loyalty, of patriotic self-sacrifice, and of law-abiding behavior. Their dearest ambition is to live in peace with all, to antagonize no class; they are conscious of no barrier separating them more than any other element of the population into a class apart. Strong in the knowledge that an overwhelming majority of their fellow-citizens understand and appreciate them, they usually ignore the occasional insults directed to them by a small and rapidly decreasing section of the community not yet emancipated from ancestral misconceptions and prejudices, and still wedded to the conviction that the Gospel is to be propagated by slander and the fomentation of religious strife.

This form of religious propaganda Catholics know to be abhorrent to the spirit of every true American; and on that spirit they rely to nullify the spasmodic efforts of bigotry; for, though a large proportion of the non-Catholics do not sympathize with Catholic doctrines, this dissent is not carried over into political or social life. Men have learned in this country to disagree profoundly without rancor or bitterness. With no compromise of principle on either side, moral worth, sterling character, kindly qualities of mind and heart bind together in goodwill, admiration and friendship the lives of those who do not worship at the same altar. The non-Catholic American would receive with a contemptuous smile or an indignant gesture any suggestion that his Catholic friend, or business associate, carried hidden in his heart some sinister tenet that gave the lie to his life, and might at any moment oblige him to turn traitor to the Republic.

The Catholic himself feels, as he has learned from the lips of his own revered and trusted teachers of religion, that the more faithful he is to his religion, the better and nobler citizen will he be. That religion and patriotism could ever come into conflict in his bosom, seems to him an utter impossibility; and in the religious principles which he has received in common with his fellow-Catholics, he sees the surest defense of the State against the forces of disorder and lawlessness, and the insidious influences that work for the overthrow of our Christian moral standards in private and public life. . . .

Of this body of American citizens living such a life and imbued with such sentiments (of which there are almost as many proofs as there are Catholics), two synods of Protestant ministers have deemed it just and wise to proclaim to the country that Catholics cannot be trusted with political office; that they cannot sincerely subscribe to the Federal Constitution; that their loyalty is illogical, being contrary to the teaching of the Church; that their religion is opposed to American liberties; and that they themselves, kept in the dark by their religious guides, are ignorant of the true nature of their Church's doctrines. In sounding forth these charges to American Catholics, and to the country in general, they declare themselves inspired, not by religious antagonism or the desire to profit by a good opportunity, but solely by patriotic solicitude for the permanence of American institutions.

Charges so contrary to the abiding convictions of American Catholics, and so hurtful to their deepest affections, are naturally resented; yet they do not appear to have excited any commotion among us. It would indeed be a grave matter if these utterances expressed the judgment of the American nation, indicated its sentiments towards our Catholic citizens, and preluded a departure from the national policy of religious liberty and equality before the law. Happily, we know this is very far from the fact. The truth is, we believe, these ministers not only do not represent the American attitude toward us, but would meet with determined opposition if they attempted to carry with them even their own congregations.* * *

The Catholic religion, as they understand it, is in conflict with the Federal Constitution, and with the object of our institutions; Catholics, then, ought not to be trusted with political office. Accordingly, Americans should seek to exclude Catholics from the chair of the President, who is called upon to enforce the Constitution; from the Supreme Bench, whose duty it is to interpret it; from the Senate and the House of Representatives, which have the power to change it. And as the chief evil dreaded from Catholics is a modification of the existing relations between Church and State, a power theoretically reserved to our State Governments, no Catholic should be chosen Governor, State legislator or judge of a supreme State Court. This is the scope of their meaning, though not all explicitly avowed. It would logically be desirable to deny Catholics the right to vote, and with men in the frame of mind their attitude suggests, the realization of this desire in the statute books, and of their complete programme, would only be a matter of their possessing sufficient power and judging the act politically expedient.

Now this proposal to exclude Catholics from office—for it is no mere theory, but a practical programme earnestly recommended to the American public by two solemn assemblies—is advocated expressly in the interest of religious liberty and for the sake of preserving the Federal Constitution. That document says: "no religious test shall ever be required as a qualification to any office or public trust under the United States." Just understand here, however, remark these Lutheran and Baptist synods, an amendment, or rather let us say, a little clause which brings out the sense with admirable clearness: "Provided, of course, that this provision be not understood to apply to Roman Catholics."

Such restrictions on religion have always been felt to be incompatible with American ideas, and have fallen, though sometimes only after a long struggle, before the force of the real American spirit.* * *

There must be no tampering with the delicate machinery by which religious liberty and equality are secured, and no fostering of any spirit which would tend to destroy that machinery. Religious passions are deep and strong; and any man in his senses who knows human nature or knows the history of Europe, and has at heart the future peace and happiness of our country, whatever his belief, will do nothing to introduce religious strife into the politics of America. Religious tolerance is not the easy superficial▸ virtue it seems in these placid days; intolerance in the dominating party tends to produce intolerance in the injured party. Then religious peace is near an end, unless strong restraints be used. The spirit of the country has changed much in half a century, and it would be very difficult to arouse such fanaticism as I saw in the Know-Nothing days. Prudent men, men who are far-sighted, especially if they are in positions of responsibility, will work for peace and harmony. Such has always been the attitude of our Catholic hierarchy, and, with few exceptions, of our priesthood. I know not what to think of men, putting themselves forward as the leaders of large religious bodies, who counsel the American people to depart from that policy which has promoted peace and good-will among us and has made use illustrious among nations for our spirit of liberty and liberality. What good can they hope to accomplish?

They say Catholicism and loyalty are logically incompatible; but if, as they acknowledge, they are felt *in fact* to be compatible, should they not rejoice? Do they wish to force Catholics to be disloyal? Or do they—ah! perhaps the motives lies here—do they wish to force Catholics to renounce the Pope and become good Protestants? But no, their motive is purely patriotic. Taking Catholicism even at their worst estimate of it, then, should they be willing to introduce into American life all the bitter and hard feeling that a political war on Catholics would certainly precipitate? Willing to incur great and inevitable present evils to ward off a danger centuries hence that they cannot believe real? Willing to punish henceforth and forever honest good Catholics whom they themselves acknowledge to be loyal Americans, because their descendants of the dim distant future might have an opportunity—they would not grasp it, confess even these fearful ones—to overturn American liberties? . . .

I am speaking in no tone of deprecation. We have nothing to fear for ourselves. We are strong, not only in our own union and strength, but in the broad American spirit of fair play and love of liberty; and, I may be permitted to add, in our confidence that God destines the Catholic Church in this country to be the bulwark of law and order, of liberty, of social justice and purity. But I speak that I may put forth whatever strength I have to crush this detestable spirit of intolerance which, if it gained strength, would wreck the peace of the country and root out charity from the hearts of men.

15

MISSIONS

OR

MORALS

THE MOST seriously divisive issues in American life are not those where the confrontation is brutal and bitter but those where no confrontation is possible. The levels on which the contenders stand do not intersect, and what is meaningful language for one is empty phraseology for the other. Like Thomas Paine and Timothy Dwight (see Chap. 7), John R. Mott and Walter Lippmann in the selections given below never meet. Part of the divergence is admittedly a function of time, for America's mood on the eve of World War I bears little resemblance to the mood of the twenties. But basic presuppositions about the kind of world into which America was moving were also undergoing radical revision.

In the early years of the present century optimism continued within the churches and without. A generalized doctrine of progress augmented the specialized sense of mission so that the very real dangers and obstacles were seen as challenges to greater dedication, as temporary interruptions in mankind's steady upward climb. In the postwar period, by contrast, disillusionment with any sort of idealism—particularly that sort cast in traditional religious terminology—pervaded American society. Contributions to missions fell away, concentration on the immediate pleasures and comforts rapidly increased, isolationism and cynicism exercised great appeal. While some called for a return to the faith of the fathers, others searched for another faith, almost any other faith, that would speak to a more critical contemporary post-Protestant era.

John R. Mott (1865–1955) ably represents that contagious confidence as well as that sense of world mission that characterized much of a nation flexing its muscles and feeling its oats. A native of New York, Mott gave untiring leadership to American mission and ecumenical enterprises around the world. Organizer, promoter, fund-raiser, and world-traveler, Mott was intimately identified with such entities as the International Missionary Council, the Student Christian Federation, and above all the Y.M.C.A. Described as the "preeminent leader of . . . world brotherhood in this century,"* Mott in 1946 shared in the Nobel Prize for Peace.

In assessing *The Present World Situation,* John Mott saw the moment of historical decision at hand. The present situation is one fraught with both opportunity and danger; men can seize the helm of history—or they can let wind and current turn the wheel at will. Western civilization has already had its impact around the world—in most cases of a detrimental sort. Now, it is time to Christianize "the impact of our Western civilization on the non-Christian world." The outbreak of World War I only lends greater urgency to the task: that of proclaiming to all men a "vital Christlike Christianity" that will "bring in a new order wherein shall dwell righteousness, love and true peace!"

When Walter Lippmann (b. 1889) wrote the book noted below—only fourteen years after Mott's—it had already become

* Richard Carey Morse (1841–1926), quoted in C. Howard Hopkins, *History of the Y.M.C.A. in North America* (New York: Association Press, 1951), p. 433.

"an unbelieving world." A graduate of Harvard (1910), Lippmann served briefly as assistant to the Secretary of War in 1917, then later helped prepare for the peace conference to follow. These and other experiences enriched his background, preparing him for an extraordinary career as journalist, lecturer, author, and Washington's philosopher-in-residence. In 1962, Walter Lippmann received the Pultizer Prize for "wise and responsible international reporting."

His *Preface to Morals* emerged as the reckless, jaded, retreating decade of the twenties came to a close. Lippmann's broad contacts had clearly also had their effect on his view of traditional religion and traditional morality. He saw Christianity—or for that matter the entire Judeo-Christian heritage—not as a great saving message to an eager, attentive world, but as an irrelevant, in-groupish anachronism. Churchmen invent "little intellectual devices for straightening out the dilemmas of biology and Genesis, history and the Gospels. . . ." But nobody listens, or cares. For Lippmann, there is only one religious issue in American history—or in mankind's history—worth talking about: the choice between salvation via obedience to a supernatural power, or salvation via allegience to an ideal of the human personality. Emerson and Bushnell would recognize the contest.

A

[The text is taken from John R. Mott, *The Present World Situation* (New York: Student Volunteer Movement for Foreign Missions, 1915), pp. 3–6; 11–16.]

The Present World Situation

The forces of pure Christianity as they face the non-Christian nations and peoples are confronting an unprecedented world situation. Certainly it is unprecedented in opportunity. In this respect there has been nothing like it in the annals of the

Christian faith. There have been times when in a few countries the doors to the friendly and constructive mission of Christianity were as wide open as they are to-day; but there never was a time when simultaneously in so many sections of the world the opportunities for the extension of the Christian religion were so numerous and so extensive as at the present time. This is true in the Far East and the Near East, in Southern Asia, in the Pacific Island world, in nearly all parts of Africa and of Latin America. Moreover, so far as one can forecast the future, there is not likely to come a time when the opportunities will be greater than those with which the Christian Church must deal to-day. Where, after China, is there another nation of four hundred million of peoples to turn from an ancient past and to swing out into the full stream of modern Christian civilization? Where after India is there another vast empire to be swept by the spirit of unrest and to be made peculiarly accessible to the reconstructive processes of Christianity? Where after Africa is there another continent for which Mohammedanism and Christianity can contend? Where after Turkey and the Nile Valley is there another keystone to the vast arch of the Mohammedan world, with seams of weakness which make possible the disrupting of the whole structure?

What lends added significance to the present situation is the fact that this unparalleled enlargement of opportunity comes at a time when the Christian Church is called upon to deal with some of the most difficult problems with which it has ever had to grapple on the home field. This is true of North America, of Western and Northern Europe, of Australasia and South Africa. Why is it that at the very time the Christian forces have more to do than ever at the home base, they are also confronted with an immeasurably greater opportunity abroad than that which has faced any preceding generation? May it not be because God sees that there are now on the earth those with whom He can trust a situation literally world-wide in its sweep? With His all-seeing eye does He not pierce beneath the surface and recognize latent in the Christians of our day capacities for vision,

for adventure, for heroism, for statesmanship and for vicarious-
ness which, if exercised and accompanied by His own superhuman forces, make possible the meeting of this absolutely new
world situation?

We are living at the most dangerous time in the history of
the world. This is due to the shrinkage of the world caused
by the greatly improved means of communication. In many ways
the whole world now is smaller than that part of the United
States east of the Mississippi River was a generation ago. It is
indeed one great community; it has become a whispering gallery.
As a result, the nations and races have been brought into the
most intimate contact. This has led to grave perils. One danger
is the great multiplication of friction points. Some hoped and
even believed that this new century might be ushered in with
universal peace and good-will among the nations and races;
but more than any preceding century has this one been characterized by national and racial misunderstandings, prejudices,
bitterness and strife. The mingling of peoples, the clash of
civilizations, and the processes which characterize this scientific
age have led to marked relaxing and weakening of the restraints
of the social customs as well as the ethical and religious systems
of non-Christian peoples. This is in itself a very grave
danger.* * *

The present world situation is unprecedented not only in
opportunity and in danger, but also in urgency. From the point
of view of the Christian Church the present moment is incom-
parably the most critical and urgent it has ever known. This is
true because so many nations just now in a plastic condition
are soon to become set unchangeably. Shall Christian or unchristian influences determine their character and destiny? The
answer to this question cannot be deferred. To delay by even a
half decade facing the situation and acting upon it comprehen-
sively would be the most serious mistake which Christian leaders
in this generation could make.

The present is a time when rising tides of nationalism and
racial patriotism are surging on every hand. Wherever the world

traveler may have gone in recent years he has become very conscious of the thrill of a new life. He has found nations being reborn; he has observed peoples coming into their own. This growing spirit of nationality and racial patriotism can no more be resisted than can the tides of the sea. If Christians show themselves sympathetic with all commendable national and racial aspirations of non-Christian countries, the progress of Christianity throughout the world will be greatly facilitated; if they do not, the mission of the Christian religion will be indefinitely retarded.

The startlingly rapid spread of the corrupt influences in our so-called Western civilization among non-Christian peoples constitutes another reason for prompt and urgent action on the part of the Christian Church. The cheek of the visitor from a Christian land blushes with shame as he sees in the port cities of Asia, Africa and Latin America the alarming prevalence of evils which have spread from his native land. Some of these evils are eating like gangrene into the less highly organized races of mankind. Christianity has a double responsibility. It must counteract these baneful influences wherever they have extended and it must preempt those regions of the world where these evils have not yet reached. Nothing but the power of the living Christ can arrest and turn back these tides of death.

On the other hand, the cancerous growths of the non-Christian civilizations are eating with great directness and deadliness toward the very vitals of Christendom. We cannot trifle with cancers nor can we safely ignore them. Now that the world has found itself in its unity as one body (and this is the first half generation in which this could be said), it can no longer be a matter of indifference to one part of the world-body what happens in any other part. If there be a plague spot in China or Turkey or Africa, sooner or later it must affect America, England and Germany. It would seem that even though a man were not a Christian he would believe in foreign missions, that is, in the spread of the knowledge and life-giving power of the Christian religion, solely on grounds of patriotism. In these days it is difficult to understand the patriotism of the citizen who does not regard with responsive sympathy every wise effort to release throughout the earth the spirit and motives of Christianity.

There is another dangerous process which greatly accentuates the urgency of the present situation—the process of syncretism. This would seek to combine certain truths of the Christian religion with certain good ideas of non-Christian systems of religion or ethics, but would leave out the superhuman aspects of Christianity. This is tantamount to leaving out Christianity itself. More difficult to counteract and overcome than the non-Christian religions themselves are the dangers growing out of eclecticism. Its confusing, unsettling and paralyzing influence is felt not only in the East but also in the West, and can be met only by bringing to bear a larger number of the strongest and best equipped minds of our generation.

The present situation is immeasurably more urgent than that of other days because of the recent unparalleled triumphs of Christianity. It is a remarkable fact that the most extensive victories of Christian missions have been those of the recent past. Not even in the early days of Christianity were such striking results achieved as have accompanied the efforts of Christian missions in Asia and Africa during the last decade. These victories have been achieved not only in the more favored parts of the world where the forces and influences of the Christian religion are most concentrated, but on some of the most difficult battle-fields of the Church. Unquestionably it is a time of rising spiritual tide. It is always wise to take advantage of a rising tide. More can be accomplished in a short time under such circumstances than in long, weary, discouraging periods of effort while the tide is falling. God seems to have done a hundred years' work within the last five years. The Christians of the West must quicken their pace. The discerning traveler returning from journeys in the Eastern world to-day must be constrained to confess solicitude, not lest the peoples of the East fail to receive Christ, but lest the Christians of the West lose Christ as a result of not passing on the knowledge of Him. The Christians now living in Western lands should have a realizing sense that this present, unparalleled world situation affords not only the greatest opportunity the Church has ever known, but also, so far as they are concerned, their best and their only opportunity.

B

[The text is taken from Walter Lippmann, *A Preface to Morals* (New York: The Macmillan Co., 1929; reprint, Boston: Beacon Press, 1960), pp. 316–19; 321–23; 325–27. Used by permission.]

The Moralist in an Unbelieving World

The moralists are not confronted with a scandal but with history. They have to come to terms with a process in the life of mankind which is working upon the inner springs of being and altering inevitably the premises of conduct. They need not suppose that their pews are empty and that their exhortations are ignored because modern men are really as wilful as the manners of the younger generation lead them to conclude. Much of what appears to be a tough self-sufficiency is protective: it is a brittle crust covering depths of uncertainty. If the advice of moralists is ignored, it is not because this generation is too proud to listen, or unaware that it has anything to learn. On the contrary there is such curiosity and questioning as never before engaged so large a number of men. The audience to which a genuine moralist might speak is there. If it is inattentive when the orthodox moralist speaks, it is because he seems to speak irrelevantly.

The trouble with the moralists is in the moralists themselves: they have failed to understand their times. They think they are dealing with a generation that refuses to believe in ancient authority. They are, in fact, dealing with a generation that cannot believe in it. They think they are confronted with men who have an irrational preference for immorality, whereas the men and women about them are ridden by doubts because they do not know what they prefer, nor why. The moralists fancy that they are standing upon the rock of eternal truth, surveying the chaos about them. They are greatly mistaken. Nothing in the modern world is more chaotic—not its politics, its business, or its sexual relations—than the minds of orthodox moralists who suppose that the problem of morals is somehow to find a way of reinforcing the sanctions which are dissolving. How can we, they say in effect, find formulas and rhetoric potent enough to make men behave? How can we revive in them that love and fear of God, that sense of the creature's dependence upon his creator, that obedience to the commands of a heavenly king, which once gave force and effect to the moral code?

They have misconceived the moral problem, and therefore they misconceive the function of the moralist. An authoritative code of morals has force and effect when it expresses the settled customs of a stable society: the pharisee can impose upon the minority only such conventions as the majority find appropriate and necessary. But when customs are unsettled, as they are in the modern world, by continual change in the circumstances of life, the pharisee is helpless. He cannot command with authority because his commands no longer imply the usages of the community: they express the prejudices of the moralist rather than the practices of men. When that happens, it is presumptuous to issue moral commandments, for in fact nobody has authority to command. It is useless to command when nobody has the disposition to obey. It is futile when nobody really knows exactly what to command. In such societies, wherever they have appeared among civilized men, the moralist has ceased to be an administrator of usages and has had to become an interpreter of human needs. For ages when custom is unsettled are necessarily ages of prophecy. The moralist cannot teach what is revealed; he must reveal what can be taught. He has to seek insight rather than to preach.

The disesteem into which moralists have fallen is due at bottom to their failure to see that in an age like this one the function of the moralist is not to exhort men to be good but to elucidate what the good is. The problem of sanctions is secondary. For sanctions cannot be artificially constructed: they are a product of agreement and usage. Where no agreement exists, where no usages are established, where ideals are not clarified and where conventions are not followed comfortably by the mass of men, there are not, and cannot be, sanctions. It is possible to command where most men are already obedient. But even the greatest general cannot discipline a whole army at once. It is only when the greater part of his army is with him that he can quell the mutiny of a faction.

The acids of modernity are dissolving the usages and the sanctions to which men once habitually conformed. It is therefore impossible for the moralist to command. He can only persuade. To persuade he must show that the course of conduct he advocates is not an arbitrary pattern to which vitality must submit, but that which vitality itself would choose if it were clearly understood. He must be able to show that goodness is victorious vitality and badness defeated vitality; that sin is the denial and virtue the fulfilment of the promise inherent in the purposes of men. The good, said the Greek moralist, is "that which all things aim at"; we may perhaps take this to mean that the good is that which men would wish to do if they knew what they were doing. * * *

What I take into account first of all is the fact, which it seems to me is indisputable, that for the modern populace the old rules are becoming progressively unsuitable and the old symbols of hope and fear progressively unreal. I ascribe that to the inherent character of the modern ways of living. I conclude from this that if the populace must be led, if it must have easily comprehended rules, if it must have common symbols of hope and fear, the question is how are its leaders to be developed, rules to be worked out, symbols created. The ultimate question is not how the populace is to be ruled, but what the teachers are to think. That is the question that has to be settled first: it is the preface to everything else.

For while moralists are at sixes and sevens in their own souls, not much can be done about morality, however high or low may be our estimates of the popular intelligence and character. If it were necessary to assume that ideals are relevant only if they are universally attainable, it would be a waste of time to discuss them. For it is evident enough that many, if not most men, must fail to comprehend what modern morality implies. But to recognize this is not to prophesy that the world is doomed unless men perform the miracle of reverting to their ancestral tradition. This is not the first time in the history of mankind when a revolution in the affairs of men has produced chaos in the human spirit. The world can endure a good deal of chaos. It always has. The ideal inherent in any age is never realized completely: Greece, which we like to idealize as an oasis of rationality, was only in some respects Hellenic; the Ages of Faith were only somewhat Christian. The processes of nature and of society go on somehow none the less. Men are born and they live and die with some happiness and some sorrow though they neither envisage wholly nor nearly approximate the ideals they pursue.

But if civilization is to be coherent and confident it must be *known* in that civilization what its ideals are. There must exist in the form of clearly available ideas an understanding of what the fulfilment of the promise of that civilization might mean, an imaginative conception of the good at which it might, and, if it is to flourish, at which it must aim. That knowledge, though no one has it perfectly, and though relatively few have it at all, is the principle of all order and certainty in the life of that people. By it they can clarify the practical conduct of life in some measure, and add immeasurably to its dignity. * * *

The crisis in the religious loyalties of mankind cannot be resolved by weariness and good nature, or by the invention of little intellectual devices for straightening out the dilemmas of biology and Genesis, history and the Gospels with which so many churchmen busy themselves. Beneath these little conflicts there is a real dilemma which modern men cannot successfully evade. "Where is the way where light dwelleth?" They are compelled to choose consciously, clearly, and with full realization of what the choice implies, between religion as a system of cosmic government and religion as insight into a cleansed and matured personality: between God conceived as the master of that fate, creator, providence, and king, and God conceived as the highest good at which they might aim. For God is the supreme symbol in which man expresses his destiny, and if that symbol is confused, his life is confused.

Men have not, hitherto, had to make that choice, for the historic churches have sheltered both kinds of religious experience, and the same mysteries have been the symbols of both. That confusion is no longer benign because men are no longer unconscious of it. They are aware that it is a confusion, and they are stultified by it. Because the popular religion of supernatural governments is undermined, the symbols of religion do not provide clear channels for religious experience. They are choked with the debris of dead notions in which men are unable to believe and unwilling to disbelieve. The result is a frustration in the inner life which will persist as long as the leaders of thought speak of God in more senses than one, and thus render all faith invalid, insincere, and faltering.

The choice is at last a personal one. The decision is rendered not by argument but by feeling. Those who believe that their salvation lies in obedience to, and communion with, the King of Creation can know how wholehearted their faith is by the confidence of their own hearts. If they are at peace, they need inquire no further. There are, however, those who do not find a principle of order in the belief that they are related to a supernatural power. They cannot be argued into the ancient belief, for it has been dissolved by the circumstances of their lives. They are deeply perplexed. They have learned that the absence of belief is vacancy; they know, from disillusionment and anxiety, that there is no freedom in mere freedom. They must find, then, some other principle which will give coherence and direction to their lives.

If the argument in these pages is sound, they need not look for and, in fact, cannot hope for, some new and unexpected revelation. Since they are unable to find a principle of order in the authority of a will outside themselves, there is no place they can find it except in an ideal of the human personality. But they do not have to invent such an ideal out of hand. The ideal way of life for men who must make their own terms with experience and find their own happiness has been stated again and again. It is that only the regenerate, the disinterested, the mature, can make use of freedom. This is the central insight of the teachers of wisdom. We can see now, I think, that it is also the mark at which the modern study of human nature points. We can see, too, that it is the pattern of successful conduct in the most advanced phases of the development of modern civilization. The ideal, then, is an old one, but its confirmation and its practical pertinence are new. The world is able at last to take seriously what its greatest teachers have said. And since all things need a name, if they are to be talked about, devotion to this ideal may properly be called by the name which these greatest teachers gave it; it may be called the religion of the spirit. At the heart of it is the knowledge that the goal of human effort is to be able, in the words I have so often quoted from Confucius, to follow what the heart desires without transgressing what is right.

16

TECHNOLOGY

OR

WISDOM

As THE post-Protestant era dissolved into the post-Christian era, Americans were inclined to grant a respect bordering on reverence to forces and institutions other than religious. Science can save, education can redeem, government can make whole again. Or else, confidence that any of these—religion included—could perform substantial miracles simply faded away. As Lippmann asked in the previous chapter, "Where is the way where light dwelleth?" The question awaited answers.

Especially in the field of education answers of some sort had to be offered, however apologetically, however provisionally. "Moral and spiritual values" were the concern and despair of school districts as committees were appointed, criteria drawn up, and mimeograph machines cranked. Church and state problems in education grew agonizingly acute. Released time, dismissed time, shared time were discussed, tried, contested, abandoned, modified. Questions of prayer and Bible-reading found their way to the nation's highest court, where these vestiges of a prepluralist

America were struck down. Considerations of sectarian or non-sectarian instruction, of teaching *about* religion versus the teaching *of* religion, of the role of religion in culture, in Western civilization, in American history—all these had their day in court, in civic hall, in ecclesiastical assembly.

Religion-and-education in America is a plethora of issues, of course, not just one. But underlying most of the public quarrels and urgent experiments was a deeply private difference about the goals of education itself. Does the school educate for ends primarily individual or social, vocational or liberal, religious or secular? Does it serve body or soul, teach values or facts?

Those very dualisms were anathema to America's most remarkable reformer of education, John Dewey (1859–1952). Logician, aesthetician, political and social theorist, and college professor, Dewey almost by accident came to be identified chiefly with the process of education. But for Dewey "education" was no narrow speciality: it was "the laboratory in which philosophic distinctions become concrete and are tested."* And a philosophy only for philosophers is not worthy of the name. Philosophy used to teach men how to endure their world or how to escape from it; now, however, philosophy must show men how to control and change that world. There is much to be done, great work to do, societies to reform, new processes to pursue. For Dewey the deadliest of the seven deadly sins was sloth.

John Dewey's *Reconstruction in Philosophy* outlines the major reorientation which must occur once one realizes that the universe is still pliable, still growing. Dewey's "new morality"—new in 1920 at any rate—is the enemy of all absolutism, all closed systems, all fixed and final revelations. Truth is not something to possess or contemplate or even to know: it is a working hypothesis, a suggested plan of action. A moral act does not arise from general supernatural stimuli nor does it seek a vague doctrinal end. It is always specific, concrete, instrumental, unique. Religious idealism or any other idealism is "thin and

* *Democracy and Education* (New York: The Macmillan Co., 1916), p. 384.

meagre or else idle and luxurious because of the separation from 'instrumental' or economic ends." There are no sacred "higher ends" or nobler goals; indeed, these become protective disguises for the "socially isolated and socially irresponsible." The chief end of man, says the Westminster Confession, is "to glorify God and enjoy him forever." The chief end of man, said Dewey, is the process of growth, "the ever-enduring process of perfecting, maturing, refining. . . ." "Growth itself is the only moral 'end.' "

Will Herberg (b. 1907) sees a shift from Dewey's understanding of man's and education's "chief end." A native of New York, Herberg early became active in the labor movement, specifically in the International Ladies Garment Workers Union (1935–48). His increasing involvement, however, with the academic and publishing world led to his joining Drew University's faculty in 1955 as graduate professor of philosophy and culture. A Conservative Jew, Herberg in that same year published *Protestant-Catholic-Jew* (Doubleday & Co.), a sociological analysis of America's pluralism that proved immensely popular. Author of four other volumes, Herberg also lectured across the country on questions political, economic, educational, philosophical, and religious.

In the essay below, Herberg reviews the relationship between religion and education in American history. Early in the present century a "new secularism" had displaced the older public-school pattern where nonsectarianism but not irreligion prevailed. "A new type of educator appeared, self-consciously secularistic, nourished on the new naturalistic educational philosophies that had already come to dominate the teachers colleges." But dissatisfactions with the "new religion of no-religion" have grown within the present generation, grown to the point where the secularist tide is now in ebb. The loss of unity, of direction, of purpose at all levels of education drove men toward other proposals, toward even—if necessary—other schools. Another kind of "reconstruction" is now called for: "It is no longer taken for granted that religion has no place in the serious business of educating the nation. . . ."

A

[The text is taken from John Dewey, *Reconstruction in Philosophy* (New York: Henry Holt & Co., 1920; reprint, Boston: Beacon Press, 1948), pp. 161–63, 169–70, 174–77, 183–86. Used by permission.]

Reconstruction in Moral Conceptions

The impact of the alteration in methods of scientific thinking upon moral ideas is, in general, obvious. Goods, ends are multiplied. Rules are softened into principles, and principles are modified into methods of understanding. Ethical theory began among the Greeks as an attempt to find a regulation for the conduct of life which should have a rational basis and purpose instead of being derived from custom. But reason as a substitute for custom was under the obligation of supplying objects and laws as fixed as those of custom had been. Ethical theory ever since has been singularly hypnotized by the notion that its business is to discover some final end or good or some ultimate and supreme law. This is the common element among the diversity of theories. Some have held that the end is loyalty or obedience to a higher power or authority; and they have variously found this higher principle in Divine Will, the will of the secular ruler, the maintenance of institutions in which the purpose of superiors is embodied, and the rational consciousness of duty. But they have differed from one another because there was one point in which they were agreed: a single and final source of law. Others have asserted that it is impossible to locate morality in conformity to law-giving power, and that it must be sought in ends that are goods. And some have sought the good in self-realization, some in holiness, some in happiness, some in the greatest possible aggregate of pleasures. And yet these schools have agreed in the assumption that there is a single, fixed and final good. They have been able to dispute with one another only because of their common premise.

The question arises whether the way out of the confusion and conflict is not to go to the root of the matter by questioning this common element. Is not the belief in the single, final and ultimate (whether conceived as good or as authoritative law) an intellectual product of that feudal organization which is disappearing historically and of that belief in a bounded, ordered cosmos, wherein rest is higher than motion, which has disappeared from natural science? It has been repeatedly suggested that the present limit of intellectual reconstruction lies in the fact that it has not as yet been seriously applied in the moral and social disciplines. Would not this further application demand precisely that we advance to a belief in a plurality of changing, moving, individualized goods and ends, and to a belief that principles, criteria, laws are intellectual instruments for analyzing individual or unique situations?

The blunt assertion that every moral situation is a unique situation having its own irreplaceable good may seem not merely blunt but preposterous. For the established tradition teaches that it is precisely the irregularity of special cases which makes necessary the guidance of conduct by universals, and that the essence of the virtuous disposition is willingness to subordinate every particular case to adjudication by a fixed principle. It would then follow that submission of a generic end and law to determination by the concrete situation entails complete confusion and unrestrained licentiousness. Let us, however, follow the pragmatic rule, and in order to discover the meaning of the idea ask for its consequences. Then it surprisingly turns out that the primary significance of the unique and morally ultimate character of the concrete situation is to transfer the weight and burden of morality to intelligence. It does not destroy responsibility; it only locates it. A moral situation is one in which judgment and choice are required antecedently to overt action. * * *

Moral goods and ends exist only when something has to be done. The fact that something has to be done proves that there are deficiencies, evils in the existent situation. This ill is just the specific ill that it is. It never is an exact duplicate of anything else. Consequently the good of the situation has to be discovered, projected and attained on the basis of the exact defect and trouble to be rectified. It cannot intelligently be injected into the situation from without. Yet it is the part of wisdom to compare different cases, to gather together the ills from which humanity suffers, and to generalize the corresponding goods into classes. Health, wealth, industry, temperance, amiability, courtesy, learning, esthetic capacity, initiative, courage, patience, enterprise, thoroughness and a multitude of other generalized ends are acknowledged as goods. But the *value* of this systematization is intellectual or analytic. Classifications *suggest* possible traits to be on the lookout for in studying a particular case; they suggest methods of action to be tried in removing the inferred causes of ill. They are tools of insight; their value is in promoting an individualized response in the individual situation.

Morals is not a catalogue of acts nor a set of rules to be applied like drugstore prescriptions or cook-book recipes. The need in morals is for specific methods of inquiry and of contrivance: Methods of inquiry to locate difficulties and evils; methods of contrivance to form plans to be used as working hypotheses in dealing with them. And the pragmatic import of the logic of individualized situations, each having its own irreplaceable good and principle, is to transfer the attention of theory from preoccupation with general conceptions to the problem of developing effective methods of inquiry. * * *

These general considerations may be amplified. First: Inquiry, discovery take the same place in morals that they have come to occupy in sciences of nature. Validation, demonstration become experimental, a matter of consequences. Reason, always an honorific term in ethics, becomes actualized in the methods by which the needs and conditions, the obstacles and resources, of situations are scrutinized in detail, and intelligent plans of improvement are worked out. Remote and abstract generalities promote jumping at conclusions, "anticipations of nature." Bad consequences are then deplored as due to natural perversity and untoward fate. But shifting the issue to analysis of a specific situation makes inquiry obligatory and alert observation of consequences imperative. No past decision nor old principle can ever be wholly relied upon to justify a course of action. No amount of pains taken in forming a purpose in a definite case is final; the consequences of its adoption must be carefully noted, and a purpose held only as a working hypothesis until results confirm its rightness. Mistakes are no longer either mere unavoidable accidents to be mourned or moral sins to be expiated and forgiven. They are lessons in wrong methods of using intelligence and instructions as to a better course in the future. They are indications of the need of revision, development, readjustment. Ends grow, standards of judgment are improved. Man is under just as much obligation to develop his most advanced standards and ideals as to use conscientiously those which he already possesses. Moral life is protected from falling into formalism and rigid repetition. It is rendered flexible, vital, growing.

In the second place, every case where moral action is required becomes of equal moral importance and urgency with every other. If the need and deficiencies of a specific situation indicate improvement of health as the end and good, then for that situation health is the ultimate and supreme good. It is no means to something else. It is a final and intrinsic value. The same thing is true of improvement of economic status, of making a living, of attending to business and family demands—all of the things which under the sanction of fixed ends have been rendered of secondary and merely instrumental value, and so relatively base and unimportant. Anything that in a given situation is an end and good at all is of equal worth, rank and dignity with every other good of any other situation, and deserves the same intelligent attention.

We note thirdly the effect in destroying the roots of Phariseeism. We are so accustomed to thinking of this as deliberate hypocrisy that we overlook its intellectual premises. The conception which looks for the end of action within the circumstances of the actual situation will not have the same measure of judgment for all cases. When one factor of the situation is a person of trained mind and large resources, more will be expected than with a person of backward mind and uncultured experience. The absurdity of applying the same standard of moral judgment to savage peoples that is used with civilized will be apparent. No individual or group will be judged by whether they come up to or fall short of some fixed result, but by the direction in which they are moving. The bad man is the man who no matter how good he *has* been is beginning to deteriorate, to grow less good. The good man is the man who no matter how morally unworthy he *has* been is moving to become better. Such a conception makes one severe in judging himself and humane in judging others. It excludes that arrogance which always accompanies judgment based on degree of approximation to fixed ends.

In the fourth place, the process of growth, of improvement and progress, rather than the static outcome and result, becomes the significant thing. Not health as an end fixed once and for all, but the needed improvement in health—a continual process—is the end and good. The end is no longer a terminus or limit to be reached. It is the active process of transforming the existent situation. Not perfection as a final goal, but the ever-enduring process of perfecting, maturing, refining is the aim in living. Honesty, industry, temperance, justice, like health, wealth and learning, are not goods to be possessed as they would be if they expressed fixed ends to be attained. They are directions of change in the quality of experience. Growth itself is the only moral "end." * * *

If a few words are added upon the topic of education, it is only for the sake of suggesting that the educative process is all one with the moral process, since the latter is a continuous passage of experience from worse to better. Education has been traditionally thought of as preparation: as learning, acquiring certain things because they will later be useful. The end is remote, and education is getting ready, is a preliminary to something more important to happen later on. Childhood is only a preparation for adult life, and adult life for another life. Always the future, not the present, has been the significant thing in education: Acquisition of knowledge and skill for future use and enjoyment; formation of habits required later in life in business, good citizenship and pursuit of science. Education is thought of also as something needed by some human beings merely because of their dependence upon others. We are born ignorant, unversed, unskilled, immature, and consequently in a state of social dependence. Instruction, training, moral discipline are processes by which the mature, the adult, gradually raise the helpless to the point where they can look out for themselves. The business of childhood is to grow into the independence of adulthood by means of the guidance of those who have already attained it. Thus the process of education as the main business of life ends when the young have arrived at emancipation from social dependence.

These two ideas, generally assumed but rarely explicitly reasoned out, contravene the conception that growing, or the continuous reconstruction of experience, is the only end. If at whatever period we choose to take a person, he is still in process of growth, then education is not, save as a by-product, a preparation for something coming later. Getting from the present the degree and kind of growth there is in it is education. This is a constant function, independent of age. The best thing that can be said about any special process of education, like that of the formal school period, is that it renders its subject capable of further education: more sensitive to conditions of growth and more able to take advantage of them. Acquisition of skill, possession of knowledge, attainment of culture are not ends: they are marks of growth and means to its continuing.

The contrast usually assumed between the period of education as one of social dependence and of maturity as one of social independence does harm. We repeat over and over that man is a social animal, and then confine the significance of this statement to the sphere in which sociality usually seems least evident, politics. The heart of the sociality of man is in education. The idea of education as preparation and of adulthood as a fixed limit of growth are two sides of the same obnoxious untruth. If the moral business of the adult as well as the young is a growing and developing experience, then the instruction that comes from social dependencies and interdependencies are as important for the adult as for the child. Moral independence for the adult means arrest of growth, isolation means induration. We exaggerate the intellectual dependence of childhood so that children are too much kept in leading strings, and then we exaggerate the independence of adult life from intimacy of contacts and communication with others. When the identity of the moral process with the processes of specific growth is realized, the more conscious and formal education of childhood will be seen to be the most economical and efficient means of social advance and reorganization, and it will also be evident that the test of all the institutions of adult life is their effect in furthering continued education. Government, business, art, religion, all social institutions have a meaning, a purpose. That purpose is to set free and to develop the capacities of human individuals without respect to race, sex, class or economic status. And this is all one with saying that the test of their value is the extent to which they educate every individual into the full stature of his possibility. Democracy has many meanings, but if it has a moral meaning, it is found in resolving that the supreme test of all political institutions and industrial arrangements shall be the contribution they make to the all-around growth of every member of society.

B

[The text, by Will Herberg, is taken from J. W. Smith and A. L. Jamison, eds., *Religious Perspectives in American Culture* (Princeton, N. J.: Princeton University Press, 1961), pp. 11–12; 20–27; 49–51. Used by permission.]

Religion and Education in America

Religion and education have been related throughout American history in a most intimate way, yet also in a way often laden with tension and ambiguity. From the seventeenth century, when the two were closely identified in purpose and content, to the twentieth, when they have become separated and sometimes even hostile, the problem of the proper relation between the two has been one of the central concerns of both. It is not easy to say whether the shift of outlook over the centuries, or the continuing preoccupation with the problem in so many different historical contexts, is the more impressive. In any case, there is perhaps no better perspective from which to assess the place of religion in American culture than that which is afforded by the eventful story of its involvement with public education, that other all-absorbing interest of the American people.

No retelling of the story will be attempted here. What will be attempted is an analysis of the underlying patterns defining the changing relation between religion and education from the time of the Puritans to the present day. Perhaps something significant may emerge from such an account, especially since religion in public education has now once again become an urgent problem agitating the American people far beyond the narrow circle of educators and religious leaders.

If we scan the three centuries that separate the establishment of common schools in New England, where religion was the heart of the venture, from the current discussions over the "crisis" in education, where religion is one of the sharpest points of controversy, we may well ask what coherence there is to observe amidst so much change and confusion. Yet I think there is one generalization we can venture which may help give some measure of meaning to the story, and cast some light on its drift and direction. Roughly, we may say that, whereas in the first period of our history education was conceived as serving the ends of religion, and in the second the two were regarded as parallel but separate enterprises equally worthy of support, today the original relation has been reversed. Religion today, where it is most highly valued and most insistently recommended, is valued and recommended precisely for its contribution to education, the goals and ends of which are defined in other terms, in terms of the culture. Somewhere between the second and third phases came the attempt to dispense with religion altogether in the educational enterprise; that experiment is now coming to an end, but its consequences are still with us, exerting a powerful influence upon our contemporary thinking on the question of religion and education.* * *

What was the place of religion in the emerging public school system? Here it is necessary to avoid two errors. The public school was "non-sectarian" from the very beginning, but this did not mean religionless, as so many latter-day secularists assume. On the other hand, we must not be misled into thinking that because religion was taken for granted in the life and work of the public school, it therefore possessed anything of the place it had enjoyed in earlier times. Religion was there in the public school, but it was there in a rather peculiar way.

There was never any intention whatever of excluding religion from the new public schools. No one could be more emphatic in affirming this than was Horace Mann, himself a Unitarian. "Horace Mann," [Raymond B.] Culver writes, "was opposed to sectarian doctrinal instruction in the schools, but he repeatedly urged the teaching of the elements of religion common to all the Christian sects. He took a firm stand against the idea of a purely secular education, and on one occasion said he was in favor of religious instruction 'to the extremest verge to which it can be carried without invading those rights of conscience which are established by the laws of God, and guaranteed by the constitution of the state.' At another time, he said that he regarded hostility to religion in the schools as the greatest crime he could commit. Lest his name go down in history as the one who had attempted to drive religious instruction from the schools [he was repeatedly accused of this by his opponents] he devoted several pages in his final report—the twelfth—to a statement in which he denied the charges of his enemies."

The public school stood for "non-sectarianism" in religion; but "non-sectarian" did not then mean non-religious. It meant non-denominational religion, and in the America of that day, non-denominational religion meant a kind of generalized Protestantism. Horace Mann feared and detested the "sectarian" wrangling that had bedeviled education for so many years and had frustrated all attempts to establish a common school. In all sincerity, he proposed a "non-sectarian" way out, a way out that seemed to him fair to all, but which was obviously a Protestant way out. "That our public schools are not theological seminaries," he declared in his Twelfth Annual Report, "is admitted. . . . But our system earnestly inculcates all Christian morals; it founds its morals on the basis of religion; it welcomes the religion of the Bible; and, in receiving the Bible, it allows it to do what it is allowed to do in no other system—*to speak for itself.*" The Bible—the King James Version, obviously—speaking for itself without comment, explanation, or interpretation as the substance of religion, is, of course, a Protestant idea; but as long as the nation remained overwhelmingly Protestant, this Protestant idea naturally appealed to all, or almost all, as a reasonable and common-sense solution of the "sectarian" problem. Even the clergy agreed, although there were those who had their qualms and reservations. Only when, in later decades, non-Protestants began to multiply into the millions, and to rise to power and influence in many parts of the country, did this "Protestant" solution cease to carry conviction. And then the public school faced another crisis.

In effect, the nineteenth-century solution was based on an unexpressed assumption that fundamentally religion and education were independent concerns, each of which should be allowed to develop in its own way, without involvement with the other. The minimum of religion included in the public school curriculum was interpreted as "character building" and was largely reduced to token Bible reading, hymn singing, and occasional holiday celebration. The business of the school was secular; religion was the business of the church and home. The former was concerned with instructing the youth in the common branches of knowledge, in the common elements of morality, and in the common principles of "republicanism" (that is, democracy); the latter's task was to inculcate Christian principles and to perpetuate the Christian religion. There was, of course, an area of overlapping since the school was concerned with "character," and American Protestantism largely interpreted its faith in practical, moralistic terms. But this common ground was so obvious that it made little impression; the day was yet far distant when the public school would be stricken with a sense of moral failure. And so this rough and ready division of labor, so characteristic of American education and American religion in the nineteenth century, became enshrined as the American system of the "separation of church and state in education."

The public school was an immense success. It made popular education possible in a land of religious diversity and cultural heterogeneity. But more: in a way that Horace Mann could only dimly foresee, it became the primary engine of the Americanization of the millions of immigrants who kept pouring into this country from all parts of the old world. And now as we look back upon it, we can see that it accomplished this work incredibly well. It took the children of the immigrants just off the boat, and, in one or at most two generations, it made real Americans out of them. The immigrant parents were not slow to realize what the public school was doing, and were deeply grateful, for despite all reservations, what the immigrant parents wanted more than anything else was that their children become Americans and make their way up the ladder of American life. The public school became almost a sacred object to the American people; it was helping to create Americans, and nothing could be more important. Americanism—if that is the proper word with which to designate this deep desire to be an American—soon came to replace religion as the urgent concern of Americans, although this devaluation of religion was masked by the new conception of religion and education as parallel enterprises meeting only at infinity. In an altogether different context, Jefferson had foreshadowed this concept of parallel coexistence when in his plan for the University of Virginia (1822, 1824) he proposed, on the one hand, that theology (or "divinity") be excluded from the official curriculum (though he had included it in 1814), and on the other, that religious schools be founded by the denominations "on the confines of the university" with "convenient access" to university facilities. The coexistence was obviously to be a cooperative one, though neither party was to do the work of the other or interfere with it in any way. And so it continued through the nineteenth century.

Yet there were problems and difficulties, and as the century wore on, these problems and difficulties became more clamant. In the first place, what about the non-Protestants who were increasing in numbers every day? The public schools to which Catholic parents were required to send their children in the latter half of the nineteenth century were, as we have seen, to all intents and purposes Protestant schools, claiming to be "non-sectarian" because they were non-denominational within Protestantism. Obviously, no believing Catholic parent could send his children to such a school without violating his religious conscience; the fact that the Protestantism of the public school was only a shallow "common-core" Protestantism did not improve matters in the least. Not every Catholic parent was equally concerned, of course; many were ready to overlook the religious deficiences of the public school for the sake of the marvelous work of Americanization it was performing. But the Catholic Church was deeply concerned, and so were many Catholic lay people. Parochial schools emerged to meet this challenge; they were designed to help preserve Catholic children in the faith, which was then generally expressed in the ethnic form in which it had been brought to this country by the immigrants. At about the same time, conservative Protestant groups, such as some of the German Lutherans, for whom a non-denominational "token" Protestantism was no Protestantism at all, set up religious schools of their own with very much the same double purpose. The emphasis on the ethnic culture declined as a new American generation appeared, but the religious urgency did not diminish. Jews . . . fell in readily with the emerging dualistic pattern of the "separation" of religion and education; Jews, also, perhaps more than any other immigrant group, cherished the public school as a vehicle of Americanization and advancement in American life.

For the time being, the Catholics could be ignored; they were building their own schools (thus once again proving their "clannishness"!), and their murmurs of discontent made no impression on the Protestant mind. But among the Protestants themselves certain misgivings began to arise. Was the secular-religious dualism upon which the "non-sectarian" public school was erected really viable? Would it not lead in the end to the total submergence of religion? Already the notion was becoming influential among educators that the government in its character and operations was obliged to be not merely "non-sectarian," but non-religious as well. In fact, to many minds "non-sectarian" was coming to mean "non-religious," and the constitutional ban on the "establishment of religion" was coming to imply a laic state on the European model. Madison had already foreshadowed this attitude when, in his later days, he expressed his qualms about the presence of chaplains in Congress as being a violation of the Constitution. Even earlier, in 1793, the Kentucky legislature, under the influence of the deist enlightenment, had dismissed its chaplain. But then came the Great Revival, taking fire in the very same Kentucky, and for some decades the evangelical movement swept everything before it. Now toward the end of the nineteenth century a new "separationist" mood began to emerge—this time, though, not merely among non-believers of Christianity, but among good conventional Christians as well. Under the Grant Administration, a constitutional amendment was sponsored to make the separation absolute, and though it failed of enactment, the support it mustered was not insignificant. Indeed, this kind of "separation" itself became a quasi-religious dogma, impervious to the criticism of fact or experience. "United with government," declared Ohio's Supreme Court in 1872, "religion never rises above the merest superstition; united with religion, government never rises above the merest despotism; and all history shows that the more widely and completely they are separated, the better it is for both." Thus according to the learned judges, virtually all governments in existence at the time, aside from that of the United States, were "despotisms," and all religions except American Protestantism were "superstitions," merely because the American system of "separation," or what they took to be the American system of "separation," did not everywhere prevail. This system was presented as one of "complete separation," the more complete the better. The logic of this position was obviously the "religion-blind" state, hitherto hardly known in American experience. No wonder many educators and religious leaders began to have their sober second thoughts.

But for the time being, the movement of de-religionization continued apace. Thought was becoming explicitly secularistic, especially on the higher levels of education. The prevailing academic ideology was a naturalistic confidence in science, technology, and progress that seemed to render much of the earlier religion meaningless and irrelevant. The fateful split between thought and emotion that had come with the revival movement now began to tell heavily against religion. Religion was either reinterpreted as a new evolutionary deism, or else it was contemptuously relegated to the realm of private feeling. In the former case, science would do just as well, if not better; in the latter case, religion obviously had no place in the life of the mind. It was in this period that many of the state universities came into being or received their definitive character; it was in this period, too, that many of the older colleges abandoned their church connections and transformed themselves into secular institutions, in this respect indistinguishable from the state universities. The emancipation of education from religion seemed to be final and complete on the university level, and was rapidly gaining ground in the elementary and secondary schools as well. A new type of educator appeared, self-consciously secularistic, nourished on the new naturalistic educational philosophies that had already come to dominate the teachers colleges.

For public education on the elementary and secondary levels, the new secularist mood meant the systematic extrusion from the schools of even the token religion that had remained from earlier times, and with it the extrusion of all religion-based moral teaching. The rapidity with which this was achieved in the larger urban communities reflected the concurrence of a number of forces—the pressures of a multi-religious community; the new naturalistic ideology of many leading educational philosophers, policy-makers, and administrators; and the "separationist" mentality among teachers. It is not without its irony that this movement was speeded by Catholic protests against the residual Protestantism of the public schools, which Catholics, of course, found unacceptable. In exchange, they got the new secularism.

This picture, however, must be greatly modified if it is not to be misleading. What has been described was characteristic of the more modern urban centers; in the rural communities and small towns, especially where the population was overwhelmingly Protestant, the older patterns continued undisturbed. The schools remained "non-sectarian" in the non-denominational sense, and thus reflected the religious ethos of the community.* * *

The place of religion in contemporary America is certainly very different from what one could have foreseen a generation ago. The older secularism is rapidly declining. Religion is enjoying a resurgence of impressive scope and proportions. Naturally, the relation between religion and education has undergone considerable change. It is no longer taken for granted that religion has no place in the serious business of educating the nation; on the contrary, the tide would seem to be running all the other way. The concern now is to bring back religion to some sort of significant relation with education, and this concern is felt in varying degrees by professional educators and the lay public, by those involved in government schools as well as by those working in independent institutions, by those responsible for elementary and secondary education as well as by those engaged in college and university education. Certainly, no one who remembers the barren and shallow secularism of a generation ago, contemptuous of everything that did not fit into its positivistic strait jacket, will fail to be grateful for this change, which makes it possible at least to try to reestablish some bond between the total educational enterprise and the deeper levels of human life and thought. Yet there is obviously another side to the story. The very resurgence of religious interest in education has brought with it certain new and pressing problems with which educator, religious leader, and concerned laymen alike will have to cope in the coming period.

1. Sentiment is now running in favor of the religious school, certainly more so than at any time in the past century. But that only makes the problem of a balance between the public school and the religious school the more urgent. Each has its own values, the religious school as well as the public school, and the one should not be overlooked for the sake of the other. The public school remains the great instrument of achieving an over-all American unity in an ethnically, racially, and religiously heterogeneous society, a training in living together that even present-day America cannot altogether do without. The religious school, aside from its primary purpose of providing an education grounded in religion, contributes that element of diversity that an increasingly conformist society so sorely needs. These two types of schools, though united in their common "Americanness" and American outlook, obviously live in a certain tension. How to achieve creative cooperation within this tension, without sacrificing the one kind of school to the other, is one of the problems for the future.

2. If the public school is to retain the support of the American people in the present period of religious upsurge, it cannot remain

religionless. This would seem to be acknowledged, in one way or another, on all sides. But what kind of religion to bring back to the schools, and how to do it without going "too far" in the direction of church-state cooperation, remains a problem. The problem is really double: on the one hand, what can be done within the basic constitutional structure of the public school as a governmental institution; and on the other hand, what can be done without stultifying and corrupting the religious traditions of the American people by reducing them to a "common-denominator" religiosity. Perhaps some combination of "teaching about" religion and creating a pro-religious atmosphere in the schools with coordinated instruction in religion by outside religious bodies will have to be worked out, but the lines are by no means clear. There are those who despair of devising any practicable program to meet current requirements, but to do so is to despair of the public school. This we surely cannot afford to do.

3. The challenge is not merely to the public school; it is a challenge to the American religious consciousness. Informed observers testify that much of the contemporary "surge of piety in America" is distressingly superficial and consists largely of a religionization of the values of our culture as expressed in the American Way of Life. The "syncretism" between traditional religion and the American Way which Sidney Mead sees emerging in the Protestantism of the latter half of the nineteenth century has now apparently become universal in our emerging three-religion America. There is real danger that the "religion" that will be reintroduced into the schools under whatever form or guise, whether as a "common-core" program or as a program of "moral and spiritual values," will be little more than this syncretistic religion of religionized American democracy. The problem is a very real one for the independent school, even the church-sponsored school, as well as for the public school, since much of even denominational or "church" religion in this country is permeated through and through with the syncretistic spirit. The change from religionlessness to religion would be

little gain—some, indeed, would put it down as a loss—if it simply meant a change from a secularized version of the "religion of democracy" to a religionized version of the same "common American faith."

17

CONSENT

OR

CONSENSUS

PLURALISM has posed many a disquieting issue in American history. In the nineteenth century, for example, religious nonconformity found its path to public acceptance paved with legal obstacles and illegal harassment. The Church of Jesus Christ of Latter-day Saints—the Mormons—conspicuously offended a prevailing American consensus: namely, that monogamy and Christianity and civilization are interdependent. When their case related to polygamy reached the U.S. Supreme Court in 1879, Chief Justice Waite ruled that government could interfere with religious practices even if it chose not to interfere with religious beliefs. Eleven years later the Court added that there was no difference of opinion on the illegality of polygamy. "Bigamy and polygamy are crimes by the laws of all civilized and Christian countries. . . . Few crimes are more pernicious to the best interests of society. . . . To extend exemption from punishment for such crimes would be to shock the moral judgment of the community. To call their advocacy a tenet of religion is to offend the common sense of mankind."*

But the "common sense of mankind" or even the common sense of Americans was not an immutable entity. By the middle of the twentieth century, the very sense of community itself appeared threatened. Traditions of belief and practice, long taken for granted, found themselves subjected to noisy challenge or quiet abandonment. Nothing was too sacred to be discussed, nothing was so widely and generally assumed as to be beyond discussion. What set of values, what hierarchy of loyalties, what frame of reference continued to define American society? Or had pluralism itself become the unique value that defined America?

The issue of voluntary consent versus enforced consensus may initially appear to be no issue at all. Bill-of-Rights-believing Americans surely would opt for the former. In wartime? Well, that may be different. In so central a matter as offering allegiance to the nation's flag? Well, there are limits. In so sensitive an area as the rights of the state itself, the welfare of the majority itself? The matter *is* debatable, and the range of issues can be very wide: compulsory vaccination, Sunday legislation, zeal in proselytizing, conscientious objection to war, birth control, censorship and morality, tax subsidies, and blasphemy. Private liberty strains against social survival.

During World War II and after, this strain was repeatedly highlighted by the activities of Jehovah's Witnesses. Founded in 1872 by Charles Taze Russell in Allegheny, Pennsylvania, this group of millennialists had grown to a worldwide membership of a million less than a century later. Jehovah's Witnesses—they did not officially adopt that name until 1931—found themselves in the hands of the law over and over again. In 1933 the group started keeping a record of their arrests, the number then being a modest 269. By 1940, however, the number had risen to over three thousand per year. The charges were varied: selling without a license, disturbing the peace, tres-

* Davis *v.* Beason 133 U.S. 333 (1890).

passing, violating local ordinances of one sort or another. But behind these minor nuisances lay a major anxiety: these troublers might be attacking or subverting the social order itself.

For it was true that Witnesses condemned American society, refused to defend it in wartime, refused even to accept responsibility for it by voting at any time. It was true that they had disturbed the peace: on quiet Sunday mornings in suburbia, on noisy afternoons in public parks or on busy corners, and for week after week in the courtrooms of America. In June 1940, the sensational Gobitis Case (Minersville School District *v*. Gobitis, 310 U.S. 586) finally reached the Supreme Court. What was to be done about two young Witnesss, William and Lillian Gobitis (ages 10 and 12), who on parental orders refused each morning in their Pennsylvania public school to salute the American flag? In introducing the opinion in the Court, Justice Frankfurter said: "A grave responsibility confronts this Court whenever in course of litigation it must reconcile the conflicting claims of liberty and authority. But when the liberty invoked is liberty of conscience, and the authority is authority to safeguard the nation's fellowship, judicial conscience is put to its severest test. Of such a nature is the present controversy."

That neat summary does not tip the Court's hand, but it does call attention to the great force of each contending tug. In this 1940 case, the Court (with Justice Harlan Stone dissenting) argued that the flag salute was a legitimate obligation for all. "The ultimate foundation of a free society is the binding tie of cohesive sentiment. Such a sentiment is fostered by all those agencies of the mind and spirit which may serve to gather up the traditions of a people, transmit them from generation to generation, and thereby create that continuity of a treasured common life which constitutes a civilization." Three years later, in the case cited below, the Court reversed its position. This time, with Justice Felix Frankfurter (1882–1965) as the eloquent dissenter, the Court weighed the guarantees of a voluntary consent against the dangers of a coerced uniformity, finding in favor of the former. Justice Robert H. Jackson (1892–1954) spoke for the Court.

Where, after all, does the enduring unity of America lie: in consent or consensus?

A

[The text is taken from *Supreme Court Reporter* (St. Paul: West Publishing Co., 1943), Vol. LXIII, pp. 1179–87. Used by permission.]

West Virginia State Board of Education v. Barnette

Mr. Justice JACKSON delivered the opinion of the Court.

Following the decision by this Court on June 3, 1940, in Minersville School District v. Gobitis, the West Virginia legislature amended its statutes to require all schools therein to conduct courses of instruction in history, civics, and in the Constitutions of the United States and of the State "for the purpose of teaching, fostering and perpetuating the ideals, principles and spirit of Americanism, and increasing the knowledge of the organization and machinery of the government." Appellant Board of Education was directed, with advice of the State Superintendent of Schools, to "prescribe the courses of study covering these subjects" for public schools. The Act made it the duty of private, parochial and denominational schools to prescribe courses of study "similar to those required for the public schools."

The Board of Education on January 9, 1942, adopted a resolution containing recitals taken largely from the Court's Gobitis opinion and ordering that the salute to the flag become "a regular part of the program of activities in the public schools," that all teachers and pupils "shall be required to participate in the salute honoring the Nation represented by the Flag; provided, however, that refusal to salute the Flag be regarded as an Act of insubordination, and shall be dealt with accordingly."

The resolution originally required the "commonly accepted salute to the Flag" which it defined. Objections to the salute as "being too much like Hitler's" were raised by the Parent and Teachers Association, the Boy and Girl Scouts, the Red Cross, and the Federation of Women's Clubs. Some modification appears to have been made in deference to these objections, but no concession was made to Jehovah's Witnesses. What is now required is the "stiff-arm" salute, the saluter to keep the right hand raised with palm turned up while the following is repeated: "I pledge allegiance to the Flag of the United States of America and to the Republic for which it stands; one Nation, indivisible, with liberty and justice for all."

Failure to conform is "insubordination" dealt with by expulsion. Readmission is denied by statute until compliance. Meanwhile the expelled child is "unlawfully absent" and may be proceeded against as a delinquent. His parents or guardians are liable to prosecution, and if convicted are subject to fine not exceeding $50 and jail term not exceeding thirty days.

Appellees, citizens of the United States and of West Virginia, brought suit in the United States District Court for themselves and others similarly situated asking its injunction to restrain enforcement of these laws and regulations against Jehovah's Witnesses. The Witnesses are an unincorporated body teaching that the obligation imposed by law of God is superior to that of laws enacted by temporal government. Their religious beliefs include a literal version of Exodus, Chapter 20, verses 4 and 5, which says: "Thou shalt not make unto thee any graven image, or any likeness of anything that is in heaven above, or that is in the earth beneath, or that is in the water under the earth; thou shalt not bow down thyself to them nor serve them." They consider that the flag is an "image" within this command. For this reason they refuse to salute it.

Children of this faith have been expelled from school and are threatened with exclusion for no other cause. Officials threaten to send them to reformatories maintained for criminally inclined juveniles. Parents of such children have been prosecuted and are threatened with prosecutions for causing delinquency.

The Board of Education moved to dismiss the complaint setting forth these facts and alleging that the law and regulations are an unconstitutional denial of religious freedom, and of freedom of speech, and are invalid under the "due process" and "equal protection" clauses of the Fourteenth Amendment to the Federal Constitution. The cause was submitted on the pleadings to a District Court of three judges. It restrained enforcement as to the plaintiffs and those of that class. The Board of Education brought the case here by direct appeal.

This case calls upon us to reconsider a precedent decision, as the Court throughout its history often has been required to do. Before turning to the Gobitis case, however, it is desirable to notice certain characteristics by which this controversy is distinguished.

The freedom asserted by these appellees does not bring them into collision with rights asserted by any other individual. It is such conflicts which most frequently require intervention of the State to determine where the rights of one end and those of another begin. But the refusal of these persons to participate in the ceremony does not interfere with or deny rights of others to do so. Nor is there any question in this case that their behavior is peaceable and orderly. The sole conflict is between authority and rights of the individual. The State asserts power to condition access to public education on making a prescribed sign and profession and at the same time to coerce attendance by punishing both parent and child. The latter stand on a right of self-determination in matters that touch individual opinion and personal attitude.

As the present Chief Justice said in dissent in the Gobitis case, the State may "require teaching by instruction and study of all in our history and in the structure and organization of our government, including the guaranties of civil liberty which tend to inspire patriotism and love of country." Here, however, we are dealing with a compulsion of students to declare a belief. They are not merely made acquainted with the flag salute so that they may be informed as to what it is or even what it means. The issue here is whether this slow and easily neglected route to aroused loyalties constitutionally may be short-cut by substituting a compulsory salute and slogan. This issue is not prejudiced by the Court's previous holding that where a State, without compelling attendance, extends college facilities to pupils who voluntarily enroll, it may prescribe military training as part of the course without offense to the Constitution. It was held that those who take advantage of its opportunities may not on ground of conscience refuse compliance with such conditions. In the present case attendance is not optional. That case is also to be distinguished from the present one because, independently of college privileges or requirements, the State has power to raise militia and impose the duties of service therein upon its citizens.

There is no doubt that, in connection with the pledges, the flag salute is a form of utterance. Symbolism is a primitive but effective way of communicating ideas. The use of an emblem or flag to symbolize some system, idea, institution, or personality, is a short cut from mind to mind. Causes and nations, political parties, lodges and ecclesiastical groups seek to knit the loyalty of their followings to a flag or banner, a color or design. The State announces rank, function, and authority through crowns and maces, uniforms and black robes; the church speaks through the Cross, the Crucifix, the altar and shrine, and clerical raiment. Symbols of State often convey political ideas just as religious symbols come to convey theological ones. Associated with many of these symbols are appropriate gestures of acceptance or respect: a salute, a bowed or bared head, a bended knee. A person gets from a symbol the meaning he puts into it, and what is one man's comfort and inspiration is another's jest and scorn.

Over a decade ago Chief Justice Hughes led this Court in holding that the display of a red flag as a symbol of opposition by peaceful and legal means to organized government was protected by the free speech guaranties of the Constitution. Here it is the State that employs a flag as a symbol of adherence to government as presently organized. It requires the individual to communicate by word and sign his acceptance of the political ideas it thus bespeaks. Objection to this form of communication when coerced is an old one, well known to the framers of the Bill of Rights.

It is also to be noted that the compulsory flag salute and pledge requires affirmation of a belief and an attitude of mind. It is not clear whether the regulation contemplates that pupils forego any contrary convictions of their own and become unwilling converts to the prescribed ceremony or whether it will be acceptable if they simulate assent by words without belief and by a gesture barren of meaning. It is now a commonplace that censorship or suppression of expression of opinion is tolerated by our Constitution only when the expression presents a clear and present danger of action of a kind the State is empowered to prevent and punish. It would seem that involuntary affirmation could be commanded only on even more immediate and urgent grounds than silence. But here the power of compulsion is invoked without any allegation that remaining passive during a flag salute ritual creates a clear and present danger that would justify an effort even to muffle expression. To sustain the compulsory flag salute we are required to say that a Bill of Rights which guards the individual's right to speak his own mind, left it open to public authorities to compel him to utter what is not in his mind.

Whether the First Amendment to the Constitution will permit officials to order observance of ritual of this nature does not depend upon whether as a voluntary exercise we would think it to be good, bad or merely innocuous. Any credo of nationalism is likely to include what some disapprove or to omit what others think essential, and to give off different overtones as it takes on different accents or interpretations. If official power exists to coerce acceptance of any patriotic creed, what it shall contain cannot be decided by courts, but must be largely discretionary with the ordaining authority, whose power to prescribe would no doubt include power to amend. Hence validity of the asserted power to force an American citizen publicly to profess any statement of belief or to engage in any ceremony of assent to one presents questions of power that must be considered independently of any idea we may have as to the utility of the ceremony in question.

Nor does the issue as we see it turn on one's possession of particular religious views or the sincerity with which they are held. While religion supplies appellees' motive for enduring the discomforts of making the issue in this case, many citizens who do not share these religious views hold such a compulsory rite to infringe constitutional liberty of the individual. It is not necessary to inquire whether non-conformist beliefs will exempt from the duty to salute unless we first find power to make the salute a legal duty.

The Gobitis decision, however, *assumed,* as did the argument in that case and in this, that power exists in the State to impose the flag salute discipline upon school children in general. The Court only examined and rejected a claim based on religious beliefs of immunity from an unquestioned general rule. The question which underlies the flag salute controversy is whether such a ceremony so touching matters of opinion and political attitude may be imposed upon the individual by official authority under powers committed to any political organization under our Constitution. We examine rather than assume existence of this power and, against this broader definition of issues in this case, re-examine specific grounds assigned for the Gobitis decision.

1. It was said that the flag-salute controversy confronted the Court with "the problem which Lincoln cast in memorable dilemma: 'Must a government of necessity be too *strong* for the liberties of its people, or too *weak* to maintain its own existence?' " and that the answer must be in favor of strength.

We think these issues may be examined free of pressure or restraint growing out of such considerations.

It may be doubted whether Mr. Lincoln would have thought that the strength of government to maintain itself would be impressively vindicated by our confirming power of the state to expel a handful of children from school. Such oversimplification, so handy in political debate, often lacks the precision necessary to postulates of judicial reasoning. If validly applied to this problem, the utterance cited would resolve every issue of power in favor of those in authority and would require us to override every liberty thought to weaken or delay execution of their policies.

Government of limited power need not be anemic government. Assurance that rights are secure tends to diminish fear and jealousy of strong government, and by making us feel safe to live under it makes for its better support. Without promise of a limiting Bill of Rights it is doubtful if our Constitution could have mustered enough strength to enable its ratification. To enforce those rights today is not to choose weak government over strong government. It is only to adhere as a means of strength to individual freedom of mind in preference to officially disciplined uniformity for which history indicates a disappointing and disastrous end.

The subject now before us exemplifies this principle. Free public education, if faithful to the ideal of secular instruction and political neutrality, will not be partisan or enemy of any class, creed, party, or faction. If it is to impose any ideological discipline, however, each party or denomination must seek to control, or failing that, to weaken the influence of the educational system. Observance of the limitations of the Constitution will not weaken government in the field appropriate for its exercise.

2. It was also considered in the Gobitis case that functions of educational officers in states, counties and school districts were such that to interfere with their authority "would in effect make us the school board for the country."

The Fourteenth Amendment, as now applied to the States, protects the citizen against the State itself and all of its creatures —Boards of Education not excepted. These have, of course, important, delicate, and highly discretionary functions, but none that they may not perform within the limits of the Bill of Rights.

That they are educating the young for citizenship is reason for scrupulous protection of Constitutional freedoms of the individual, if we are not to strangle the free mind at its source and teach youth to discount important principles of our government as mere platitudes.

Such Boards are numerous and their territorial jurisdiction often small. But small and local authority may feel less sense of responsibility to the Constitution, and agencies of publicity may be less vigilant in calling it to account. The action of Congress in making flag observance voluntary and respecting the conscience of the objector in a matter so vital as raising the Army contrasts sharply with these local regulations in matters relatively trivial to the welfare of the nation. There are village tyrants as well as village Hampdens, but none who acts under color of law is beyond reach of the Constitution.

3. The Gobitis opinion reasoned that this is a field "where courts possess no marked and certainly no controlling competence," that it is committed to the legislatures as well as the courts to guard cherished liberties and that it is constitutionally appropriate to "fight out the wise use of legislative authority in the forum of public opinion and before legislative assemblies rather than to transfer such a contest to the judicial arena," since all the "effective means of inducing political changes are left free."

The very purpose of a Bill of Rights was to withdraw certain subjects from the vicissitudes of political controversy, to place them beyond the reach of majorities and officials and to establish them as legal principles to be applied by the courts. One's right to life, liberty, and property, to free speech, a free press, freedom of worship and assembly, and other fundamental rights may not be submitted to vote; they depend on the outcome of no elections.

In weighing arguments of the parties it is important to distinguish between the due process clause of the Fourteenth Amendment as an instrument for transmitting the principles of the First Amendment and those cases in which it is applied for its own sake. The test of legislation which collides with the

Fourteenth Amendment, because it also collides with the principles of the First, is much more definite than the test when only the Fourteenth is involved. Much of the vagueness of the due process clause disappears when the specific prohibitions of the First become its standard. The right of a State to regulate, for example, a public utility may well include, so far as the due process test is concerned, power to impose all of the restrictions which a legislature may have a "rational basis" for adopting. But freedoms of speech and of press, of assembly, and of worship may not be infringed on such slender grounds. They are susceptible of restriction only to prevent grave and immediate danger to interests which the state may lawfully protect. It is important to note that while it is the Fourteenth Amendment which bears directly upon the State it is the more specific limiting principles of the First Amendment that finally govern this case.

Nor does our duty to apply the Bill of Rights to assertions of official authority depend upon our possession of marked competence in the field where the invasion of rights occurs. True, the task of translating the majestic generalities of the Bill of Rights, conceived as part of the pattern of liberal government in the eighteenth century, into concrete restraints on officials dealing with the problems of the twentieth century, is one to disturb self-confidence. These principles grew in soil which also produced a philosophy that the individual was the center of society, that his liberty was attainable through mere absence of governmental restraints, and that government should be entrusted with few controls and only the mildest supervision over men's affairs. We must transplant these rights to a soil in which the *laissez-faire* concept or principle of non-interference has withered at least as to economic affairs, and social advancements are increasingly sought through closer integration of society and through expanded and strengthened governmental controls. These changed conditions often deprive precedents of reliability and cast us more than we would choose upon our own judgment. But we act in these matters not by authority of our competence but by force of our commissions. We cannot, because of modest estimates of our competence in such specialities as public education, withhold the judgment that history authenticates as the function of this Court when liberty is infringed.

4. Lastly, and this is the very heart of the Gobitis opinion, it reasons that "National unity is the basis of national security," that the authorities have "the right to select appropriate means for its attainment," and hence reaches the conclusion that such compulsory measures toward "national unity" are constitutional. Upon the verity of this assumption depends our answer in this case.

National unity as an end which officials may foster by persuasion and example is not in question. The problem is whether under our Constitution compulsion as here employed is a permissible means for its achievement.

Struggles to coerce uniformity of sentiment in support of some end thought essential to their time and country have been waged by many good as well as by evil men. Nationalism is a relatively recent phenomenon but at other times and places the ends have been racial or territorial security, support of a dynasty or regime, and particular plans for saving souls. As first and moderate methods to attain unity have failed, those bent on its accomplishment must resort to an ever-increasing severity. As governmental pressure toward unity becomes greater, so strife becomes more bitter as to whose unity it shall be. Probably no deeper division of our people could proceed from any provocation than from finding it necessarry to choose what doctrine and whose program public educational officials shall compel youth to unite in embracing. Ultimate futility of such attempts to compel coherence is the lesson of every such effort from the Roman drive to stamp out Christianity as a disturber of its pagan unity, the Inquisition, as a means to religious and dynastic unity, the Siberian exiles as a means to Russian unity, down to the fast failing efforts of our present totalitarian enemies. Those who begin coercive elimination of dissent soon find themselves exterminating dissenters. Compulsory unification of opinion achieves only the unanimity of the graveyard.

It seems trite but necessary to say that the First Amendment to our Constitution was designed to avoid these ends by avoiding these beginnings. There is no mysticism in the American concept of the State or of the nature or origin of its authority. We set up government by consent of the governed, and the Bill of Rights denies those in power any legal opportunity to coerce that consent. Authority here is to be controlled by public opinion, not public opinion by authority.

The case is made difficult not because the principles of its decision are obscure but because the flag involved is our own. Nevertheless, we apply the limitations of the Constitution with no fear that freedom to be intellectually and spiritually diverse or even contrary will disintegrate the social organization. To believe that patriotism will not flourish if patriotic ceremonies are voluntary and spontaneous instead of a compulsory routine is to make an unflattering estimate of the appeal of our institutions to free minds. We can have intellectual individualism and the rich cultural diversities that we owe to exceptional minds only at the price of occasional eccentricity and abnormal attitudes. When they are so harmless to others or to the State as those we deal with here, the price is not too great. But freedom to differ is not limited to things that do not matter much. That would be a mere shadow of freedom. The test of its substance is the right to differ as to things that touch the heart of the existing order.

If there is any fixed star in our constitutional constellation, it is that no official, high or petty, can prescribe what shall be orthodox in politics, nationalism, religion, or other matters of opinion or force citizens to confess by word or act their faith therein. If there are any circumstances which permit an exception, they do not now occur to us.

We think the action of the local authorities in compelling the flag salute and pledge transcends constitutional limitations on their power and invades the sphere of intellect and spirit which it is the purpose of the First Amendment to our Constitution to reserve from all official control.

The decision of this Court in Minersville School District v. Gobitis and the holdings of those few per curiam decisions which preceded and foreshadowed it are over-ruled, and the judgment enjoining enforcement of the West Virginia Regulation is affirmed.

Affirmed.

B

[The text is taken from *Supreme Court Reporter* (St. Paul: West Publishing Co., 1943), Vol. LXIII, pp. 1189–90, 1191, 1192–93, 1194–96, 1197–98, 1200. Used by permission.]

West Virginia Board of Education *v.* Barnette

Mr. Justice FRANKFURTER, dissenting.

One who belongs to the most vilified and persecuted minority in history is not likely to be insensible to the freedoms guaranteed by our Constitution. Were my purely personal attitude relevant I should wholeheartedly associate myself with the general libertarian views in the Court's opinion, representing as they do the thought and action of a lifetime. But as judges we are neither Jew nor Gentile, neither Catholic nor agnostic. We owe equal attachment to the Constitution and are equally bound by our judicial obligations whether we derive our citizenship from the earliest or the latest immigrants to these shores. As a member of this Court I am not justified in writing my private notions of policy into the Constitution, no matter how deeply I may cherish them or how mischievous I may deem their disregard. The duty of a judge who must decide which of two claims before the Court shall prevail, that of a State to enact and enforce laws within its general competence or that of an individual to refuse obedience because of the demands of his conscience, is not that of the ordinary person. It can never be emphasized too much that one's own opinion about the wisdom or evil of a law should be excluded altogether when one is doing one's duty on the bench.

The only opinion of our own even looking in that direction that is material is our opinion whether legislators could in reason have enacted such a law. In the light of all the circumstances, including the history of this question in this Court, it would require more daring than I possess to deny that reasonable legislators could have taken the action which is before us for review. Most unwillingly, therefore, I must differ from my brethren with regard to legislation like this. I cannot bring my mind to believe that the "liberty" secured by the Due Process Clause gives this Court authority to deny to the State of West Virginia the attainment of that which we all recognize as a legitimate legislative end, namely, the promotion of good citizenship, by employment of the means here chosen. * * *

The precise scope of the question before us defines the limits of the constitutional power that is in issue. The State of West Virginia requires all pupils to share in the salute to the flag as part of school training in citizenship. The present action is one to enjoin the enforcement of this requirement by those in school attendance. We have not before us any attempt by the State to punish disobedient children or visit penal consequences on their parents. All that is in question is the right of the state to compel participation in this exercise by those who choose to attend the public schools.

We are not reviewing merely the action of a local school board. The flag salute requirement in this case comes before us with the full authority of the State of West Virginia. We are in fact passing judgment on "the power of the State as a whole". Practically we are passing upon the political power of each of the forty-eight states. Moreover, since the First Amendment has been read into the Fourteenth, our problem is precisely the same as it would be if we had before us an Act of Congress for the District of Columbia. To suggest that we are here concerned with the heedless action of some village tyrants is to distort the augustness of the constitutional issue and the reach of the consequences of our decision.

Under our constitutional system the legislature is charged

solely with civil concerns of society. If the avowed or intrinsic legislative purpose is either to promote or to discourage some religious community or creed, it is clearly within the constitutional restrictions imposed on legislatures and cannot stand. But it by no means follows that legislative power is wanting whenever a general non-discriminatory civil regulation in fact touches conscientious scruples or religious beliefs of an individual or a group. Regard for such scruples or beliefs undoubtedly presents one of the most reasonable claims for the exertion of legislative accommodation. It is, of course, beyond our power to rewrite the state's requirement, by providing exemptions for those who do not wish to participate in the flag salute or by making some other accommodations to meet their scruples. That wisdom might suggest the making of such accommodations and that school administration would not find it too difficult to make them and yet maintain the ceremony for those not refusing to conform, is outside our province to suggest. Tact, respect, and generosity toward variant views will always commend themselves to those charged with the duties of legislation so as to achieve a maximum of good will and to require a minimum of unwilling submission to a general law. But the real question is, who is to make such accommodations, the courts or the legislature?

This is no dry, technical matter. It cuts deep into one's conception of the democratic process—it concerns no less the practical differences between the means for making these accommodations that are open to courts and to legislatures. A court can only strike down. It can only say "This or that law is void." It cannot modify or qualify, it cannot make exceptions to a general requirement. And it strikes down not merely for a day. At least the finding of unconstitutionality ought not to have ephemeral significance unless the Constitution is to be reduced to the fugitive importance of mere legislation. When we are dealing with the Constitution of the United States, and more particularly with the great safeguards of the Bill of Rights, we are dealing with principles of liberty and justice "so rooted in the traditions and conscience of our people as to be ranked as fundamental"—something without which "a fair and enlightened system of justice would be impossible." * * *

The constitutional protection of religious freedom terminated disabilities, it did not create new privileges. It gave religious equality, not civil immunity. Its essence is freedom from conformity to religious dogma, not freedom from conformity to law because of religious dogma. Religious loyalties may be exercised without hindrance from the state, [but] the state may not exercise that which except by leave of religious loyalties is within the domain of temporal power. Otherwise each individual could set up his own censor against obedience to laws conscientiously deemed for the public good by those whose business it is to make laws.

The prohibition against any religious establishment by the government placed denominations on an equal footing—it assured freedom from support by the government to any mode of worship and the freedom of individuals to support any mode of worship. Any person may therefore believe or disbelieve what he pleases. He may practice what he will in his own house of worship or publicly within the limits of public order. But the lawmaking authority is not circumscribed by the variety of religious beliefs, otherwise the constitutional guaranty would be not a protection of the free exercise of religion but a denial of the exercise of legislation.

The essence of the religious freedom guaranteed by our Constitution is therefore this: no religion shall either receive the state's support or incur its hostility. Religion is outside the sphere of political government. This does not mean that all matters on which religious organizations or beliefs may pronounce are outside the sphere of government. Were this so, instead of the separation of church and state, there would be the subordination of the state on any matter deemed within the sovereignty of the religious conscience. Much that is the concern of temporal authority affects the spiritual interests of men. But it is not enough to strike down a non-discriminatory law that it may hurt or offend some dissident view. It would be too easy to cite numerous prohibitions and injunctions to which laws run counter if the variant interpretations of the Bible were made the tests of obedience to law. The validity of secular laws cannot be measured by their conformity to religious doctrines. It is only in a theocratic state that ecclesiastical doctrines measure legal right or wrong.

An act compelling profession of allegiance to a religion, no matter how subtly or tenuously promoted, is bad. But an act promoting good citizenship and national allegiance is within the domain of governmental authority and is therefore to be judged by the same considerations of power and of constitutionality as those involved in the many claims of immunity from civil obedience because of religious scruples.

That claims are pressed on behalf of sincere religious convictions does not of itself establish their constitutional validity. Nor does waving the banner of religious freedom relieve us from examining into the power we are asked to deny the states. Otherwise the doctrine of separation of church and state, so cardinal in the history of this nation and for the liberty of our people, would mean not the disestablishment of a state church but the establishment of all churches and of all religious groups.

The subjection of dissidents to the general requirement of saluting the flag, as a measure conducive to the training of children in good citizenship, is very far from being the first instance of exacting obedience to general laws that have offended deep religious scruples. Compulsory vaccination, food inspection regulations, obligation to bear arms, testimonial duties, compulsory medical treatment—these are but illustrations of conduct that has often been compelled in the enforcement of legislation of general applicability even though the religious consciences of particular individuals rebelled at the exaction. * * *

When dealing with religious scruples we are dealing with an almost numberless variety of doctrines and beliefs entertained with equal sincerity by the particular groups for which they satisfy man's needs in his relation to the mysteries of the uni-

verse. There are in the United States more than 250 distinctive
established religious denominations. In the state of Pennsylvania there are 120 of these, and in West Virginia as many as 65.
But if religious scruples afford immunity from civic obedience to
laws, they may be invoked by the religious beliefs of any individual even though he holds no membership in any sect or
organized denomination. Certainly this Court cannot be called
upon to determine what claims of conscience should be recognized and what should be rejected as satisfying the "religion"
which the Constitution protects. That would indeed resurrect the
very discriminatory treatment of religion which the Constitution
sought forever to forbid. And so, when confronted with the task
of considering the claims of immunity from obedience to a law
dealing with civil affairs because of religious scruples, we cannot
conceive religion more narrowly than in the terms in which
Judge Augustus N. Hand recently characterized it:

"It is unnecessary to attempt a definition of religion; the content of the term is found in the history of the human race and is
incapable of compression into a few words. Religious belief arises
from a sense of the inadequacy of reason as a means of relating
the individual to his fellow-men and to his universe. * * * [It]
may justly be regarded as a response of the individual to an inward mentor, call it conscience or God, that is for many persons
at the present time the equivalent of what has always been
thought a religious impulse."

Consider the controversial issue of compulsory Bible-reading
in public schools. The educational policies of the states are in great
conflict over this, and the state courts are divided in their decisions
on the issue whether the requirement of Bible-reading offends constitutional provisions dealing with religious freedom. The requirement of Bible-reading has been justified by various state courts
as an appropriate means of inculcating ethical precepts and
familiarizing pupils with the most lasting expression of great
English literature. Is this Court to overthrow such variant state
educational policies by denying states the right to entertain such
convictions in regard to their school systems because of a belief

that the King James version is in fact a sectarian text to which parents of the Catholic and Jewish faiths and of some Protestant persuasions may rightly object to having their children exposed? On the other hand the religious consciences of some parents may rebel at the absence of any Bible-reading in the schools. Or is this Court to enter the old controversy between science and religion by unduly defining the limits within which a state may experiment with its school curricula? The religious consciences of some parents may be offended by subjecting their children to the Biblical account of creation, while another state may offend parents by prohibiting a teaching of biology that contradicts such Biblical account. What of conscientious objections to what is devoutly felt by parents to be the poisoning of impressionable minds of children by chauvinistic teaching of history? This is very far from a fanciful suggestion for in the belief of many thoughtful people nationalism is the seed-bed of war.

There are other issues in the offing which admonish us of the difficulties and complexities that confront states in the duty of administering their local school systems. All citizens are taxed for the support of public schools although this Court has denied the right of a state to compel all children to go to such schools and has recognized the right of parents to send children to privately maintained schools. Parents who are dissatisfied with the public schools thus carry a double educational burden. Children who go to public school enjoy in many states derivative advantages such as free text books, free lunch, and free transportation in going to and from school. What of the claims for equality of treatment of those parents who, because of religious scruples, cannot send their children to public schools? What of the claim that if the right to send children to privately maintained schools is partly an exercise of religious conviction, to render effective this right it should be accompanied by a quality of treatment by the state in supplying free textbooks, free lunch, and free transportation to children who go to private schools? What of the claim that such grants are offensive to the cardinal constitutional doctrine of separation of church and state?

These questions assume increasing importance in view of the steady growth of parochial schools both in number and in population. I am not borrowing trouble by adumbrating these issues nor am I parading horrible examples of the consequences of today's decision. I am aware that we must decide the case before us and not some other case. But that does not mean that a case is dissociated from the past and unrelated to the future. We must decide this case with due regard for what went before and no less regard for what may come after. Is it really a fair construction of such a fundamental concept as the right freely to exercise one's religion that a state cannot choose to require all children who attend public school to make the same gesture of allegiance to the symbol of our national life because it may offend the conscience of some children, but that it may compel all children to attend public school to listen to the King James version although it may offend the consciences of their parents? And what of the larger issue of claiming immunity from obedience to a general civil regulation that has a reasonable relation to a public purpose within the general competence of the state? Another member of the sect now before us insisted that in forbidding her two little girls, aged nine and twelve, to distribute pamphlets Oregon infringed her and their freedom of religion in that the children were engaged in "preaching the gospel of God's Kingdom". A procedural technicality led to the dismissal of the case, but the problem remains.

These questions are not lightly stirred. They touch the most delicate issues and their solution challenges the best wisdom of political and religious statesmen. But it presents awful possibilities to try to encase the solution of these problems within the rigid prohibitions of unconstitutionality.

We are told that a flag is a doubtful substitute for adequate understanding of our institutions. The states that require such a school exercise do not have to justify it as the only means for promoting good citizenship in children, but merely as one of diverse means for accomplishing a worthy end. We may deem it a foolish measure, but the point is that this Court is not the organ of government to resolve doubts as to whether it will fulfill its purpose. Only if there be no doubt that any reasonable mind could entertain can we deny to the states the right to resolve doubts their way and not ours. * * *

The flag salute exercise has no kinship whatever to the oath tests so odious in history. For the oath test was one of the instruments for suppressing heretical beliefs. Saluting the flag suppresses no belief nor curbs it. Children and their parents may believe what they please, avow their belief and practice it. It is not even remotely suggested that the requirement for saluting the flag involves the slightest restriction against the fullest opportunity on the part both of the children and of their parents to disavow as publicly as they choose to do so the meaning that others attach to the gesture of salute. All channels of affirmative free expression are open to both children and parents. Had we before us any act of the state putting the slightest curbs upon such free expression, I should not lag behind any member of this Court in striking down such an invasion of the right to freedom of thought and freedom of speech protected by the Constitution.

I am fortified in my view of this case by the history of the flag salute controversy in this Court. Five times has the precise question now before us been adjudicated. Four times the Court unanimously found that the requirement of such a school exercise was not beyond the powers of the states. Indeed in the first three cases to come before the Court the constitutional claim now sustained was deemed so clearly unmeritorious that this Court dismissed the appeals for want of a substantial federal question. In the fourth case the judgment of the district court upholding the state law was summarily affirmed on the authority of the earlier cases. The fifth case, Minersville District v. Gobitis, was brought here because the decision of the Circuit Court of Appeals for the Third Circuit ran counter to our rulings. They were reaffirmed after full consideration, with one Justice dissenting.

What may be even more significant than this uniform recognition of state authority is the fact that every Justice—thirteen in all—who has hitherto participated in judging this matter has at one or more times found no constitutional infirmity in what is now condemned. Only the two Justices sitting for the first time on this matter have not heretofore found this legislation inoffensive to the "liberty" guaranteed by the Constitution. And among the Justices who sustained this measure were outstanding judicial leaders in the zealous enforcement of constitutional safeguards of civil liberties—men like Chief Justice Hughes, Mr. Justice Brandeis, and Mr. Justice Cardozo, to mention only those no longer on the Court.

One's conception of the Constitution cannot be severed from one's conception of a judge's function in applying it. The Court has no reason for existence if it merely reflects the pressures of the day. Our system is built on the faith that men set apart for this special function, freed from the influences of immediacy and from the deflections of worldly ambition, will become able to take a view of longer range than the period of responsibility entrusted to Congress and legislatures. We are dealing with matters as to which legislators and voters have conflicting views. Are we as judges to impose our strong convictions on where wisdom lies? That which three years ago had seemed to five successive Courts to live within permissible areas of legislation is now outlawed by the deciding shift of opinion of two Justices. What reason is there to believe that they or their successors may not have another view a few years hence? Is that which was deemed to be of so fundamental a nature as to be written into the Constitution to endure for all times to be the sport of shifting winds of doctrine? Of course, judicial opinions, even as to questions of constitutionality, are not immutable. As has been true in the past, the Court will from time to time reverse its position. But I believe that never before these Jehovah's Witnesses cases (except for minor deviations subsequently retraced) has this Court overruled decisions so as to restrict the powers of democratic government. Always heretofore, it has withdrawn narrow views of legislative authority so as to authorize what formerly it had denied.

In view of this history it must be plain that what thirteen Justices found to be within the constitutional authority of a state, legislators can not be deemed unreasonable in enacting. Therefore, in denying to the states what heretofore has received such impressive judicial sanction, some other tests of unconstitutionality must surely be guiding the Court than the absence of a rational justification for the legislation. But I know of no other test which this Court is authorized to apply in nullifying legislation.

In the past this Court has from time to time set its views of policy against that embodied in legislation by finding laws in conflict with what was called the "spirit of the Constitution." Such undefined destructive power was not conferred on this Court by the Constitution. Before a duly enacted law can be judicially nullified, it must be forbidden by some explicit restriction upon political authority in the Constitution. Equally inadmissible is the claim to strike down legislation because to us as individuals it seems opposed to the "plan and purpose" of the Constitution. That is too tempting a basis for finding in one's personal views the purposes of the Founders.

The uncontrollable power wielded by this Court brings it very close to the most sensitive areas of public affairs. As appeal from legislation to adjudication becomes more frequent, and its consequences more far-reaching, judicial self-restraint becomes more and not less important, lest we unwarrantably enter social and political domains wholly outside our concern. I think I appreciate fully the objections to the law before us. But to deny that it presents a question upon which men might reasonably differ appears to me to be intolerance. And since men may so reasonably differ, I deem it beyond my constitutional power to assert my view of the wisdom of this law against the view of the State of West Virginia.* * *

Of course patriotism cannot be enforced by the flag salute. But neither can the liberal spirit be enforced by judicial invalidation of illiberal legislation. Our constant preoccupation with the constitutionality of legislation rather than with its wisdom tends to preoccupation of the American mind with a false value. The tendency of focusing attention on constitutionality is to make constitutionality synonymous with wisdom, to regard a law as all right if it is constitutional. Such an attitude is a great enemy of liberalism. Particularly in legislation affecting freedom of thought and freedom of speech much which should offend a free-spirited society is constitutional. Reliance for the most precious interests of civilization, therefore, must be found outside of their vindication in courts of law. Only a persistent positive translation of the faith of a free society into the convictions and habits and actions of a community is the ultimate reliance against unabated temptations to fetter the human spirit.

18

AGELESS WORLD
OR
WORLD COME OF AGE

THE ISSUE which life forces upon the individual, which history presses upon the nation, is how faithfully to preserve the past, how freely to adjust to the present. To discard ancient wisdom merely because it is ancient is folly for certain. To live in a past that disdains to acknowledge new discoveries and insights, new techniques and interests, is to court irrelevance or death. To which path does wisdom point as one chooses for the future?

The issue comes, of course, in many forms: technological innovations versus proved methods; sociological experimentation versus established custom; psychological emancipation versus a rootage that may nourish as well as restrict. In the philosophical and theological realm, the process of demythologizing, of exchanging old for new, is an ancient one. Remythologizing is equally ancient and equally necessary. St. Augustine acknowledged that the world may indeed be only a dream, but, he concluded, that dream is my world. So if one finds the imprecision and nonlaboratory quality of the philosophical-theological enterprise disquieting, if one finds overly ambitious talk about Truth not to his liking, then the discussion can be in other terms. If capitalized Truth is a snare and delusion, we can then ask by what illusions do men or nations live. What myth is most meaningful, most supportive? And this issue does crowd in upon contemporary America.

Both Judaism and Christianity are richly historical; neither treats the past lightly. But both seek relevance in the present, unwilling to preside over museums dedicated to a harmless antiquarianism. In that unrelenting tension, some theologians find truth—or indispensable illusion—more obscured than revealed in the pyrotechnics of contemporaneity. They turn with some assurance to historical plateaus of understanding, to men of judicious learning, for guidance and inspiration. Other theologians see in the dazzling excitement of the present far more promise and challenge than a murky stream of history could possibly offer. They look confidently to an environment pregnant with possibility, to a future freed of burdening myth.

John Courtney Murray, S.J. (1904–1967) is hardly an unreconstructed reactionary, but an imaginative liberal who finds usefulness in ancient doctrine. A graduate of Boston College in 1927 and of Woodstock College (Maryland) in 1934, Murray completed his formal education at Gregorian University in Rome. In 1937, he returned to the Jesuit seminary, Woodstock College, where—with some interruptions—he taught theology for thirty years. An author and teacher of international repute, Murray probably had his greatest impact in shepherding the Decree on Religious Liberty through Vatican Council II.

In the pivotal volume excerpted below, the Jesuit theologian learnedly reviews the tortuous path by which modern man has arrived at his present position of cosmic confusion and ethical relativism. In retracing those steps, he comes across many ideas outmoded, archaic, and inadequate. But in the concept of natural law he finds an enduring vitality. That it is hoary with age is no liability: "Only the old idea is adequate in the face of the new problem." The idea of natural law has a timeliness superior to the old liberal individualism, superior to Marxism, superior to "modern evolutionary scientific humanism," i.e., the "new rationalism." It preserves what is "good and valid" in these competing systems but rejects what is "weak and false." The result, says John Courtney Murray, is a dynamic for a new "age of order," an order in man and society which arises from and reflects the eternal order of God.

William Hamilton (b. 1924) speaks a different language and looks for understanding in other locales. For many years professor of theology at Colgate Rochester Divinity School (Rochester, New York), Hamilton taught such courses as the "Theology of Karl Barth," the "Theology of Bonhoeffer," and his own "Radical Theology." In 1967 he left the seminary for New College (Sarasota, Florida) where he is professor of religion in the division of humanities. Along with Thomas J. Altizer (Emory University) and Paul van Buren (Temple University), William Hamilton is an effective spokesman within the contemporary "death of God" movement in American theology.

In the article abridged below, Hamilton scans the enveloping, inviting world with a wide-angle lens: Continental theology, current novels and poetry, psychoanalysis and philosophy—even the movies. While he does not cast history altogether aside, he finds a far greater suggestiveness in the present. In urging men to move from the cloister to the world, to "put a Protestant 'yes' to the world," Hamilton is not writing only for Protestants any more than Murray was writing only for Catholics. Each calls for what he sees to be modern man's appropriate if not mandatory response to the surrounding chaos. For Hamilton, the response is to grow up and assume one's manly place in a world come of age. ". . . we do not ask God to do for us what the world is qualified to do." Rather we affirm the world, learn from it, love it. "We move to our neighbor, to the city and to the world out of a sense of the loss of God."

A

[The text is taken from John Courtney Murray, *We Hold These Truths* (New York: Sheed & Ward, 1960; reprint, New York: Doubleday Image, 1964), pp. 299–300, 302–303, 310–12, 314–317. Used by permission.]

The Uses of Doctrine

The eighteenth-century gospel, based on the individualistic law of nature, could not at the time fail to be popular. For the primary drive then was toward destruction, and the law of nature concept of human rights was an appropriate dynamism of destruction, precisely because of the philosophical nonsense it enshrined. I mean that its individualistic rationalistic nominalism, precisely because it disregarded the organic character of society, and precisely because its concept of "progress" entailed a complete denial of the past and of the continuity of human effort, was an effective solvent of the corporate institutional structure of society as it then was. It could not (in France, at least) initiate simply a movement of reform; it could only operate as an engine of destruction. In the same way, its rationalistic secularism was effective against the usurping theory of divine right on which sovereignty at the time was based. And its mobilization of the "power of the people," under the nominalist slogan of the "rights of man," was an effective counterpoise to the unendurable centralization of power in king and nobles. This theory, therefore, could ride against the evils of the time with all the force, not only of truth but of error itself. Its theoretic dogmas were, as theories, false; but, as dogmas, powerful. Its exclusive attention to the problem of politics, and its attempt to solve it by violently creating an artificial "equality of citizens" (free, supposedly, as men, because equal as citizens), could end, as it did, only in dictatorship. But at least it could accomplish the social ruin that made dictatorship inevitable. And for the moment, a work of ruin was the immediate objective; for anger was abroad as well as reason, and it was not averse to using "reason" as its instrument.

On the other hand, the theory of natural rights, based on a law of nature, had also a measure of constructive dynamism—this time, not by reason of the philosophical nonsense involved in its theoretical scaffolding, but by reason of the intuition of truth that even the scaffolding could not wholly obscure. By nature all men are, as Bergbohm despairingly said, natural-law jurists. Intuitively they reach the essential imperatives of their own nature and know them to be unthwartably imperative—however much they may subsequently deform them, and destroy their proper bases, by uninformed or prejudiced reflective thought. And just as all men by nature—by the native power of moral intelligence—know that there is a difference between the *iustum naturale* and the *iustum legale* (the one based on natural law, the other on positive law), so, too, they naturally "see" the natural-law truth that "sovereignty is from the people," however much they may then go on falsely to conceptualize this truth. Usually the suffering of injustice is needed to bring the vision, just as immunity from suffering may obscure it. It is, as Pascal said, "the passions that make us think." And in those days the theory of divine right, together with the oppressive weight of the remnants of the feudal system, generated enough passion to make men think—furiously. In their fury, they thought of the truth anciently deposited in the *lex regia* of Justinian's *Institutes,* and elaborated by the Christian intelligence since the eleventh century. * * *

If one were, in fine, to sum up its [the doctrine of natural rights] political significance, one would have to say, I think, that it was able to destroy an order of political privilege and inaugurate an era of political equality; but it was not able to erect an order of social justice or inaugurate an order of human freedom. The testimony to the fact is the contemporary protest, in the name of "human rights," against the order (if one can call it an order) which is our heritage from the law of nature of the eighteenth and nineteenth centuries. The characteristics of the law of nature—its rationalism, individualism, and nominalism—made it an effective force for dissolution in its time; but today we are not looking for forces of dissolution, but for constructive forces. Similarly, its power as a solvent made it a force for liberty, in the thin and bloodless, individualist and negative nineteenth-century concept of liberty; but today we are looking for liberation and liberty in something better than this purely formal sense. We want liberty with a positive content within an order of liberty of rational design. Rousseau's "man everywhere in chains" is still too largely a fact. Our problem is still that of human freedom, or, in juridical terms, human rights. It is a problem of the definition of freedom, and then, more importantly, its institutionalization.

But the statement of the problem that we have in common with Locke and with the men of Paris and Philadelphia in 1789 has greatly changed. It is now seen to have a social dimension that no longer permits its statement in the old individualistic terms. Its multiple facors are now grasped with a realism that will not suffer its solution in the old nominalistic categories. And its background now has a new depth that the old one-dimensional, rationalistic thought never penetrated. The background is an idea of man in his nature, history, and psychology, that transcends the limited horizons of the rationalist mind. Finally, the growing conviction as to the ultimate impotence of the old attempts to solve the problem of human liberty and social order in purely secularistic, positivist terms had created a new openness to the world of metaphysical and religious values. If these alterations in the statement of the problem of freedom and human rights have in fact come about, as I think they have, they will explain the contemporary *Wiederkehr* of the ancient natural law of the Greek, Roman, and Christian traditions. Only the old idea is adequate in the face of the new problem. It alone affords the dynamic basis from which to attack the problem of freedom as posited in the "age of order" on whose threshold we stand. And it is such a basis because it is metaphysical in its foundations, because it is asserted within a religious framework, and because it is realist (not nominalist), societal (not individualist), and integrally human (not rationalist) in its outlook on man and society. In other words, the structure of the old idea of natural law follows exactly the structure of the new problem of human liberty. * * *

The whole metaphysic involved in the idea of natural law may seem alarmingly complicated; in a sense it is. Natural law supposes a realist epistemology, that asserts the real to be the measure of knowledge, and also asserts the possibility of intelligence reaching the real, i.e., the nature of things—in the case, the nature of man as a unitary and constant concept beneath all individual differences. Secondly, it supposes a metaphysic of nature, especially the idea that nature is a teleological concept, that the "form" of a thing is its "final cause," the goal of its becoming; in the case, that there is a natural inclination in man to become what in nature and destination he is—to achieve the fullness of his own being. Thirdly, it supposes a natural theology, asserting that there is a God, Who is eternal Reason, *Nous* at the summit of the order of being, Who is the author of all nature, and Who wills that the order of nature be fulfilled in all its purposes, as these are inherent in the natures found in the order. Finally, it supposes a morality, especially the principle that for man, a rational being, the order of nature is not an order of necessity, to be fulfilled blindly, but an order of reason and therefore of freedom. The order of being that confronts his intelligence is an order of "oughtness" for his will; the moral order is a prolongation of the metaphysical order into the dimensions of human freedom.

This sounds frightfully abstract; but it is simply the elaboration by the reflective intelligence of a set of data that are at bottom empirical. Consider, for instance, the contents of the consciousness of a man who is protesting against injustice, let us say, in a case where his own interests are not touched and where the injustice is wrought by technically correct legislation. The contents of his consciously protesting mind would be something like these. He is asserting that there is an idea of justice; that this idea is transcendent to the actually expressed will of the legislator; that it is rooted somehow in the nature of things; that he really *knows* this idea; that it is not made by his judgment but is the measure of his judgment; that this idea is of the kind that ought to be realized in law and action; that its violation is injury, which his mind rejects as unreason; that this unreason is an offense not only against his own intelligence but against God, Who commands justice and forbids injustice.

Actually, this man, who may be no philosopher, is thinking in the categories of natural law and in the sequence of ideas that the natural-law mentality (which is the human mentality) follows. He has an objective idea of the "just" in contrast to the "legal." His theoretical reason perceives the idea as true; his practical reason accepts the truth as good, therefore as law; his will acknowledges the law as normative of action. Moreover, this man will doubtless seek to ally others in his protest, in the conviction that they will think the same as he does. In other words, this man, whether he be protesting against the Taft-Hartley Act or the Nazi genocidal laws, is making in his own way all the metaphysical affirmations that undergird the concept of natural law. In this matter philosophical reflection does not augment the data of common sense. It merely analyzes, penetrates, and organizes them in their full abstractness; this does not, however, remove them from vital contact with their primitive source in experience.

From the metaphysical premises of natural law follow its two characteristics. It is a law immanent in the nature of man, but transcendent in its reference. It is rational, not rationalist. It is the work of reason, but not of an absolutely autonomous reason. It is immanent in nature in the sense that it consists in the dictates of human reason that are uttered as reason confronts the fundamental moral problems of human existence. These are the problems of what I, simply because I am a man and apart from all other considerations, ought to do or avoid in the basic situations in which I, again simply because I am a man, find myself. My situation is that of a creature before God; that of a "self" possessed of freedom to realize its "self"; that of a man living

among other men, possessing what is mine as the other possesses
what is his. In the face of these situations, certain imperatives
"emerge" (if you like) from human nature. They are the product
of its inclinations, as these are recognized by reason to be conformed to my rational nature. And they are formed by reason
into dictates that present themselves as demanding obedience.
Appearing, as they do, as dictates, these judgments of reason are
law. Appearing, as they do, in consequence of an inclination that
reason recognizes authentically human, they are "natural" law.

However, these dictates are not simply emergent in the rationalist sense. Reason does not create its own laws, any more
than man creates himself. Man has the laws of his nature given
to him, as nature itself is given. By nature he is the image of
God, eternal Reason; and so his reason reflects a higher reason;
therein consists its rightness and its power to oblige. Above the
natural law immanent in man stands the eternal law immanent
in God transcendent; and the two laws are in intimate corre-
spondence, as the image is to the exemplar. The eternal law is
the Uncreated Reason of God; it appoints an order of nature—
an order of beings, each of which carries in its very nature also
its end and purposes; and it commands that this order of nature
be preserved by the steady pursuit of their ends on the part of
all the natures within the order. Every created nature has this
eternal law, this transcendent order of reason, imprinted on it by
the very fact that it is a nature, a purposeful dynamism striving
for the fullness of its own being. In the irrational creation, the
immanence of the eternal law is unconscious; the law itself is a
law of necessity. But in the rational creature the immanent law
is knowable and known; it is a moral law that authoritatively
solicits the consent of freedom. St. Thomas, then, defines the
natural law as the "rational creature's participation in the eternal
law." The participation consists in man's possession of reason,
the godlike faculty, whereby man knows himself—his own nature
and end—and directs himself freely, in something of divine
fashion but under God, to the plenitude of self-realization of his
rational and social being. * * *

This carries us on to the function of natural law in political philosophy—its solution to the eternally crucial problem of the legitimacy of power, its value as a norm for, and its dictates in regard of, the structures and processes of society. The subject is much too immense. Let me say, first, that the initial claim of natural-law doctrine is to make political life part of the moral universe, instead of leaving it to wander as it too long has, like St. Augustine's sinner, in *regione dissimilitudinis*. There are doubtless a considerable number of people not of the Catholic Church who would incline to agree with Pius XII's round statement in *Summi Pontificatus* that the "prime and most profound root of all the evils with which the City is today beset" is a "heedlessness and forgetfulness of natural law." Secretary of State Marshall said practically the same thing, but in contemporary idiom, when remarked that all our political troubles go back to a neglect or violation of human rights.

For the rest, I shall simply state the major contents of the political ideal as it emerges from natural law.

One set of principles is that which the Carlyles and others have pointed out as having ruled (amid whatever violations) the political life of the Middle Ages. First, there is the supremacy of law, and of law as reason, not will. With this is connected the idea of the ethical nature and function of the state (*regnum* or *imperium* in medieval terminology), and the educative character of its laws as directive of man to "the virtuous life" and not simply protective of particular interests. Secondly, there is the principle that the source of political authority is in the community. Political society as such is natural and necessary to man, but its form is the product of reason and free choice; no ruler has a right to govern that is inalienable and independent of human agency. Thirdly, there is the principle that the authority of the ruler is limited; its scope is only political, and the whole of human life is not absorbed in the polls. The power of the ruler is limited, as it were, from above by the law of justice, from below by systems of private right, and from the sides by the public right of the Church. Fourthly, there is the principle of the contractual nature of the relations between ruler and ruled. The latter are not simply material organized for rule by the *rex legibus solutus,* but human agents who agree to be ruled constitutionally, in accordance with law.

A second set of principles is of later development, as ideas and in their institutional form, although their roots are in the natural-law theories of the Middle Ages.

The first is the principle of subsidiarity. It asserts the organic character of the state—the right to existence and autonomous functioning of various sub-political groups, which unite in the organic unity of the state without losing their own identity or suffering infringement of their own ends or having their functions assumed by the state. These groups include the family, the local community, the professions, the occupational groups, the minority cultural or linguistic groups within the nation, etc. Here on the basis of natural law is the denial of the false French revolutionary antithesis, individual *versus* state, as the principle of political organization. Here too is the denial of all forms of state totalitarian monism, as well as of Liberalistic atomism that would remove all forms of social or economic life from any measure of political control. This principle is likewise the assertion of the fact that the freedom of the individual is secured at the interior of institutions intermediate between himself and the state(e.g., trade unions) or beyond the state (the church).

The second principle is that of popular sharing in the formation of the collective will, as expressed in legislation or in executive policy. It is a natural-law principle inasmuch as it asserts the dignity of the human person as an active co-participant in the political decisions that concern him, and in the pursuit of the end of the state, the common good. It is also related to all the natural-law principles cited in the first group above. For instance, the idea that law is reason is fortified in legislative assemblies that discuss the reasons for laws. So, too, the other principles are fortified, as is evident.

Here then in briefest compass are some of the resources resident in natural law, that would make it the dynamic of a new "age of order." It does not indeed furnish a detailed blueprint of the order; that is not its function. Nor does it pretend to settle the enormously complicated technical problems, especially in the economic order, that confront us today. It can claim to be only a "skeleton law," to which flesh and blood must be added by that heart of the political process, the rational activity of man, aided by experience and by high professional competence. But today it is perhaps the skeleton that we mostly need, since it is precisely the structural foundations of the political, social, and economic orders that are being most anxiously questioned. In this situation the doctrine of natural law can claim to offer all that is good and valid in competing systems, at the same time that it avoids all that is weak and false in them.

Its concern for the rights of the individual human person is no less than that shown in the school of individualist Liberalism with its "law of nature" theory of rights, at the same time that its sense of the organic character of the community, as the flowering in ascending forms of sociality of the social nature of man, is far greater and more realistic. It can match Marxism in its concern for man as worker and for the just organization of economic society, at the same time that it forbids the absorption of man in matter and its determinisms. Finally, it does not bow to the new rationalism in regard of a sense of history and progress, the emerging potentialities of human nature, the value of experience in settling the forms of social life, the relative primacy in certain respects of the empirical fact over the preconceived theory; at the same time it does not succumb to the doctrinaire relativism, or to the narrowing of the object of human intelligence, that cripple at their root the high aspirations of evolutionary scientific humanism. In a word, the doctrine of natural law offers a more profound metaphysic, a more integral humanism, a fuller rationality, a more complete philosophy of man in his nature and history.

I might say, too, that it furnishes the basis for a firmer faith and a more tranquil, because more reasoned, hope in the future. If there is a law immanent in man—a dynamic, constructive force for rationality in human affairs, that works itself out, because it is a natural law, in spite of contravention by passion and evil and all the corruptions of power—one may with sober reason believe in, and hope for, a future of rational progress. And this belief and hope is strengthened when one considers that this dynamic order of reason in man, that clamors for expression with all the imperiousness of law, has its origin and sanction in an eternal order of reason whose fulfillment is the object of God's majestic will.

B

[The text, by William Hamilton, is taken from *The Christian Scholar*, Vol. XLVIII, No. 1 (Spring, 1965), pp. 30–31, 36–41, 44–46. Used by permission. Reprinted in Thomas J. J. Altizer and William Hamilton, *Radical Theology and the Death of God* (Indianapolis: Bobbs-Merrill Co., 1966).]

The Death of God Theology

What does it mean to say that God is dead? Is this any more than a rather romantic way of pointing to the traditional diffi-culty of speaking about the holy God in human terms? Is it any more than a warning against all idols, all divinities fashioned out of human need, human ideologies? Does it perhaps not just mean that "existence is not an appropriate word to ascribe to God, that therefore He cannot be said to exist, and He is in that sense dead"? It surely means all this, and more. The hypo-thetical meanings suggested still all life within the safe boun-daries of the neo-orthodox or biblical-theology tradition, and the death of God group wants clearly to break away from that. It used to live rather comfortably there, and does so no longer. Perhaps we can put it this way; the neo-orthodox reconstruction of the Christian doctrine of revelation seems to have broken down for some. It used to be possible to say: we cannot know God but He has made himself known to us, and at that point analogies from the world of personal relations would enter the scene and help us out. But somehow, the situation has deteriorated; as before, we cannot know, but now it seems that He does not make himself known, even as enemy. This is more than the old protest against natural theology or metaphysics; more than the usual assurance that before the holy God all our language gets broken and diffracted into paradox. It is really that we do not know, do not adore, do not possess, do not believe in God. It is not just that a capacity has dried up within us; we do not take all this as merely a statement about our frail psyches, we take it as a statement about the nature of the world and we try to convince others. God is dead. We are not talking about the absence of the experience of God, but about the experience of the absence of God. Yet the death of God theologians claim to be theologians, to be Christians, to be speaking out of a community to a community. They do not grant that their view is really a complicated sort of atheism dressed in a new spring bonnet. * * *

I would like to move now from the fairly invulnerable task of reporting the views of others, to the task of laying out my own point of view, which I believe belongs in this general tradition. If [Thomas] Altizer begins with the cosmic event of the disappearance of the sacred, and if [Paul] van Buren begins with the language problem, my starting point may be said to have two parts, one negative, the other positive.

The negative part is the perception, already referred to, of the deterioration of the portrait of the God-man relation as found in biblical theology and the neo-orthodox tradition. This theological tradition was able to portray a striking and even heroic sort of faith, a sort of holding on by the fingernails to the cliff of faith, a standing terrified before the enemy-God, present to man as terror or threat, comforting only in that he kept us from the worse terrors of life without Him. This God, we used to say, will never let us go. But He has, or we have Him, or something, and in any case this whole picture has lost its power to persuade some in our time.

But our negations are never very important or interesting. There is a positive affirmation or starting point by which I enter into the country inhabited by the death of God settlers. It has to do with the problem of the Reformation or being a Protestant today. This is what I mean. At the end of the last century the Reformation was interpreted as a victory for the autonomous religious personality, freed from the tyranny of hierarchy and institution, while man's relation to God was described as unmediated and available to all. This is what the Reformation means, for example, in Harnack's *What Is Christianity?* it was characteristic of liberal Protestantism as a whole, and it achieves its symbolic expression in Luther, standing alone at Worms, refusing to go against his conscience.

As the century wore on, and wars, depressions, bombs and anxieties came our way, we found ourselves seeing the Reformation in a new light. The old approach was not wrong, it was just that the new approach fitted our experience better. In this new approach, which we might call yesterday's understanding of the Reformation, the central fact was not the autonomous religious personality; it was the theological discovery of the righteous God. In that portion of our century when men and nations knew trouble, sin, and guilt, we needed to receive this theological truth of the Reformation, just as earlier the psychological truth needed to be heard. Thus, we learned to say that the Reformation was a theological event, it centered in Luther's discovery of the meaning of justification or forgiveness, and its symbol proved to be Luther, storming about his room in Wittenberg, cursing the God who demands righteousness of men.

Today we may need to look at the Reformation in a third sense, no more or less true than the earlier approaches, but perhaps needing special emphasis just now and fitting new experiences in both church and world. This approach is more ethical than psychological or theological, and its focus is not on the free personality or on justification by faith, but on the movement from the cloister to the world. Of course, there is no specific event in Luther's life that can be so described, but the movement is there in his life nonetheless, and it is a movement we need to study. From cloister to world means from church, from place of protection and security, of order and beauty, to the bustling middle class world of the new university, of politics, princes, and peasants. Far more important than any particular ethical teaching of Luther is this fundamental ethical movement. Here I touch some of Altizer's concerns, but I am not as anxious to recover the sacred, since I am starting with a definition of Protestantism as a movement away from the sacred place.

This view of the Reformation, along with my preliminary negative comment, does allow a kind of picture of faith. It is not, this time, holding on by the fingernails, and it is not a terror-struck confession before the enemy God. It is not even, one can almost say, a means of apprehending God at all. This faith is more like a place, a being with or standing beside the neighbor. Faith, one might suggest, has almost become collapsed into love, and the Protestant is no longer defined as the forgiven sinner, the *simul justus et peccator,* but as the one beside the neighbor, beside the enemy, at the disposal of the man in need. The connection between holding to the neighbor and holding to Jesus will be dealt with in a moment.

At this point I am inclined to reflect the later [Dietrich] Bonhoeffer more than either van Buren or Altizer want or need to. The Protestant I am describing has no God, has no faith in God, and affirms both the death of God and the death of all the forms of theism. Even so, he is not primarily a man of negation, for if there is a movement away from God and religion, there is the more important movement into, for, towards the world, worldly life, and the neighbor as the bearer of the worldly Jesus. We must look more carefully at these two movements: toward the world and away from religion.

We need to be very careful in how we put this Protestant "yes" to the world. It is not the same kind of "yes" that one finds in that tradition of theology of culture today that makes use of the world as illustrations for its doctrines of sin and redemption. This "yes" is also in considerable tension with a num-

ber of themes in modern literature. Recently, Lionel Trilling
called attention to Thomas Mann's remark that all his work was
an effort to free himself from the middle class, and to this
Trilling added the comment that all truly modern literature can
be so described. Indeed, he goes on, modern literature is not
only asking for a freedom from the middle class, but from society itself. It is this conception of the modern, I am saying, that
should be opposed by the Protestant. Who are the characteris-
tically modern writers in this sense I am criticising? Any such
list would surely include Henry James, Eliot, Yeats, Pound,
Joyce, Lawrence, Kafka, Faulkner, Beckett. Is it possible to
affirm the value of the technological revolution, the legitimacy of
the hopes and claims of the dispossessed, most of all, of the
moral centrality of the Negro revolution in America today—is
it possible to affirm all these values and still to live comfortably
in the modern world as these writers portray it? Surely not, in
some important senses.

When I state that there is something in the essence of Protestantism itself that drives us into the world, it is not to the
world of these "modern" writers, but in many ways it is into
the world they reject—to the world of technology, power,
money, sex, culture, race, poverty, and the city. Lawrence's
protest against the mechanization of life now seems a bit archaic
and piquant, and his aristocratic hostility to the democratic
ethos of Christianity is rather more than piquant, it is irrelevant
and false. In a way, I am describing not a move away from
Puritanism, but a move to it, and to the middle class and to the
city. Perhaps the time has come when Protestants no longer
need to make ritual acts of hostility to Puritanism, moralism,
and to all the hypocrisies and prohibitions of middle class culture. The chronicle of middle class hypocrisy may well be
complete, with no more work on it necessary. There are those
in our world today who would like to be a little closer to the
securities of middle class existence so they too might become
free to criticise them, and who must indeed be granted political,
economic, and psychological admission to that world. Attacks

on the silliness of middle class morality have almost always had an antipolitical character, and it is to that element in the modern sensibility that the Protestant takes exception. Thus the worldliness affirmed by Protestantism has a post-modern, pro-bourgeois, urban and political character. This may mean a loosening of the ties between the Protestant intellectual and avant-garde modernism, and it might even mean the start of some interesting work in the shaping of a radical ethic today.

The Protestant protest against religion is related to, but it must not be confused with, this affirmation of the world. (Both are clearly implied by our formula, from church to world.) Assertions that Protestantism is against religion, or that Christianity or revelation is an attack on religion, have, of course, been with us for a considerable time now, and nearly everybody has had a word to say on the subject. Karl Barth's long discussion of the subject in *Church Dogmatics* I/2 has had a massive and perhaps undeserved influence. Barth defines religion, in his attack on it, as something like man's arrogant and grasping attempt to become God, so it is hard to see what all the posturing is about. If by definition religion equals sin, and you then say revelation ought to be against religion, you may cause some shuddering frissons of delight among careless readers, but you have not forwarded theological clarity very much.

More immediate in influence, of course, is the plea for a religionless Christianity in the prison letters of Bonhoeffer. We really don't know what Bonhoeffer meant by religion, though long articles have been written on the subject, and our modern study of the problem of religionlessness must be carried on quite independent of the task, probably fruitless, of establishing just what Bonhoeffer meant.

There are two schools of interpretation of Protestant religionlessness. One might be called the moderate, Honest-to-God, ecclesiastical interpretation. In this, religion generally means "religious activities" like liturgy, counselling, going to church, saying your prayers. To be religionless in this sense is to affirm that the way we have done these things in the past may not be the only way, or may not be worth doing at all, and that radical experiments ought to be attempted in the forms of the church and ministry. Bishop Robinson's lectures on "The New Reformation" delivered in America in the spring of 1964 are an able presentation of this moderate radicalism. A good deal of the material out of Geneva, New York, and the denominational headquarters on the church and ministry reflects this promising line, and a good many religious sociologists, and radical religious leaders on the race issue tend to use Bonhoeffer and religionlessness in this way.

This is an important trend, and we need more and not less experimentation on these matters of the ministry, for we are well into the opening phase of the breakdown of organized religion in American life, well beyond the time when ecumenical dialogues or denominational mergers can be expected to arrest the breakdown.

The religionlessness I wish to defend, however, is not of this practical type. At no point is the later Bonhoeffer of greater importance to the death of God theology than right here, in helping us work out a truly theological understanding of the problem of religionlessness. I take religion to mean not man's arrogant grasping for God (Barth) and not assorted Sabbath activities usually performed by ordained males (the moderate radicals), but any system of thought or action in which God or the gods serve as fulfiller of needs or solver of problems. Thus I am asserting with Bonhoeffer the breakdown of the religious a priori and the coming of age of man.

The breakdown of the religious a priori means that there is no way, ontological, cultural, or psychological, to locate a part of the self or a part of human experience that needs God. There is no God-shaped blank within man. Man's heart may or may not be restless until it rests in God. It is not necessarily so. God is not in the realm of the necessary at all; he is not necessary being, he is not necessary to avoid despair or self-righteousness. He is one of the possibles in a radically pluralistic spiritual and intellectual milieu.

This is just what man's coming of age is taken to mean. It is not true to say, with Luther, *entweder Gott oder Abgott* [either God or idol]. It is not true to say, with Ingmar Bergman, who probably didn't mean it, "Without God, life is an outrageous terror." It is not true to say that there are certain areas, problems, dimensions to life today that can only be faced, solved, illumined, dealt with, by a religious perspective.

I am defining religion as the assumption in theology, preaching, apologetics, evangelism, counselling, that man needs God, and that there are certain things that God alone can do for him. I am denying that religion is necessary and saying that the movement from the church to the world that we have taken as definitive of Protestantism not only permits but requires this denial. To assert that we are men moving from cloister to world, church to world, to say that we are secular men, is to say that we do not ask God to do for us what the world is qualified to do. Really to travel along this road means that we trust the world, not God, to be our need fulfiller and problem solver, and God, if he is to be for us at all, must come in some other role.

This combination of a certain kind of God-rejection with a certain kind of world-affirmation is the point where I join the death of God movement. At this point, I would like to formulate a question directed against what I have been saying. What distinguishes this position I have been sketching out from ordinary Feuerbachian atheism? Earlier we distinguished between mysticism and Christological ethics as ways of handling the historical experience of the death of God. I think both of these responses are valid and useful, and in answering the question about atheism I would like to propose my version of them.

I am in full sympathy with much of the mystical imagery used by Altizer, perhaps most of all with the idea of "waiting." There is an element of expectation, even hope, that removes my position from classical atheisms and that even removes from it a large amount of anguish and gloom. In addition to the idea of waiting for God, I am interested in the search for a language that does not depend on need or problem. . . . If God is not needed, if it is to the world and not God that we repair for our needs and problems, then perhaps we may come to see that He is to be enjoyed and delighted in. Part of the meaning of waiting for God is found in this attempt to understand what delighting in Him might mean.

To the valid theme of the Christological ethic worked out by van Buren I am adding the emphasis on Protestant worldliness both as an interpretation of the Reformation and as an attack on certain forms of modern sensibility.

By way of a provisional summary: the death of God must be affirmed; the confidence with which we thought we could speak of God is gone, and our faith, belief, experience of Him are very poor things indeed. Along with this goes a sharp attack on religion which we have defined as any system using God to meet a need or to solve a problem, even the problem of not having a God. Our waiting for God, our godlessness, is partly a search for a language and a style by which we might be enabled to stand before Him once again, delighting in His presence.

In the time of waiting we have a place to be. It is not before an altar, it is in the world, in the city, with both the needy neighbor and the enemy. This place really defines our faith, for faith and love have come together in the interim of waiting. This place, as we shall see, is not only the place for the waiting for God, it is also a way to Jesus Christ.* * *

I must now attempt to draw some of the themes of this essay together, so that I may be attacked and assented to for the proper reasons, and so this death of God tradition may have as good a chance as possible of taking on a theological life of its own along with the other theological styles and visions that we are beginning to discern in this new post-existentialist, post-European period. In a recent critical review of Julian Huxley's *Essays of a Humanist,* Philip Toynbee makes an attack on all psychologically inclined Christians, biologists who listen to Bach, mystical astronomers and humane Catholics. What can we put in their place, he asks.

And the answer? Simply to wait—on God or whatever it may be, and in the meantime to leave the general alone and to concentrate all our natural energies and curiosities on the specific, the idiosyncratic, the personal.

This combination of waiting and attention on the concrete and personal is precisely the theological point I have been trying to make. Waiting here refers to the whole experience I have called "the death of God," including the attack on religion and the search for a means by which God, not needed, may be enjoyed. We have insisted all along that "death of God" must not be taken as symbolic rhetoric for something else. There really is a sense of not-having, of not believing, or having lost, not just the idols or the gods of religion, but God Himself. And this is an experience that is not peculiar to a neurotic few, nor is it private or inward. Death of God is a public event in our history, we are saying.

Thus we wait, we try out new words, we pray for God to return, and we seem to be willing to descend into the darkness of unfaith and doubt that something may emerge on the other side. In this way, we have tried to interpret and confirm the mystical images that are so central to the thought of Altizer.

But we do more than play the waiting game. We concentrate our energy and passion on the specific, the concrete, the personal. We turn from the problems of faith to the reality of love. We walk away from the inner anguish of a Hamlet or an Oedipus, and take up our worldly responsibility with Prospero and Orestes. As Protestants, we push the movement from church to world as far as it can go and become frankly worldly men. And in this world, as we have seen, there is no need for religion and no need for God. This means that we refuse to consent to that traditional interpretation of the world as a shadow-screen of unreality, masking or concealing the eternal which is the only true reality. This refusal is made inevitable by the scientific revolution of the seventeenth century, and it is this refusal that stands, as a troublesome shadow, between ourselves and the Reformation of the sixteenth. The world of experience is real, and it is necessary and right to be actively engaged in changing its patterns and structures.

This concentration on the concrete and the worldly says

something about the expected context of theology in America today. It means, I think, that the theological work that is to be truly helpful—at least for a while—is more likely to come from worldly contexts than ecclesiastical ones, more likely to come from participation in the Negro revolution than from the work of faith and order. But this is no surprise, for ever since the Civil War, ever since the Second Inaugural of Lincoln we might even say, the really creative American theological expressions have been worldly rather than ecclesiastical: the work of Walter Rauschenbusch and the work of Reinhold Niebuhr are surely evidence for this.

The death of God Protestant, it can be seen, has somewhat inverted the usual relation between faith and love, theology and ethics, God and the neighbor. We are not proceeding from God and faith to neighbor and love, loving in such and such a way because we are loved in such and such a way. We move to our neighbor, to the city and to the world out of a sense of the loss of God. We set aside this sense of loss or death, we note it and allow it to be, neither glad for it, not insistent that it must be so for all, nor sorry for ourselves. And, for the time of our waiting we place ourselves with our neighbor and enemy in the world.

ACKNOWLEDGMENTS

It is a pleasure to express appreciation to the John Randolph Haynes and Dora Haynes Foundation for a summer fellowship which gave initial impetus to the present volume. A University of California intramural grant also assisted in securing some of the scarcer items.

The courtesy of publishers or individuals who have graciously permitted the reprinting of materials on which they hold the copyright is also gratefully acknowledged. These include the following:

Harvard University Press for Charles Finney's *Lecturers on Revivals of Religion* (see Chap. 8) and for Josiah Strong's *Our Country* (see Chap. 14);

Alexander L. Abbott for Lyman Abbott's *Reminiscences* (see Chap. 12);

The Macmillan Company (Crowell-Collier) for Walter Lippmann's *Preface to Morals* (see Chap. 15);

Beacon Press for John Dewey's *Reconstruction in Philosophy* (see Chap. 16);

Princeton University Press for Will Herberg's essay in *Religious Perspectives in American Culture* (see Chap. 16);

West Publishing Company for the texts of United States Supreme Court decisions (see Chap. 17);

Sheed and Ward for John C. Murray's *We Hold These Truths* (see Chap. 18);

The Christian Scholar and William Hamilton for an essay reprinted in *Radical Theology and the Death of God* (see Chap. 18).